The
AMERICAN DUCHESS
Guide to
18th Century Dressmaking

How to Hand Sew Georgian Gowns and
Wear Them with Style

Lauren Stowell
Founder of American Duchess

Abby *and* Cox

PAGE STREET
PUBLISHING CO.

PAGE STREET
PUBLISHING CO.

First published in 2017 by
Page Street Publishing Co.
27 Congress Street, Suite 105
Salem, MA 01970
www.pagestreetpublishing.com

Distributed by Macmillan, sales in Canada by The Canadian Manda Group.

23   22   21   20   5   6   7   8

ISBN-13: 978-1-62414-453-0

ISBN-10: 1-62414-453-5

Library of Congress Control Number: 2017942125

Cover and book design by Page Street Publishing Co.

Photography by Lauren Stowell, Abby Cox and Chris Stowell

Printed and bound in China

Dedication

This book is dedicated to all the nameless dressmakers and milliners throughout history. Thank you.

Contents

What This Book Is All About

Dear Reader,

Welcome to the wild world of eighteenth-century historical costuming. Within these pages we will take you on a dressmaking journey through the Georgian era, helping you to learn about, create and dress in four types of gowns and their accessories.

Our goal with *The American Duchess Guide to 18th Century Dressmaking* is to turn our research and experience into an accessible book that will take you from your first project to that fabulous finished ensemble. We encourage you to use our instructions stitch-for-stitch or as jumping-off points for creating outfits that represent your unique style.

Finally, when we set out to write this book, we wanted above all else to show how fun and exciting the eighteenth century can be. Though it might seem intimidating, we *know* you can do it!

Stay fabulous and sew fearlessly!

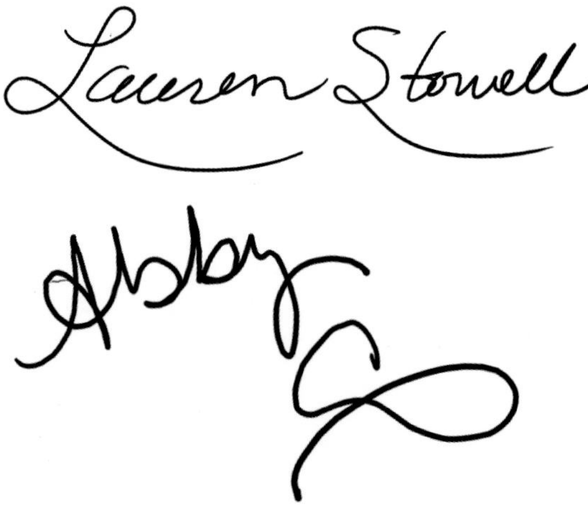

Lauren Stowell

Abby

So You Want to Sew an Eighteenth-Century Gown, Eh?

The American Duchess Guide to 18th Century Dressmaking is divided into four beefy chapters, each representing a different type of gown common in the eighteenth century. We've also included the accompanying accessories, or millinery, needed to create a full, accurate ensemble for each gown. You will find caps, hats, aprons, mitts, kerchiefs, muffs and more, plus a section at the end of each chapter showing how to get fully dressed in all the wonderful things you just made. Our intent is to illustrate how important the combination of all of these pieces is in creating that "stepped out of a portrait" look.

All of the projects in this book are hand sewn with period-correct methods, which differ greatly from modern techniques. Scary though it may be, we encourage you to learn and follow the hand-stitching techniques. For Georgian gowns, these methods genuinely make construction easier, and the resulting gown and accessories are more accurate, attractive and well-made than those sewn on a machine. Time-consuming? Yes. Worth it? Absolutely.

With hand sewing in mind, you will notice that we use thread of two different weights. The choice to use "quilter" weight (#30) thread for our seams and bodice construction and the more normal weight (#50) for hems and finer sewing, follows the same decisions made by eighteenth-century dressmakers. You will also notice that we used silk almost exclusively, but it is just as accurate to use cotton or linen thread for your gown construction.

We've chosen linen for all the gown linings in this book, as it was ubiquitous in its use as lining fabric for women's gowns during the eighteenth century. While we talk about the benefits of linen as a textile on page 171, using linen for your linings will help provide a stable and authentic structure for your gowns.

Finally, we have not included patterns or instructions for making your own stays (corset). Stay making is a complicated and time-consuming endeavor that warrants even more publications than what already exist. For every gown in this book, we wear a different style of stay, essential in creating the specific silhouette of each time period. Though we could not include stay making here, you *will* need to have stays before making your gown.

Just remember to have fun, be bold and sew without fear!

PATTERNS: PAPER OR GRIDDED OR DRAPED? OH MY!

While we all strive to be as historically accurate as possible, sometimes modernity and life make it borderline impossible. For example, one of the biggest issues with eighteenth-century dressmaking is finding the balance between paper patterns and draping. Most modern seamstresses prefer to use paper patterns, but in the eighteenth century, mantua makers cut and fit the gowns directly on their clients. It doesn't mean that paper patterns didn't exist; tailors used paper shapes when constructing men's garments, and milliners used them for different accessories. Mantua makers did not seem to work this way, though.

But that doesn't always work for us, does it? Sometimes finding that balance between accessibility and accuracy is a struggle. When we made the gowns for this book, we used gridded or scaled patterns in published books or websites for our starting points, noted at the start of each chapter, and then draped the shapes directly on the model.

We realize that draping is an advanced, complex technique in itself, so to help find a balance between paper patterns and draping, we have included gridded patterns of the linings used in our gowns. This way, you can see the shape of the gown lining you will need, scale or drape and adjust them to fit you and build the gown upon your fitted lining. It's important to note that these patterns are direct copies of our linings, and they reflect our different proportions, measurements and quirks. You *will* need to make adjustments for your own proportions, measurements and quirks.

FITTING YOUR MOCK-UP

When starting with our lining shapes or a paper pattern, it is essential to first create a muslin mock-up to sort out any major fitting issues. Below, we walk you through how to fit a mock-up using our gridded patterns. If you choose to use a preprinted paper pattern, cut out the larger size to fit your mock-up. This reference can also be used in correspondence with the fitting guides seen throughout the book.

1. Measure yourself (or your model) and compare the measurements to that of the lining you wish to use. Adjust the lines accordingly to better accommodate your shape.

2. Cut out the lining shapes in muslin, adding 1 to 2 inches (2.5 to 5 cm) seam allowance on *all* sides. Check grain lines to make sure they correspond with the pattern.

3. Roughly pin the seams together and try the mock-up on over all the underpinnings. Pin the front in place.

4. With a pencil, mark and/or adjust where the muslin bodice is too short or too long, if the shoulder straps are too loose or the neckline gapes open, if the armscyes are too low and open, and if the fit is too loose or too tight. Refer to the Troubleshooting Guide (page 230) for common fitting wrinkles and rumples.

5. Smooth the bodice, pinching up the seams and repinning to adjust the fit. If needed, clip into the waist edge, pulling down on the bodice while folding the excess upward, and pin. Smooth the excess toward the center front and center back seams, repinning and marking as you go.

6. With a pencil, sketch along the waist fold, the base of all the seams on both sides and the shoulder straps. Also take this opportunity to draw the neckline just as you want it.

7. Need to extend or fill in a bit? If the waist is too short, shoulder straps too broad or your armscye too low and wide, pin a scrap of muslin in and redraw the lines. Be sure not to remove these pins when taking the muslin mock-up off the body.

8. Check the placement of the side seam line on the body and redraw the new seam line in the correct place if needed. Reference original gowns, but don't become paralyzed by exact placement—go for the general area. Hatch mark across this new line to create match points. Side seams are placed farther to the back than modern placement. A deeper, curvier side seam helps flatter the wearer and creates a prettier line.

9. Unpin the front closure of the mock-up and remove from the body. Double-check that your new seam lines, waist edge, armscye and neckline are adequately marked, then unpin all the pieces and lay flat.

10. You will see quite a few scratchy lines. True these lines up with a ruler and French curve. Cut all the pieces out on the seam and edge lines.

11. This is now your new pattern. If you like, trace it onto paper and add seam allowance. You're now ready to cut!

Armscyes in the eighteenth century were much higher than today. Though it may be a tad uncomfortable during fittings, it is better to have a too-tight armscye that you will cut out after your sleeves are set than having an armscye that is too big and needs to be pieced.

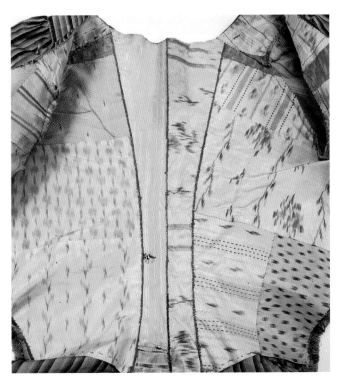

Jacket (Detail), late 18th century, The Metropolitan Museum of Art, New York, 2010.151

Dress (Back Detail), 1775–85, The Metropolitan Museum of Art, New York, 2009.300.1340

PIECING IS PERIOD, PERIOD

In the eighteenth century, fabric was expensive and labor was cheap. It was standard practice for old gowns to be deconstructed and made anew. Economical construction was essential, and it was the goal of early mantua makers to avoid cutting the fabric whenever possible, favoring tucks, pleats and folds to preserve whole widths and lengths. While this cutting style evolves and changes through the eighteenth century, the desire to be as economical as possible with fabric does not.

Almost every original eighteenth-century gown we have studied in museums features piecing, whether it's from remaking, mistakes or fabric conservation. Piecing can be found in every component of an eighteenth-century gown: sleeves, bodices, skirts and even linings. The eighteenth-century mantua maker did not view having to piece as a mistake, but rather as the best way to make the most of the textile and meet the customer's needs. In turn, it does not appear that customers cared if their gowns had been pieced; it was just a normal part of clothing manufacture. So if you end up running short on fabric or make a cutting mistake—it's OK! Just piece in what's missing and appreciate the air of authenticity that piecing lends to your garment.

The first step is to save your fabric scraps. When piecing, try to match the grainline and any nap or directional elements, particularly with shot silks where the warp and weft are two different colors. Try to pattern match if you can, but even Georgian mantua makers sometimes didn't. Pieces can be prick stitched, applique stitched or sewn right sides together.

Throughout the projects in this book, we have had to piece parts of the gowns, whether to extend a sleeve head, lengthen a train, let out a bodice or build enough yardage for a petticoat. Clever piecing can take a "stuck" project to a finished one and adds a twist of Georgian authenticity that makes your gown not only more accurate but unique to you.

CHAPTER ONE

Historic Stitches and How to Sew Them

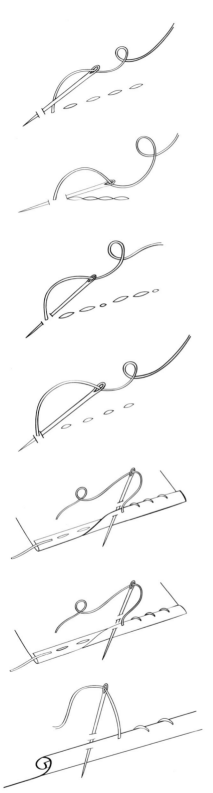

Running Stitch

Working from right to left, weave the needle up and down through all layers. When you're using running stitches for hemming or a seam, make sure that the visible stitch is very fine. Basting stitches should be long and even.

Backstitch

Working right to left, anchor the knot on the wrong side of the fabric, bringing the needle up through all layers. Travel a couple of threads to the right of where your needle came through, push the needle through all the layers, and bring it back up equidistant from the first puncture. Bring the needle to that same thread entry point, pushing down through all layers, traveling equidistant to the left, bring the needle up through and repeat. This is the strongest stitch, ideal for seams.

Running Backstitch

Using the instructions above, combine the running and backstitch. Stitch two or three running stitches and then a backstitch for strength. This stitch is commonly used in skirt and petticoat seams.

Prick Stitch

Working from right to left, anchor the knot on the wrong side of the fabric, and come straight up through all layers. Bring your needle down 1 or 2 threads to the right, making sure the needle goes through all the layers. Bring the needle up equidistant from how far you spaced the stitches from the seam edge. For example, if you're sewing ¼ inch (6 mm) in from the folded edge, space your stitches ¼ inch (6 mm) apart. This careful and visible spaced backstitch is used most often on side seams.

Hem Stitch with Basting

Working left to right, turn up half of the seam allowance on the edge of your fabric and baste with long running stitches. Turn up the remaining seam allowance again to encase the raw edge. To hem stitch, bury your knot between the fold and fabric, bringing the needle out toward you. Travel a little bit to the left and pass the needle through the outer fabric, bringing it back in through the folded layers. The resulting stitch is visible on the outside of the garment, and should be small and fine.

Narrow Hem

Working left to right, turn up a narrow seam allowance (⅛ to ¼ inch [3 to 6 mm]) on the edge of your fabric and baste with long running stitches. Then fold this edge up again in *half* so the finished hem is between ¹⁄₁₆ and ⅛ inch (1 to 3 mm) wide. Hem stitch from right to left in the same technique explained above.

Rolled Hem

Keeping tension with your dominant hand, roll the raw edge back and forth between your fingers until the edge tightly rolls over itself at least twice. Hold the rolled edge between your fingers to keep it in place as you hem stitch it all together. It will take a bit of time before it starts to look small and even. Licking your fingers can help make this process easier.

Edge Stitch / Edge Hem Stitch

This stitch is commonly used to join the fashion fabric and the lining. Before stitching, turn in the seam allowances on both pieces and baste. With the two pieces placed wrong sides together, offset the fashion fabric to be slightly above the lining fabric and pin into place. With the lining side facing you, bury your knot between the two layers with the needle coming out toward you through the lining. Travel a small amount to the left and make a small stitch catching all layers, and bring the needle back toward you. Repeat. This stitch is visible on the outside and should be small.

Applique Stitch

This is performed just like the hem stitch *except* that the travel and catches are in reverse. The small stitch is the one you see, and you will travel on the underside. This is used when you're sewing from the right side of the fabric.

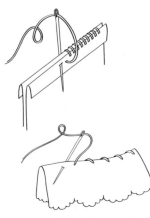

Whipstitch

This stitch is commonly used over an edge, either raw or finished. Place the two pieces of fabric right sides together and pin. Working right to left, work with the needle pointing toward you, passing through all layers. Bring the needle back around to the far layer, passing through the layers with the needle facing you. Repeat.

Whip Gather

Working right to left, whip over the edge of the fabric a determined distance. Then pull the thread gathering up the fabric to the desired length, and knot the thread (but do not cut) before moving on to the next section.

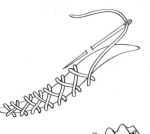

Herringbone Stitch

First, you will work from left to right. Pass your needle through the fabric a couple of threads toward the left. Bring the needle up and then angle it down and to the right. Bring the needle down and travel a couple of threads to the left, bringing the needle back up. Repeat.

Stroked Gathers

This technique is used for your aprons and 1790s ensemble. It consists of three evenly spaced and stitched running stitches that are then gathered up to fit the desired space. The gathers are then carefully stitched with a hem or whipstitch, making sure that you catch every bump in the gathers.

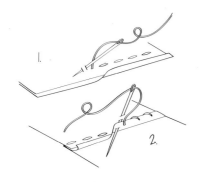

FELLING

This technique cleanly joins two pieces of fabric in an encased seam. With right sides together, offset one edge by ¼ inch (6 mm) and running stitch to join. Open the seam out flat with the seam allowance facing up. Fold up the longer edge of the seam allowance over the shorter raw edge by ¼ inch (6 mm), finger press, then fold over again along the seam line. Running stitch or hem stitch the folded, clean edge down, then press the seam flat.

THE ENGLISH STITCH

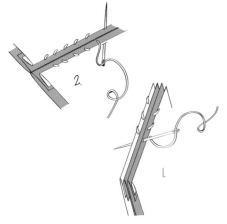

This stitch/seaming technique is probably one of the weirdest things you will come across in this book. However, it is extremely common and useful in eighteenth-century dressmaking, perfect for seaming together the lining and fashion fabric of bodice seams in one stitch instead of two. Though the name of this stitch has previously been shrouded in mystery, Pernilla Rasmussen found evidence of it being known as the "English Stitch" in the 1824 tailoring book by F. Heyder.[1] While there are many places this seaming technique could be useful, it is most represented in original bodices of Italian gowns, but also sometimes makes an appearance in sacques and other extant bodices too.

Working right to left, you will have the two pieces you are seaming with all their edges basted into place facing right side to right side. Make a quick stitch on the lining fabric closest to your person, burying the knot between the fashion fabric and the lining fabric. Then pass the needle through the fashion fabrics and lining to the other side. Bring the needle up and point it back at you, passing through both fashion fabrics and the lining on the side closest to you (see illustration 1). Repeat. Keep your stitches very small and tight here, about 12 stitches per inch (2.5 cm). You should have a neat, finished seam when opened flat (see illustration 2).

MANTUA MAKER'S SEAM

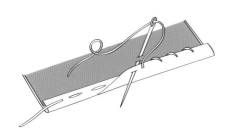

This seaming technique is not as scary as you might think. In fact, it's deceptively easy. It's known as a mantua maker's seam or mantua maker's hemming, and it dominates women's clothing in this time period and even into the nineteenth century. According to *The Workwoman's Guide* from 1838,

> *"This is often used instead of sewing, for bags and sleeves that have no linings, or skirts of petticoats &c., and the work is prepared as follows. Lay the raw edges of one piece a little below that of the other, then turn the upper edge over the lower, twice, as in hemming, and fell it securely down."*[2]

The mantua maker's seam is an ingenious, efficient way to connect and encase raw edges on skirt panels in gowns, and we even use it in our 1790s reticules. Though similar to a modern French seam or felled seam, the mantua maker's seam is fast, easy and period correct.

To work a mantua maker's seam, start with two layers of fabric, right side to right side. Offset the bottom fabric by ⅛ to ¼ inch (3 to 6 mm), depending on how wide you need this seam to be. Fold the bottom fabric up and over the top fabric once and baste into place sewing from right to left. Next, fold the baste edge up once more and hem stitch through all layers. When you're finished, you will open up this seam and have a clean finish on the outside and an encased raw edge on the interior.

CHAPTER TWO

The English Gown, 1740s

Based on Diagram XIV from *Cut of Women's Clothing* by Norah Waugh [1]

The first gown in our book is rooted in one of the most fundamental moments in fashion and women's history. This gown, what we will refer to as the "English gown," is based on the groundbreaking mantua, or manteaux, gown. The mantua allowed women the chance to step out of the shadow of male tailors and create their own trade, ushering in a new era of fashion and dressmaking with the new century.[2]

A more informal style of gown worn by women of all social classes, the mantua came into fashion during the last quarter of the seventeenth century and developed over time into what was called the "night-gown," "gown" and/or "mantua." While this gown may have been called *Robe a l'Anglaise* in French, this term is uncommon in eighteenth-century English and American sources. For the sake of clarity, we will simply call it the English gown.

The gown we re-create in this chapter is representative of the period from 1740 to 1750. The close-fitting pleated back, separate stomacher front, robings cut-in-one and large full sleeves are all style hallmarks of this decade. Over time, this type of gown changes, exhibiting smaller back pleats, a closed front and narrower sleeves, before falling out of fashion in the 1780s.

A Rake's Progress, Plate 4, William Hogarth, June 25, 1735, The Metropolitan Museum of Art, New York, 32.35(31)

Robe à l'Anglaise (Back), 1770–75, Brooklyn Museum Costume Collection at The Metropolitan Museum of Art, 2009.300.648

OUR CHOICES FOR THE ENGLISH GOWN

To achieve the appropriate silhouette of the 1740s, the correct undergarments are essential. Shifts had large full sleeves to fill out and decorate the gown sleeves. Stays were often fully boned, straight and long in the torso. These pieces must come first—we know, you want to jump right into making the dress, but don't skip your underpinnings!

While we do not provide instructions for shifts or stays in this book, you will find in this chapter the instructions for making a basic under-petticoat, a standard underpinning that may be used for all of your other gown projects before the 1790s. It's a good starter project and will serve you well.

For this project, we've chosen to portray a working woman's ensemble and so have styled our gown without a hoop or false rump. However, this very same design made in silk, fitted over hoops (see page 75 for pocket hoops), would create a fashionable aristocratic look.

Finally, this gown is made from a medium-weight blue worsted wool. While wool is a great fiber for women's gowns, all the other historic fibers are open to you: learn about silk (page 73), linen (page 171) and cotton (page 129).

AN ODE TO WOOL

Wool, commonly called "stuff" in the eighteenth century, was arguably the most common fiber type worn by women below a certain social class in the eighteenth century.[6] While spun and woven wools, such as worsteds, were extremely common, there was a huge variety of woven wools and wool blends used for clothing: glazed calamanco, camlet, bombazine, baize, cassimere, linsey-woolsey and more.[7] Here are a few great reasons why we strongly recommend a dress-weight worsted wool for the English, Italian and even the 1790s gowns:

1. Wool isn't actually that hot...unless it needs to be. Wool naturally reacts to the environment to regulate your body temperature. Wool will keep a dry layer close to the skin while still being able to withstand cold, moist climates, and when it's hot, it will wick away your perspiration.[8]

2. Since wool is so good at wicking away moisture, it makes for an antimicrobial, antibacterial fabric. It's hard to make it stinky and gross.[8]

3. Wool is amazing to work with. It doesn't wrinkle or show fitting faults in the same way that silk, linen or cotton does. It's a very forgiving fabric to work with, resulting in a better-looking gown without the heartache of fighting with a slippery silk or wiggly linen.

4. Wool is hard-wearing and durable. This gown will last you a long time, and you'll get your money's worth.

5. Wool doesn't combust into flame—it smolders. If you are working near an open fire, wool is your safest textile choice.

6. A wool gown is easy to dress up or dress down with millinery. Crisp white accessories in cotton or silk will go far in making a "plain ol' wool gown" look very fashionable. Alternatively, the same wool gown paired with a checked apron and printed kerchief does well for common impressions and dirty work.

7. Wearing wool could be very patriotic. Wool fabrics were a cornerstone of English manufacturing, and it was imperative to support one's home industry.[9]

Working with wool isn't without challenges, but it does create amazing textiles that are great to sew with. We especially recommend wool to beginning historical costumers as an excellent choice for that first gown.

1740s Undies
Basic Under-Petticoat

This petticoat is an example of the most basic and common underpinning, second only to the shift. This under-petticoat can and should be worn with the English Gown (page 15), Sacque (page 71) and Italian Gown (page 127). Making it out of a matelassé cotton will help give it extra body and loftiness without the weight. You can also make it out of a sturdy linen, cotton, or wool flannel. This petticoat should be on the shorter side; the hem should be somewhere between below your knee and lower calf.

Under-petticoats don't have to be as full as outer petticoats. The fullness of the petticoat depends on your size. You want enough room for your legs to move freely. A good rule of thumb is to aim for about 100 inches (2.5 meters).

For the under-petticoat, we use just one seam to close the skirt. Depending on your fabric width, you may need to join panels together to achieve the needed hem circumference. Also assess the seaming technique needed according to your fabric edges. If they are selvage edges, carry on with assembly steps 4 through 6; if they are raw cut edges, you will want to use the mantua maker's seam (page 13).

MATERIALS

- 2–3 yards (2–3 m) of cotton matelassé, sturdy linen or wool flannel
- Heavy-weight sewing thread (35/2 linen or #30 silk)
- 1.5–2 yards (1.5–2 m) ¾–1" (1.9–2.5-cm)-wide linen or cotton tape

ASSEMBLY

1. Use a soft tape measure at your natural waist point (usually around your belly button, just below your ribs) and note the number. Measure down the approximate hem length (waist to somewhere below your knee and above lower calf).

2. Cut out the fabric, measuring the length of the waist to calf on the straight of the grain and cutting selvage to selvage.

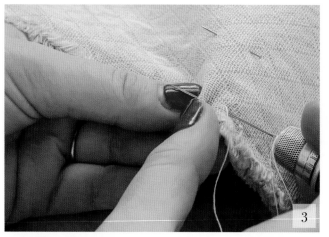

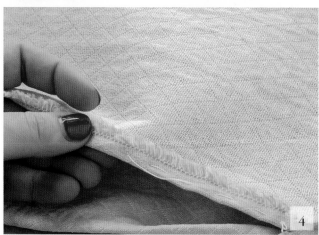

3. Pin one petticoat seam right sides together, leaving 10 inches (25.5 cm) free at the top for the opening. Stitch the seam using a running backstitch for selvage edges or a mantua maker's seam (6 to 8 stitches per inch [2.5 cm]) for raw cut edges (page 13).

4. Baste, then hem the edges of the opening (8 stitches per inch [2.5 cm]).

5. With the petticoat opened out flat, hem at ½-inch (1.2-cm) wide (8 to 10 stitches per inch [2.5 cm]).

6. Find the center of the front panel and mark.

7. Time to pleat. On the front, make one large box pleat at the center front, about 3 to 6 inches (7 to 15 cm) wide and between 1 to 3 inches (2.5 to 7.6 cm) deep. Then knife pleat each side of the front petticoat panel toward the back, checking the circumference against your waist measurement. Pleating was not an exact science in the eighteenth century, and it doesn't need to be today. Just pleat to fit with 1- to 2-inch (2.5- to 5-cm)-wide pleats on the visible side; they can be as deep as needed on the underside. Don't worry if they are not perfect.

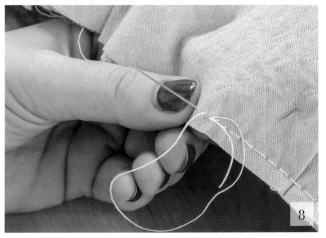

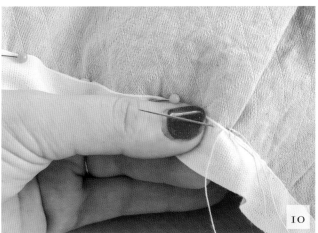

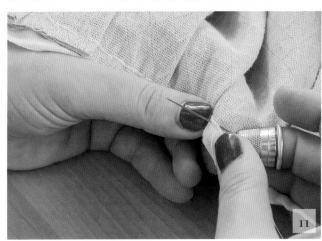

8. Backstitch the pleats down about ¼ to ½ inch (6 mm to 1 cm) from the edge, stitching through all layers to secure (6 to 8 stitches per inch [2.5 cm]).

9. Find the center point of your waist tape, pin to the center front of your petticoat. Then working from the center front around to the back, pin the waist tape halfway over the raw edge of the petticoat, leaving the other half to fold over and bind the edge.

10. Finely hem stitch the waist tape down on the right side of the fabric (10 to 12 stitches per inch [2.5 cm]).

11. Fold the waist tape over the raw edge and finely hem stitch it into place.

12. Once both sides are attached, whip the tape together at both ends to keep it secure.

Done!

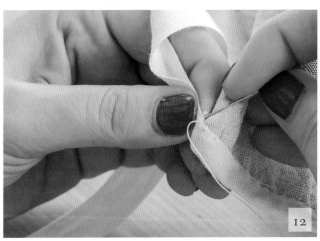

1740s
The English Gown
Petticoat

This petticoat is made to go with the 1740s English gown. Constructed in a typical eighteenth-century way, the petticoat is open at both sides to allow the wearer to reach her pockets and is tied at the front and back. For the portrayal of common dress in this period, neither the petticoat waist nor hem is adjusted over any additional underpinnings such as a false rump or hoop. The length of a petticoat depends on what is fashionable for the period and what the woman will be doing. For example, if the woman will be doing more physical labor, she would want her petticoat hem to be a bit above the ankle to prevent tripping. Finally, plain petticoats like this were worn throughout most of the eighteenth century, so you can wear this same petticoat with a later gown as long as the gown doesn't need to be worn over a hoop or false rump.

MATERIALS

- *2–3 yards (2–3 m) of fabric, enough to have a circumference of 108–120 inches (2.7–3 m) (Note: This example uses 60" (1.5-m)-wide fabric with a panel for the front and one for the back. If you are using narrower fabric, you might need to add extra panels to your petticoat.)*
- *Silk thread (#30 for construction and #50 for hemming)*
- *2.5–4 yards (2.5–4 m) of 1" (2.5-cm)-wide linen or cotton tape*

ASSEMBLY

1. Cut out your petticoat according to your desired length and fullness. For 60-inch (1.5-m)-wide fabric, two panels are required—front and back—for a 120-inch (3-m) hem.

2. With right sides together, selvage-to-selvage, pin one side seam. Leave open 10 inches (25.5 cm) from the top for the pocket slit.

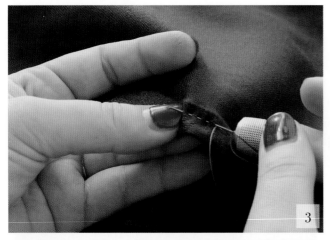

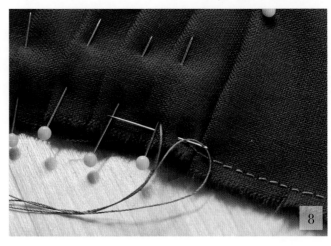

3. For the pocket slit, turn back the edges of the opening and hem stitch. For selvage edges, only turning back once will suffice; for raw edges, turn double to enclose. Press.

4. Starting from the hem, sew the side seam with a running backstitch (6 to 8 stitches per inch [2.5 cm]). Stop at the bottom of the pocket slit. Press open the seam.

5. Each side of the petticoat will be pleated to half the waist measurement. For example, the waistband of our petticoat will be pleated to fit a 28-inch (71-cm) waist. Therefore, the front and back each need to be pleated to 14 inches (35 cm), respectively. The size and depth of the knife pleats will be in part determined by your size and the amount of fabric in the petticoat. There is no need for the pleats to be even—feel your way through, striving for a uniform look on the exterior, but not worrying about the interior measurements of each pleat. Check against your measuring tape regularly and adjust the pleats as needed. This might take a couple of tries, and that's OK. You'll get there.

6. Fold the front panel of the petticoat in half to find the center front. Mark with a pin.

7. Starting 3 inches (7 cm) from the center mark, begin to knife pleat in the direction of the side seams. This will form a box pleat at the center front that is 6 inches (15 cm) wide.

8. Backstitch the pleats in place, close to the edge (6 to 8 stitches per inch [2.5 cm]).

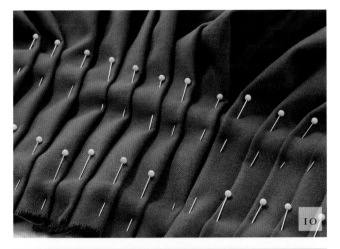

9. Fold the back panel of the petticoat in half to find the center back. Mark with a pin.

10. Begin to pleat toward the center back, forming an inverted box pleat. Continue to knife pleat in the direction of the center back.

11. Backstitch the pleats in place, close to the edge.

12. With right sides together, lay the front and back panels together at the remaining side seam. Pin, leaving open 10 inches (25.5 cm) from the top for the pocket slit.

13. For the pocket slit, turn back the edges of the opening and hem stitch (6 to 8 stitches per inch [2.5 cm]). For selvage edges, only turning back once will suffice; for raw edges, turn double to enclose. Press.

14. Starting from the hem, sew the side seam with a running backstitch. Stop at the bottom of the pocket slit (6 to 8 stitches per inch [2.5 cm]). Press open the seam.

15. Cut two lengths of linen tape approximately double your total waist circumference. Fold each tape in half to mark the center points. Match these center points to the center points of each petticoat panel. Pin along the waist edge with the tape ½ inch (1.2 cm) deep, leaving ½ inch (1.2 cm) free to fold over to the inside later. Applique stitch the edge of the tape in place, making sure to catch all the layers (12 stitches per inch [2.5 cm]).

16. Fold the tape to the inside, pin, and hem stitch in place. Secure with several strong stitches at each side seam. The remaining tape forms the ties.

17. Hem the petticoat either ¼ inch or ½ inch wide (8 to 12 stitches per inch [2.5 cm]).

Done!

1740S
The English Gown
Stomacher

We know you want to jump right into making your English Gown (page 29), but just as with the petticoat, you need one more piece first: the stomacher. In the 1740s, stomachers could be simple or very decorative for higher-class ensembles. A plain self-fabric or hand-embroidered linen design works a treat for a common woman's gown, while metallic lace, embroidery or beribboned stomachers are en vogue for the fashionable lady.

MATERIALS
- *½ yard (0.5 m) of fabric*
- *½ yard (0.5 m) of stiffened linen buckram*
- *Silk thread #30*

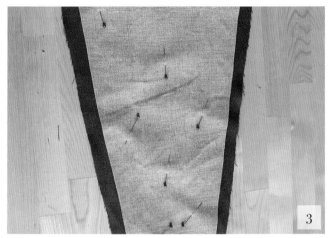

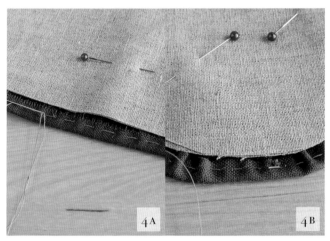

ASSEMBLY

1. Measure the length and width needed for the stomacher, or see pattern on page 30. The length should be from the top edge of the stays to just below the "points" of the bodice front edges. The width should be across the bust and across the waist with additional width added for the gown front edges to overlap. Add ½ to ¾ inch (1.2 to 2 cm) seam allowance.

2. Cut one layer of fashion fabric, one layer of linen and one layer of linen buckram. To make linen buckram, liberally paint medium-weight linen with gum tragacanth and allow to dry in the sun. You'll want to do this outside—gum tragacanth stinks.

3. Cut off the seam allowance of the linen and linen buckram pieces and pin or baste both layers together.

4. Turn up half of the seam allowance on the fashion fabric and baste.

5. Center the linen pieces on the fashion fabric with even seam allowance on all edges. Pin to hold.

6. Work the sides and bottom curve of the stomacher first. Fold in the remaining seam allowance, covering the raw edge of the linen buckram. At the bottom curve, with a loose running stitch, gather and ease the fashion fabric around the bottom. Pin as you go, then hem stitch in place (8 to 10 stitches per inch [2.5 cm]), catching just the linen buckram.

7. Fold over the top edge and hem stitch in place. Be sure to work the stomacher absolutely flat, being careful not to pull or create tension in the fashion fabric in any way.

8. Optional: Stitch a small tab of cotton or linen tape to the sides of the stomacher at the top. This helps with pinning the stomacher to the stays when dressing.

1740S
The English Gown

To begin the English gown, we will demonstrate how to pattern, cut and assemble robings that are all-in-one with the body. This technique produces the double robings seen in 1740s portraits and makes use of a hidden dart to manipulate the straight-cut fabric over the bust and shoulder.

Another unique design in the first half of the eighteenth century was the broad and roomy sleeve. These sleeves were cut straight with a single seam and decorated with pleated cuffs, winged cuffs or ruffled flounces. Sleeves become narrower later on in the eighteenth century, so keep this in mind if you want to make your gown to a later fashion.

Finally, early eighteenth-century cuffs could be large or small, winged or open. With the very broad sleeves on our working woman's gown, we've chosen a large open cuff only slightly bigger than the sleeve itself. Winged cuffs are constructed exactly the same way but with the addition of a tacking stitch at the back of the elbow to close the loop and create the wing.

MATERIALS

- 4–6 yards (4–6 m) of gown fabric
- 2–2.5 yards (2–2.5 m) unbleached linen
- Silk thread (#30 for gathers and topstitching and #50 for hemming)

THE BODICE

We will begin the English gown by constructing the pleated front and back pieces separately, in preparation for later joining the two together. The pleating on this gown is no easy thing, but the results are beautiful and come with a sense of accomplishment.

1740s English Gown Bodice Lining, Stomacher & Sleeve

Use this pattern for the lining pieces upon which to build your pleated-back English Gown.

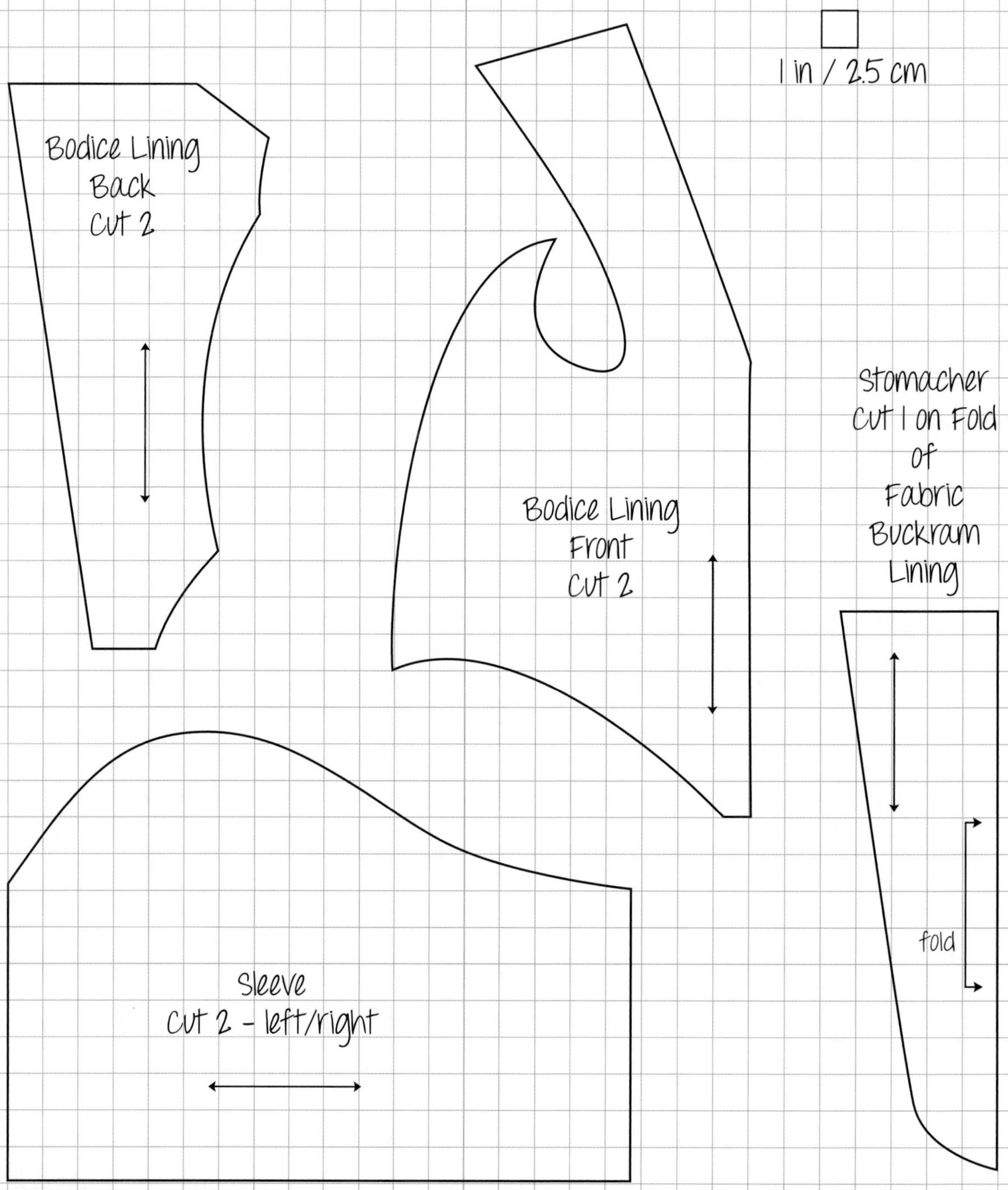

1 in / 2.5 cm

Bodice Lining
Back
Cut 2

Bodice Lining
Front
Cut 2

Stomacher
Cut 1 on Fold
of
Fabric
Buckram
Lining

fold

Sleeve
Cut 2 - left/right

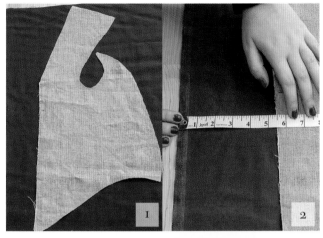

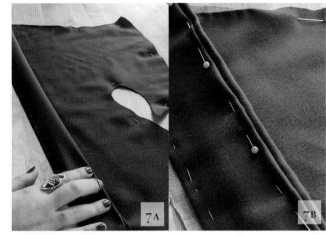

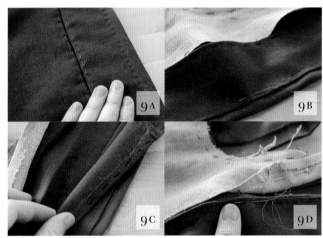

1. Determine the approximate length of the robings by measuring from roughly the shoulder seam on your back over the bust and just past the waist. Add seam allowance at both ends.

2. Place the bodice front lining atop your fashion fabric and 4 to 6 inches (10 to 15 cm) from the straight edge.

3. At the bottom of your robings, draw a perpendicular line from the straight front edge to about the width of your top pleat once pleated.

4. Now trace the waist curve of the bodice lining and extend the line downward toward the center front edge, meeting the straight line from the previous step. A French curve will help place this line.

5. Baste up the seam allowance along the curved waist edge from where the skirts will attach, around the squared bottom and the front edge of the robings.

6. Turn up and narrow hem the curved waist edge from where the skirts will attach, around the squared bottom, and the front edge of the robings just to where the front edge will meet the center point of the bodice lining.

7. Now pleat the robings, keeping the lines on the straight. The top pleat does not need to be deep, but the second/bottom pleat must be the full width, allowing you to reach the front edge of the bodice beneath. This is vital to pinning the gown when dressing.

8. Pin and press the pleats in place. Do not stitch.

9. With the pleated robings folded out flat away from the bodice, prick stitch the robings together along both edges of the top pleat. Space your stitches ¼ inch (6 mm) apart and ¼ inch (6 mm) from the edge. This stitch connects the top pleat to the one below it only—do not stitch the pleats to the bodice!

10. Turn up the seam allowance on the neck edge, front edge and waist edge of the bodice lining and baste.

1740s English Gown Bodice - Robings Cut in One

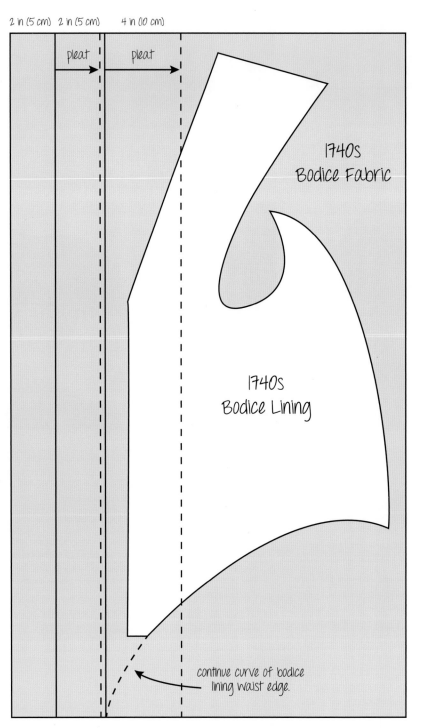

2 in (5 cm)   2 in (5 cm)   4 in (10 cm)

pleat   pleat

1740s
Bodice Fabric

1740s
Bodice Lining

continue curve of bodice
lining waist edge.

Cut the fashion fabric
away from the armscye
and the side back
seam after pleating
the robings.

11

13A | 13B

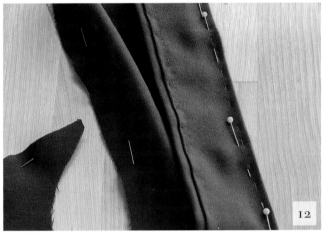

12

14A | 14B

11. Place the lining onto the bodice outer fabric, lining up the front edge of the lining below the bust point with the fold line of the robings and about ¼ inch (6 mm) back. Use a spaced prick stitch along the bodice lining edge, through all layers, securing the bodice lining and outer fabric together and leaving 2 to 3 inches (5 to 8 cm) unhemmed at the shoulder. The robings are now held in place on the outside, but the underside of the pleats is still accessible.

12. Lay the bodice front piece out flat and smooth the outer fabric to the lining. Pin the raw edges of the bodice together at the side seam and armscye. You will see that you have excess fabric in the shoulder area.

13. Pinch up the "wedge" of excess fabric in the shoulder area, folding, finger pressing and pinning as needed toward the front edge and tapering down to a point. If the wedge is too deep, you can cut some of the excess fabric to make it easier and less bulky. The placement of this dart is variable but should be covered by the robings.

14. Applique stitch the dart seam from shoulder down to the point on the fashion fabric only (10 stitches per inch [2.5 cm]). Do not stitch it to the lining.

15. While optional, the interior lacing strips on stomacher-front gowns assist greatly in closing the gown with more than just pins. This lacing keeps the back well-fitted while also allowing ease of dressing. To create your lacing strips, measure from just below your bust to just above your waist. Add seam allowance. Cut a strip of linen this length and about 4 inches (10 cm) wide.

16. Fold in and baste all the raw edges on each strip, then fold each lacing strip in half lengthwise and press.

Spiral Lacing

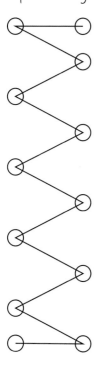

Cross Lacing

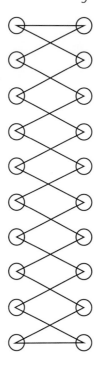

17

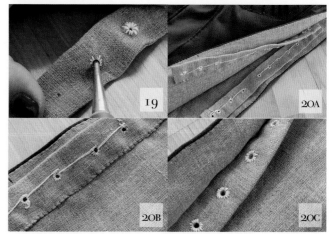

17. Mark the holes for spiral lacing on both pieces about 1 inch (2.5 cm) apart. Make sure you have a right and left side.

18. Pierce the hole with your awl. With heavy linen thread, well waxed and doubled, whipstitch the raw edge of the hole, working around and pulling the thread snug to create your eyelets. Eyelets weren't perfect in the eighteenth century and yours don't have to be either. The sewn threads are merely there to keep the hole open, so don't worry if they're not densely sewn.

19. When you've stitched around the eyelet, poke through the hole with the awl once more to reopen the eyelet.

20. With the lacing strips complete, pin them to the bodice front lining and hem stitch in place, careful to catch only the lining fabric. The placement of the lacing strips needs to be far enough apart when laced securely to allow the edges of the stomacher to tuck in between the lacing strips and the bodice front edges.

21. Now we will pleat the back of the gown bodice. Determine the full length of the back of your gown by measuring from the nape of the neck to the floor over your underpinnings and with your proper shoes on. Cut this length of fabric the full width from selvage to selvage. This begins the back of your gown.

22. Cut the linen bodice lining pieces according to your pattern.

23. Backstitch the center back seam of the lining with your seam allowance (10 to 12 stitches per inch [2.5 cm]). Press open the seam.

24. With the back piece of the gown fabric and your lining both folded lengthwise, place the lining atop the gown fabric, matching the top edge on the straight. The lining will sit at an angle to the fold of the gown fabric. Pin.

25. To help manage the volume of fabric, we will cut away some of the excess before pleating the back. To do this, measure across the back of the lining at the neckline, double it and add 2 inches (5 cm) for safety's sake. Mark with a pin, then measure straight down and mark this line.

26. At the center back waist edge of the lining, measure down 2 inches (5 cm) and mark with a pin. Measure straight out across the fabric to meet the vertical line and mark. Don't cut it yet!

27. Trace the angle of the lining center back seam, then measure up 2 inches (5 cm) from the bottom and mark that too.

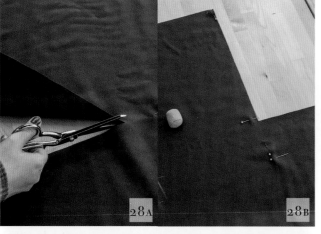

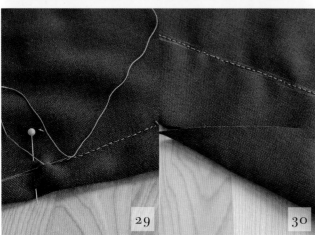

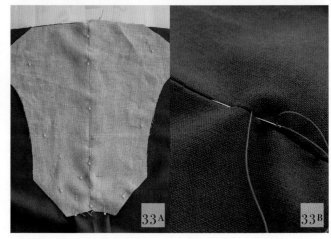

28. Now cut out the excess fabric rectangle measured out earlier. Measure twice, cut once! If you're anywhere near the lining, stop and triple check everything. We used 60-inch (1.5-m)-wide fabric for this gown. If you have narrower fabric, you might not need to cut anything away, but you may need to add extra panels in the skirt later on.

29. Now it's time to get stitching. Backstitch the gown fabric along the angled center back seam line previously marked (10 to 12 stitches per inch [2.5 cm]).

30. Here's the secret sauce: just above the small mark 2 inches (5 cm) above the waist edge of the center back seam (remember that mark?), make an angled cut, stopping about an inch (2.5 cm) above the mark.

31. Cut open the back seam along the fold until you meet the angled cut.

32. Press open the back seam. You can now see how the angled cut plays nice with the open seam. On the outside, a tuck is formed—the beginning of your back pleats.

33. Next, place the lining wrong sides together over the gown fabric, matching the top neck edges and the center back seams. Prick stitch "in the ditch" through both layers of the center back seams, matching the seam lines on both sides (8 to 10 stitches per inch [2.5cm]).

34. Lastly, mark the bottom of the center seam 2 inches (5 cm) up from the bottom of the lining raw edge. Ready to pleat? We bet you are. Let's do it.

35. Pleating the back of an English gown is a fiddly business. Stick with it, though, and your results will be stunning! Determine the width and style of your pleats for your time period and aesthetic look—earlier gowns tend to have wider back pleats while later gowns tend to have narrower back pleats.

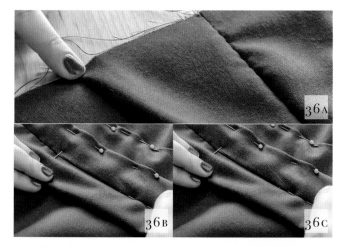

36. Start the pleats at the top, pinching up several inches of fabric to get the depth and width you want. Work the first pleat from the center back seam, pinning as you go.

37. Work the second pleat from the center back. This second pleat can be any distance from the first—we recommend 1 to 1.5 inches (2.5 to 4 cm) or so. Work this pleat from neck to waist, pinning as you go. Nope, we're not going to stitch it down yet.

38. Time to work the pleats on the other side. For the top pleats, to get those two sides of the pleats even, pinch up and fold over the center back seam, matching the opposite pleat. Fold back into position and pin in place. Measure as needed to check your work. Pin, pin, adjust, pin!

39. Now, we know you really want to stitch this down, but before you do, make one last check on the body. Hold up the back piece or pin it in place on the model. Check the proportion, placement of the waist seam and overall effect. Adjust as necessary.

40. Prick stitch the pleats to the lining, about ¼ inch (6 mm) apart and ¼ inch (6 mm) from the edge. About 2 inches (5 cm) from the bottom waist edge of the lining, continue to stitch the pleats through the gown fabric, but not the lining. End your stitching about ½ inch (1.25 cm) below the lining waist edge.

41. If you have a lot of excess fabric on the side seams of the back panel, you can cut this away. Do not cut along the bottom waist edge yet— that comes later!—just cut straight out at a right angle, meeting up with the previous straight cut.

First Fitting and Attaching the Skirts

Next, we will fit the bodice on the body to achieve that perfect, unique fit. With the English gown, the first fitting can be unwieldy, with the back skirt hanging from the stitched bodice back pleats. Be careful with the skirt in this step—you don't want to tear or stretch it.

1. First, following the shape of the lining, cut the fashion fabric with seam allowance at the same angle on both sides. Cut beneath the back pleats just a smidge. Be very careful with how you handle the gown at this point because there is a lot of stress on the fabric now and you don't want to accidentally tear anything.

2. With the model in all of her underpinnings, pin the back of the gown to the stays, lining up the center back seam with the center back of the model and securely pin in place.

3. Pin the stomacher to the stays, lining up the center front of the stomacher with the center front of the model.

4. Roughly pin the bodice fronts on the model, noting the angle of the bodice and where the waist is sitting. You do not want your waist to be too short! It can help to pin the waist to the petticoat so it doesn't ride up in the fitting process.

5. Securely pin the bodice to the stomacher on the edge of or beneath the robings, making sure each side is even.

6. Roughly pin the shoulder strap lining to the back piece. This is not your final shoulder strap fitting. This is just to help keep the bodice in place.

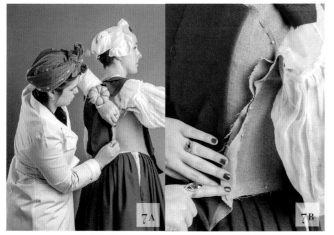

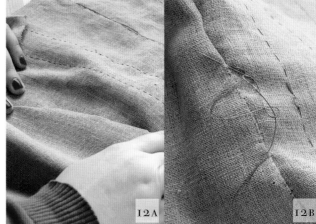

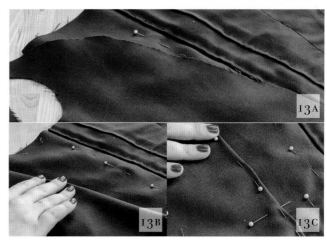

7. Begin fitting the side back seams by pulling and pinching the linen linings of the back and front pieces together and pinning. Keep the lining taut and smooth and even on both sides. Don't trim anything away unless it is absolutely vital, including the armscyes—these will be trimmed away later.

8. If the waist is too low, you will see wrinkles there. Remove any basting and fold the seam allowance up or slice the teeniest tiniest cuts into the seam allowance to release the wrinkles.

9. Continually check throughout the fitting that nothing has gone wonky. It's a good rule of thumb to check your center front, center back and sides as you go. Don't hyper focus on one spot for too long without checking how that fitting is affecting the rest of the gown.

10. Mark/pin/baste the final waist point. If this is different from the basted waist edge of the lining front from step 10 (The Bodice, page 31), remove the basting stitch, fiddle and baste again.

11. When finished, make sure you and your model are both happy with the overall look and fit. Then carefully remove the gown from the model by unpinning the stomacher, fronts and shoulder straps. Leave the side seams and waist pins and markings in place.

12. Lay the gown and bodice out open and flat. Stitch the linings together at the marked, fitted side back seams from the inside using a hem stitch (10 to 12 stitches per inch [2.5 cm]), avoiding the fashion fabric. Press the seams open and trim seam allowance to ¾ to 1 inch (2 to 2.5 cm).

13. Now from the outside, smooth and pin the fashion fabric toward the side back seam, folding under the seam allowance to create the pretty curving side seams seen in originals. You want the side back seams to be flattering and even on both sides. It does not have to match the lining side back seams. One of the easiest ways to match the side back seams is to do one side first, get it exactly how you like it, and then copy it on the other side by doing a point-for-point measure and marking the points with pins, pencil or chalk. Measure one final time after everything is pinned into place to check that your curves are even.

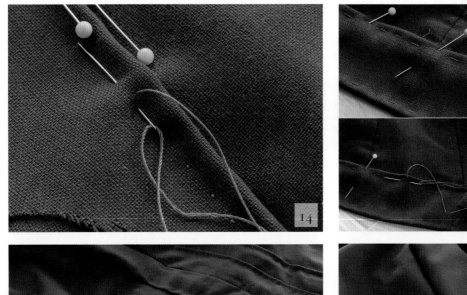

14. Prick stitch the side back seams into place using the same distance/method that was used for the robings and back pleats (page 31).

15. Baste up the fashion fabric waist seam according to your pins or other marking method. Baste up the waist edge of the fashion fabric as best you can beneath the bodice pleats at the back—it may taper to nothing, but be sure this rawness is hidden under the bodice pleats.

16. Original English gowns show a number of treatments for the top of the bodice back. The most common finishing is to bind the edge with a strip of self-fabric, sometimes done before the shoulder straps are set and sometimes afterward. We've chosen to bind first, bypassing the tricky angles and fussy stitching that come with binding the top edge last. To do this, cut a strip of self-fabric on the straight, the length of your bodice top edge, and your desired width doubled. Add seam allowance to the long edges.

17. Apply half the width of the binding to the top edge of the bodice, over the pleats. Prick stitch the binding on the exterior (¼ x ¼ inch [6 x 6 mm]), then fold the remaining width over the edge and to the inside of the bodice. Hem stitch the edge to the lining on the inside (8 stitches per inch [2.5 cm]). Don't worry about finishing the short edges on the ends of the binding—these will be covered by the robings later.

18. Next, we will attach the rest of the gown skirting. Sew the additional side skirt panels to the back of the gown using a mantua maker's seam for raw cut edges or a running back stitch for selvage edges (6 to 8 stitches per inch [2.5 cm]).

19. Leave 10 inches (25.5 cm) from the top of skirts open at that seam for the pocket openings. Turn back and running stitch selvage edges or baste and hem stitch the opening on raw cut edges (6 to 8 stitches per inch [2.5 cm]).

20. Before pleating the skirt, mark the placement of your pocket slits on the waist edge of your bodice. It's usually just a little forward of the center of your underarm. Keep it even on both sides.

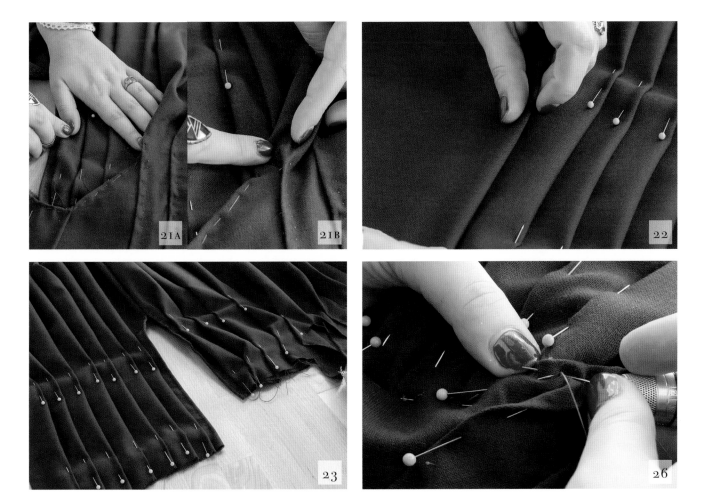

21. Now we're going to knife pleat all this skirt into the bodice. The first couple pleats starting at the center back of the gown are tricky. The bodice pleats flowing from the back into the skirt must overlay the skirt pleats. To do this, scooch the pre-pleated skirt panel toward the center back, under the bodice pleats, to form one hidden knife pleat. Pin.

22. Continue to pleat and pin the side back skirts, working the knife pleats from the center back toward the front. Adjust as needed, then baste.

23. Pleat and pin the skirt front panels, working the knife pleats from the front toward the back, and checking the length against the bodice waist measurement the skirt needs to fit into. Adjust as needed, then baste. The size and number of pleats are dependent on how much fabric you have, your waist size and your target time period: larger pleats for earlier; smaller pleats for later. We cannot give you a formula for pleating your Georgian gown. You just need to embrace your inner eighteenth-century mantua-maker. Make it work. Make them pretty,

but don't waste your time with math and perfection. If one side has an extra pleat in it, that's fine—originals did too—and nobody will be counting them.

24. Pull back the lining from the waist edge on the inside and pin out of the way.

25. Working flat from the outside, lap the basted bodice waist edge over the pleats of the side back skirt and pin. Check that nothing is pulling or rumpled, especially where the bodice back pleats transition into the skirt pleats. All should lie smooth and flat.

26. From the outside, prick stitch the pleats to the waist edge through all fashion fabric layers, catching each pleat as you go. Aim for a ⅛-inch (3-mm) square prick stitch and don't fuss too much trying to get it perfect. Stitch from the back pleats to the pocket slit mark. Leave the pleated front skirts free at this point.

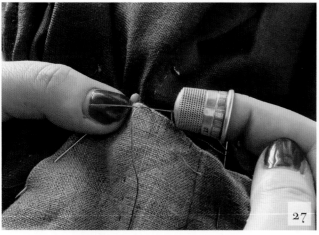

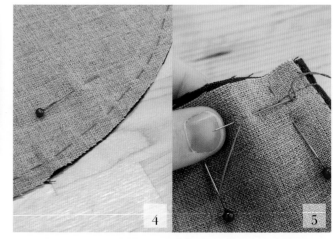

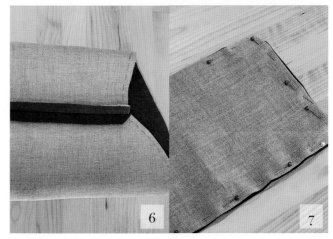

27. Flip the gown to the inside and unpin the lining. Working flat, smooth the lining, fold under the seam allowance on the raw waist edge at the back half of the bodice, and hem stitch over the pleats (8 to 10 stitches per inch [2.5 cm]). Don't worry about catching all the layers—the pleats are now secured on both the exterior and interior.

SLEEVES AND CUFFS

During the great span of years the English gown was in fashion, various cuff treatments came in and out of style. Early English gowns had large open cuffs while winged cuffs and ruffled sleeve flounces (page 119) came into style later. We've chosen large pleated cuffs to pair with the broad, early-style sleeves. Winged cuffs are made with the same method in varying sizes and flares.

1. Cut out the lining and the fashion fabric for both sleeves, making sure you have a left sleeve and a right sleeve. It helps to work both sleeves together to make sure you have a left and right.

2. Baste up the fashion fabric seam allowance on the cuff edge of the sleeve.

3. Place the lining on the fashion fabric wrong sides together. Fold the lining seam allowance in to sit just below the fashion fabric, and edge hem stitch (6 to 8 stitches per inch [2.5 cm]). It's okay if the stitch is visible from the outside.

4. Baste the sleeve head lining and fashion fabric together to help with fitting later.

5. Fold the sleeve in half, matching the raw edges, and pin all four layers together. Backstitch together (6 to 8 stitches per inch [2.5 cm]).

6. Press the seam allowance open or to one side.

7. Now we will construct the cuffs. Fold and baste up all four sides of the fashion fabric cuff.

8. Place the cuff lining on the fashion fabric, wrong side together. Pin through the middle to hold the lining in place, then turn each edge of the lining to sit slightly inside the outer fabric edge, pin and hem stitch around all four sides (8 stitches per inch [2.5 cm]).

1740s Pleated Cuffs

Double check the long edge of your cuffs against the width of your sleeves. The cuff must be longer than the sleeve is wide to make open-backed or winged cuffs

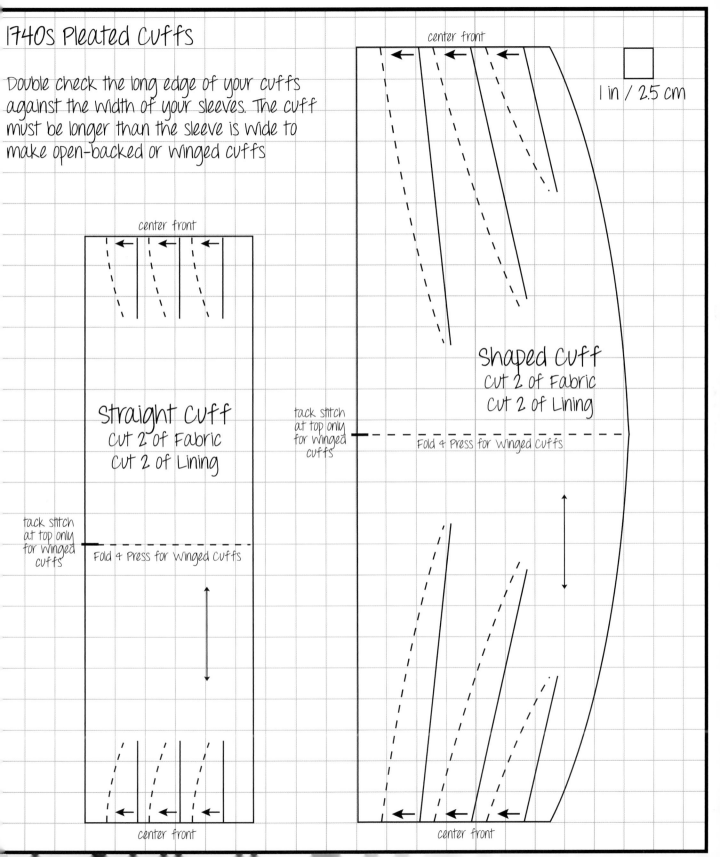

center front

1 in / 2.5 cm

Straight Cuff
Cut 2 of Fabric
Cut 2 of Lining

center front

tack stitch at top only for winged cuffs

Fold & Press for Winged Cuffs

Shaped Cuff
Cut 2 of Fabric
Cut 2 of Lining

tack stitch at top only for winged cuffs

Fold & Press for Winged Cuffs

center front

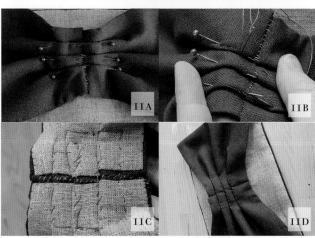

9. With the lining and outer fabric attached, mark the pleats on the outside with chalk or washable/removable ink.

10. Fold the cuff in half, right sides together, matching the short edges, and whipstitch together (8 to 10 stitches per inch [2.5 cm]).

11. From the outside of the cuff, pleat upward three times according to your marks. Be sure to line up the vertical seam. Pin into position and tack each pleat down with small prick stitches (5 to 6 stitches per inch [2.5 cm]) to secure the pleats for at least 1 inch (2.5 cm) on each side of the center seam.

Second Fitting and Finishing Up

The eighteenth-century method for setting sleeves differed greatly from today's techniques. Sleeves were set on the body, working from the outside, to achieve comfort and mobility. This method is used through all the projects in this book.

1. Put the gown on over all underpinnings and with your proper shoes on. At this point you can use the lacing strips to close the gown, keeping the back well-fitted. Place the stomacher over the lacing strip, then pin the gown to the stomacher, placing the pins beneath the robings.

2. Pull the lining of the shoulder strap very snugly over the model's shoulder. Pinch the raw edges of the strap and back shoulder seam together, pin, then allow to lie flat, with the seam allowance facing upward. Balance is important, but nothing is worse than poorly fitted shoulder straps that fall off. They need to be tight! Depending on the shape of your shoulders, your straps may need to be set narrowly or broadly in the back. Adjust as needed until the straps are secure and the front and back bodice pieces do not gape along the neckline.

3. Repeat for the other shoulder strap, matching the angles as best you can. Almost everyone has a shoulder they hold up higher than the other—that's normal, but try to make the shoulder straps appear even from the outside. Don't worry about the seam allowance being even on the interior—fit and outward appearance is most important.

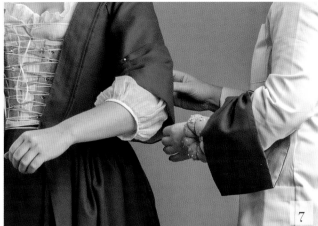

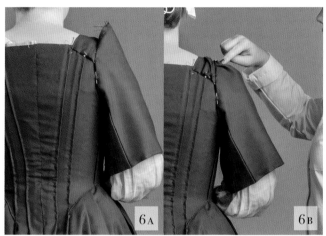

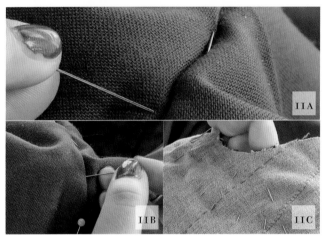

4. Pull the first sleeve onto the model's arm, roughly pinning the sleeve seam and shoulder point. Many eighteenth-century sleeve seams usually sit somewhere between the true underarm and almost visible back of the arm.

5. Working from roughly where your armpit starts in front, fit the underside of the sleeve, folding up the seam allowance and carefully pinning into place.

6. With the underarm pinned, work the top of the sleeve, tucking and pleating at the top of the shoulder and working toward the back to make the extra volume of the sleeve head fit. Turn the seam allowance under and pin as you go. Earlier gowns are commonly fit over the shoulder straps but under the robings, with the seam allowance turned under, but raw edges may also be left, to be covered later by the robings.

7. With both sleeves set, pull the cuffs over the sleeves and pin into position all around the top of the cuff. When you reach the back of the arm, you will have extra length in the cuff versus the circumference of the sleeve. For open cuffs, like ours, just leave this extra bit to "float." For winged cuffs, pinch the excess at the top just where the cuff meets the sleeve and pin.

8. Next, we will fit the skirt panels. We have found it easiest to fit the front skirt panels of most gowns on the body, over all underpinnings and with your proper shoes on. Tuck the prepleated and basted skirt front panel between the outer fabric and the lining of the bodice front. Adjust the length and angle as needed until the skirt pleats fall gracefully over the petticoat with no twisting, collapsing or buckling. Pin.

9. Mark the skirt hem length, then carefully remove the gown from the model.

10. Inside the bodice, where the shoulder strap attaches to the back of the bodice, carefully stitch down the strap to the lining of the gown using small hemming stitches.

11. Now it's time for the magical armscye pinning trick. To make it easier to backstitch the underarm of the sleeves, the pins are adjusted to go into the armscye. Pin the entire underarm this way from where it starts at the front crease to where the shoulder strap will begin in the back of the gown.

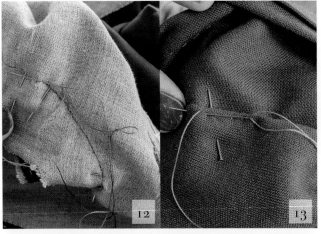

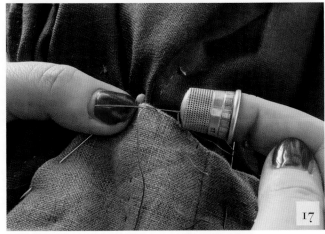

12. After perfecting your pinning, draw a pencil line to show the curve of the armscye, matching both sides. Tightly backstitch along this line (12 to 14 stitches per inch [2.5 cm]).

13. Moving on to the top of the sleeve, prick stitch the sleeve (⅛ x ⅛ inch [3 x 3 mm]) into place through all layers, over the top of the shoulder strap. The top of the sleeve will be covered by the robing.

14. On the inside, cut out the excess fabric in the armscye, leaving about ¼ to ½ inch (6.3 to 12.7 mm) raw seam allowance.

15. On the cuffs, do a spaced prick stitch around just the top edge. Allow any excess to "fly" at the back. For winged cuffs, make a few stitches at just the top where you pinned the cuff in back.

16. Next lay the shoulder strap over top of the binding in back, turn the raw edges under, and make sure that the angles and match points are the same on both sides of the gown. Prick stitch into place (⅛ x ⅛ inch [3 x 3 mm]). This can be tricky, especially if your shoulders are uneven. Power through! You can do it!

17. Hem stitch closed any remaining opening along the neckline (8 to 10 stitches per inch [2.5 cm]).

18. At the waist edge, turn back the lining and pin to keep it out of the way. Then prick stitch the bodice and skirt together catching in each pleat through all layers (⅛ x ⅛ inch [3 x 3 mm]).

19. Release the bodice lining. Smooth toward the waist edge, then turn under the seam allowance and hem stitch over the skirt front pleats (8 to 10 stitches per inch [2.5 cm]).

20. Finally, hem your gown. The size of the hem should be between ¼ (6 mm) and ½ inch (1.3 cm) wide (8 to 10 stitches per inch [2.5 cm]). No more or it starts to look too modern. Your hem may be longer in back, angled up at the front, or even all the way around, depending on your figure, underpinnings and stylistic preferences.

Congratulations! You did it! The English gown is done!

1740S
Neck Handkerchief

Neck handkerchiefs in the 1740s were large and full. They could be squares folded in half or triangular with slits or shaping on the long edge. Some kerchiefs were trimmed with lace while others were simple and plain. This kerchief has some shaping in the neck, and is in possession of longer "tails" to fill out the stomacher section of the 1740s gown. This project is another great practice piece for fine hemming, and you can also make it out of fancier fabric to make it a more fashionable piece.

MATERIALS
- *1 yard (1 m) of lightweight linen*
- *Linen (60/2) or cotton thread*

1740s Neck Handkerchief

Neck Handkerchiefs in the 1740s were quite large, often worn tucked into bands on the gown stomacher.
The slit at the neck will help the kerchief fold around the neck and lay smoothly.

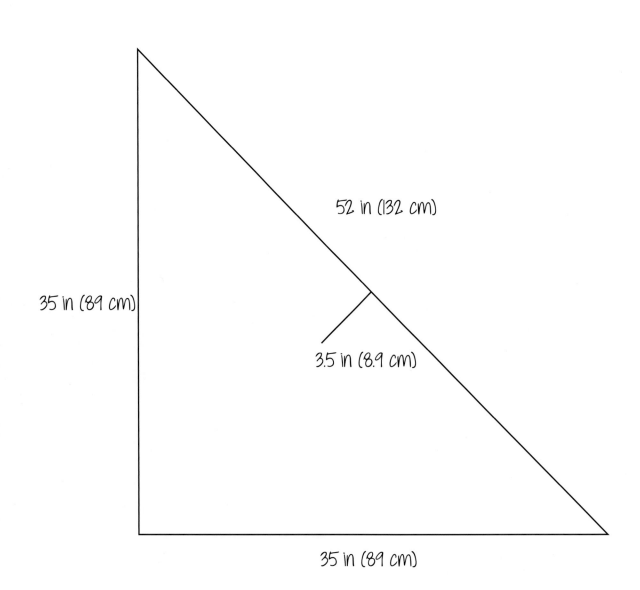

52 in (132 cm)

35 in (89 cm)

3.5 in (8.9 cm)

35 in (89 cm)

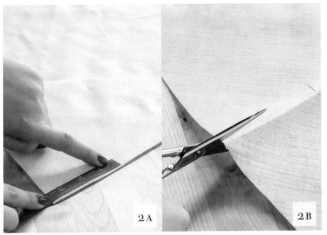

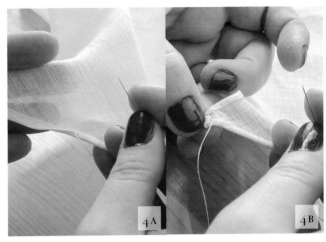

ASSEMBLY

1. Iron and starch the kerchief piece. Fold it in half, matching corners, and press again. Open and lay flat.

2. From the long edge, measure down into the body of the neck handkerchief 3.5 inches (8.9 cm) along the center crease and mark with a pin. Cut open along this line to the pin.

3. Turn up ¼ inch (6 mm) on all edges, including the slit and baste. The point where the neck slit ends and the neck handkerchief body starts will not baste back. Leave it free for now.

4. Turn up all edges again, folding the ¼ inch (6 mm) basted edge in half to create a ⅛-inch (3-mm)-wide narrow hem. Hem stitch (12 to 16 stitches per inch [2.5 cm]).

5. At the raw end point of the slit, closely whipstitch over the raw edge to finish.

1740s
Apron

Made out of a plain woven white linen, this project is excellent practice for your fine hemming and stroke gathers. We've shaped the top of the apron with a dip, which accommodates the robings and presents that nice tidy appearance when worn. As with all the accessories, you can dress it up or down with your fabric choices.

MATERIALS

- *1 yard (1 m) Irish linen, cotton or silk organza*
- *Linen (60/2) or cotton thread*
- *2.5 yards (2.5 m) ½–1" (1.3–2.5-cm) wide linen or cotton tape*

ASSEMBLY

1. Cut out the body of the apron according to the cutting diagram (page 52).

2. Baste and hem stitch three sides of the apron, leaving the waist edge raw (12 to 14 stitches per inch [2.5 cm]).

3. Starting from the outside edge, running stitch to the center of the apron, spacing your running stitches about ¼ inch (6 mm) apart. Continue with two additional rows of running stitches about ⅛ inch (3 mm) below this first row, following the spacing.

1740s Apron

Aprons in the 1740s were made to be tucked under the gown robings. To keep the hem straight, the waist was cut with a dip and the apron worn loosely around the waist.

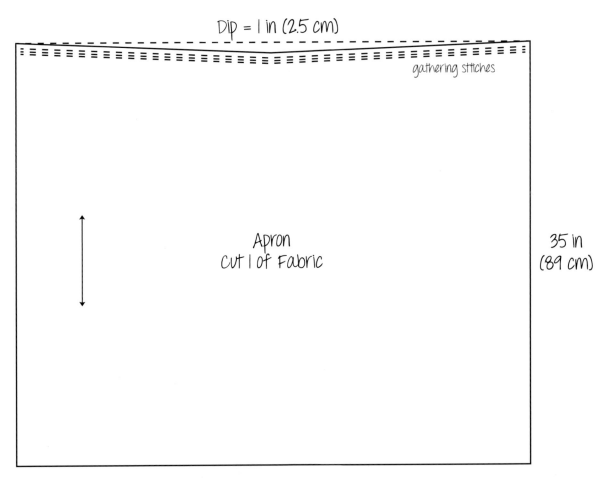

Dip = 1 in (2.5 cm)

gathering stitches

Apron
Cut 1 of Fabric

35 in
(89 cm)

48 in (122 cm)

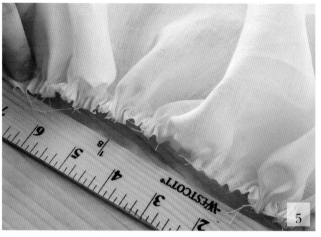

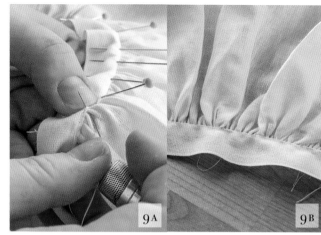

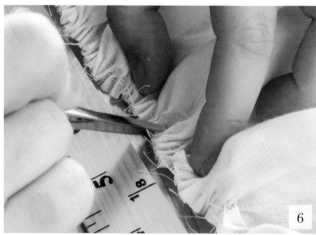

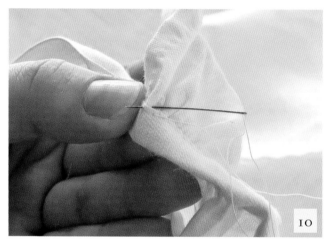

4. Repeat step three, this time starting from the center and stitching toward the outside edge.

5. With the three ends of the thread held together, draw up the running stitches to the needed width, approximately a quarter of your waist measurement. Anchor the threads by wrapping them in a figure eight around a pin. Repeat for the second half.

6. Keep the gathers even. "Stroke" each bump of the gathers with the point of your scissors, or a similar tool, to space each gather evenly. Work one side of the apron, then the other. To help control the fullness, shoot a little steam from the iron onto the gathers and tap with your fingers.

7. Cut the waist tape approximately double your waist circumference plus enough to tie a bow. Fold this length in half and mark the center with a pin.

8. Matching the center of the apron top to the center of the waist tape, lay the edge of the waist tape over the waist edge of the apron approximately half the width of the tape. Pin. Leave the other half of the waist tape to fold over.

9. Hem stitch the edge of the waist tape to the apron, catching every "bump" of the gathers.

10. On the inside, fold the remaining waist tape over the raw edge and hem stitch to the apron, again catching every bump of the gathers.

Done!

1740S
Cap

This cute little cap is based on fashion prints from the 1740s.[10] We consider it a "Lappet Cap Lite" as it has tiny lappet-like shapes at the side of the face but does not tie under the chin. The mini-lappets can also be pinned up out of the way, which was common during the 1740s–1750s. We've opted to make the cap out of a plain white linen to match our other working-class millinery, but this pattern can easily be made in cotton organdy or silk gauze for a more fashionable look.

MATERIALS
- *½–1 yard (0.5–1 m) Irish linen, cotton organdy or silk organza*
- *Linen thread (60/2 & 35/2)*
- *20" (51 cm) of ¼" (6-mm)-wide fine cotton tape or candlewicking*
- *1+ yard (1+ m) of 1" (2.5-cm)-wide silk ribbon for decoration*

1749 Cap

Ruffle for Cap

Self-fabric Ruffle:
Cut a strip of self fabric 49.5 in (125.7 cm) long
1.75 in (4.5 cm) – 2 in (5 cm) wide when hemmed

Your cap may also be trimmed
in a lace ruffle of about
the same length and width.

1 in / 2.5 cm

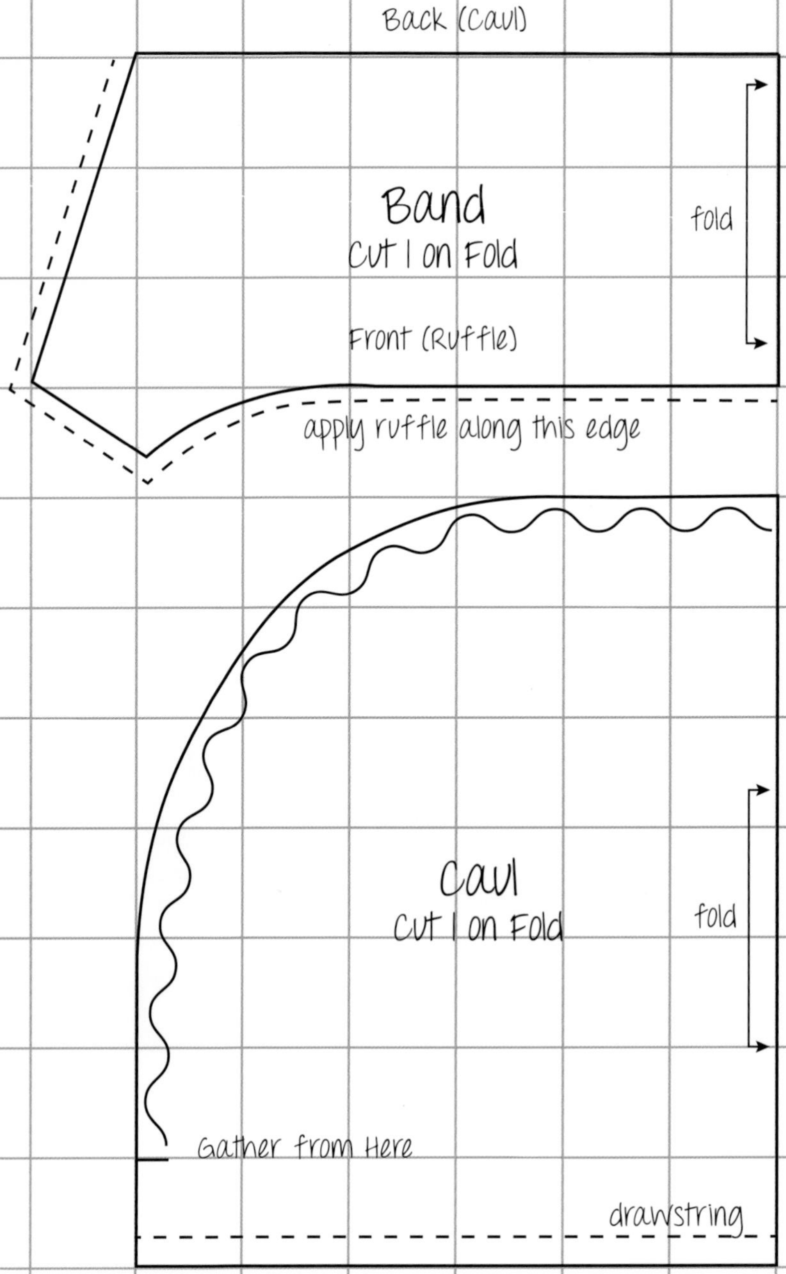

Back (Caul)

Band
Cut 1 on Fold

fold

Front (Ruffle)

apply ruffle along this edge

Caul
Cut 1 on Fold

fold

Gather from Here

drawstring

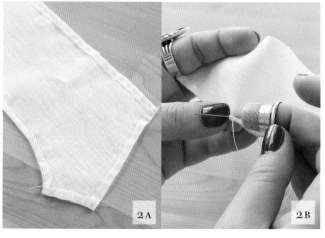

2 A 2 B

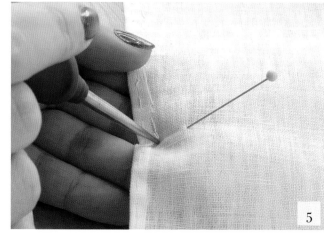

5

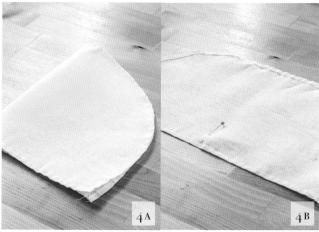

4 A 4 B

6

ASSEMBLY

1. Lightly starch and iron the pieces. This helps avoid the wibbly-wobbly of linen.

2. Turn up ¼ inch (6 mm) on all sides of the band and ruffle of the cap and baste. Fold this ¼ inch (6 mm) in half again to create a ⅛-inch (3-mm)-wide narrow hem. Hem stitch (12 to 16 stitches per inch [2.5 cm]).

3. Turn up ¼ inch (6 mm) on the edges of the caul and baste.

4. Fold the caul piece in half to find the center back. Mark with a pin.

5. Using an awl, work a hole at the center of the bottom edge of the caul just above the basting.

6. Use waxed linen thread, doubled, to overcast the edges of the hole. When complete, poke with the awl again to open and shape the eyelet.

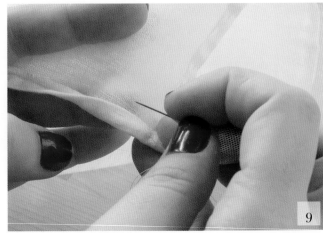

7. Atop the turned and basted edge, secure the tape to the base of the caul piece on each end using a few strong backstitches.

8. Pull the excess tape through the eyelet, using an awl or pin to push the tape through. Cut the tape at the center.

9. Fold up the straight bottom edge of the caul piece over the tape. Finely hem, making sure not to catch the tape in the stitches.

10. Fine hem the remaining basted edges of the caul (see step 2).

11. With a pin, mark where the gathering should start on each side of the caul of the cap so that it will fit into the band. This is about 1 to 1.5 inches (2.5 to 3.8 cm) up on each side.

12. Fold the caul in half to find the top center point and mark with a pin.

13. Fold the band in half to find the top center point and mark with a pin.

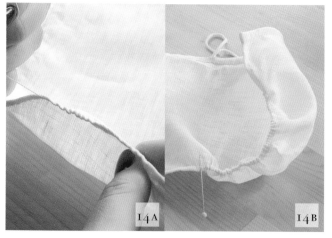

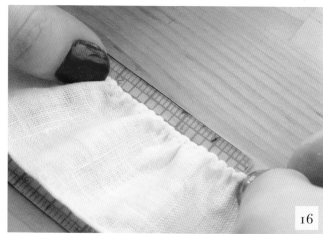

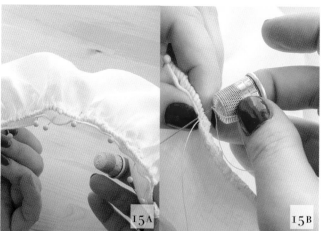

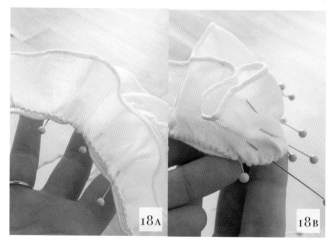

14. Using a heavier thread, loosely whip over the curved hemmed edge of the caul from one side to the center point, about 4 to 6 stitches per inch (2.5 cm). Pull up this thread to gather half of the caul to approximately half the length of the band and tie off. Repeat step 14 for the other side of the caul.

15. Pin the caul to the band with right sides together, matching the center marks. Whip stitch the two pieces together, catching every bump of the gathers. When complete, open out the seam, press and pull flat with your fingers.

16. The ruffle is approximately 1.5 times the length of the band. The ruffle is not as tightly gathered as the caul. Start the gathering by loosely whipping over one long edge of ruffle, stopping 3 inches (8 cm) in. Pull the gathering thread up to reduce this 3-inch (8-cm) section to 2 inches (6 cm), then tack stitch the end to secure the gathered section. Do not cut the thread.

17. Continue along the length of the band in 3-inch (8-cm) sections, each time whipping 3 inches (8 cm), gathering to 2 inches (5 cm), then tack stitching before continuing.

18. With right sides together, pin the ruffle to the band. Whip stitch the edges together, being sure to catch every bump of the gathers then tie off. Open out the seam, finger press and pull to set the stitching.

19. Iron the seams so everything lays smoothly and restarch as needed.

20. Add the silk ribbon as decoration.

1740S
Mitts

Mitts were a good way to keep your forearms warm in the eighteenth century. They could be fancy or plain and unlike gloves, were open on the ends. These mitts are a simple design made from lightweight wool, cut on the bias to provide stretch and fit to the intended wearer's arms.

MATERIALS
- *½–1 yard (0.5–1 m) worsted wool*
- *Silk thread #30*
- *Small scrap in complementary silk taffeta*

18th Century Mitts

Measuring for the Thumb

Length - Length of your thumb
Width - Circumference of the base of your thumb.

The thumb piece needs to be larger than the thumb hole.

Find where your thumb sits in proximity to your wrist and knuckles. Draw the shape at the fold point.

Be sure to include the "dip" in the circular shape — this is important!

Measuring for the Mitts

Knuckles circumference halved
Wrist circumference halved
Forearm circumference halved

Lengths
A to B - Finger knuckle to Hand Knuckle
B to C - Hand knuckle to Wrist
C to D - Wrist to Inner Elbow

Mark the fold line first (circumferences halved), then plot the top side and underside points.
"Connect the dots" to create the shape.

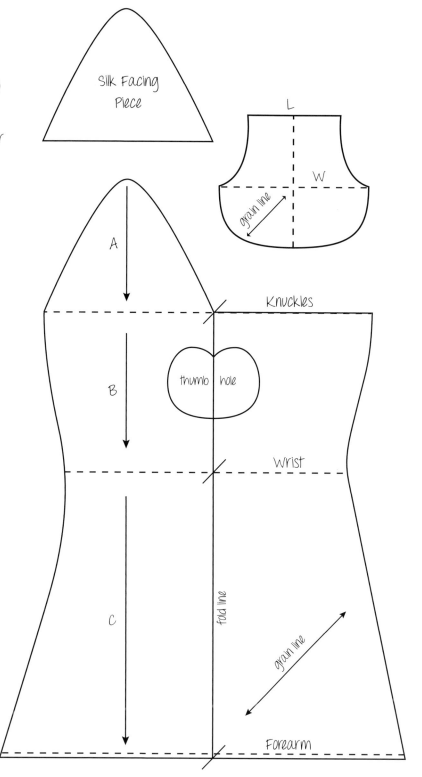

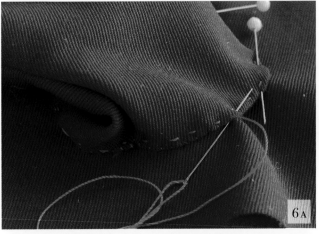

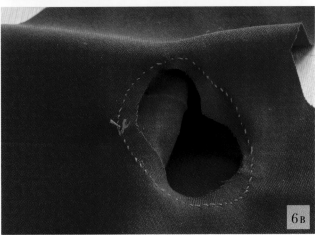

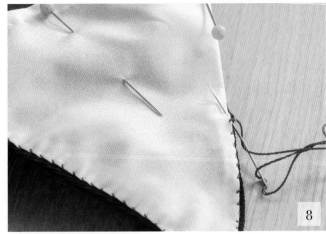

ASSEMBLY

1. Hem the bottom edge of the silk facing piece (6 to 8 stitches per inch [2.5 cm]). Set aside.

2. Cut the thumb hole with seam allowance in the body piece of the mitts. Set aside.

3. Hem the top edge of the thumb piece (6 to 8 stitches per inch [2.5 cm]).

4. Stitch the seam of the thumb piece using a backstitch (8 to 10 stitches per inch [2.5 cm]).

5. Turn up the seam allowance on the base of the thumb piece and baste.

6. Pin the base of the thumb piece around the hole in the body of the mitts on the right side. This is a topical application and will be stitched from the outside. Match the seam of the thumb piece to the peak of the thumb hole. Applique stitch the thumb piece to the body of the mitts from the outside (10 stitches per inch [2.5 cm]). Keep your stitches small and neat.

7. With the thumb piece applied but the body of the mitts still flat, turn under and baste half of the seam allowance along the top edge of the mitts.

8. With wrong sides together, match the point of the mitts and the point of the facing piece. Turn under the seam allowance of the facing piece to match the basted edge of the mitts, and hem stitch in place (8 to 10 stitches per inch [2.5 cm]). Leave the previously hemmed bottom edge of the mitts free.

9. Turn and hem stitch the remaining, unfaced top edge of the mitts (the underside of the hand).

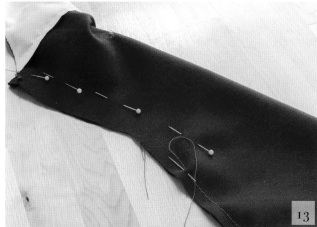

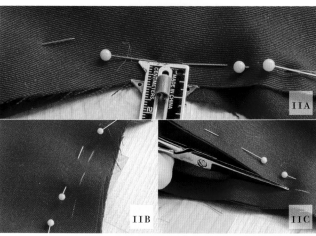

10. Now we will have a mitt-fit. With wrong sides together, match the side seams of the body of the mitts and pin lengthwise. Then with the mitts on the model right-side-out and the seam allowance on the outside, adjust the pins along the seam until the fit is smooth and closely fitted. Avoid making the mitts too tight, especially around the wrist. Test your pinning by taking the mitts on and off, adjusting anywhere that may be too tight or too loose.

11. Remove the mitts, lay flat, and mark ¼ inch (6 mm) seam allowance out from the pin marks. Cut off the excess.

12. Unpin and turn the mitts inside out, matching the seams right-sides together.

13. Backstitch along the seam line (10 to 12 stitches per inch [2.5 cm]), leaving the ¼ inch (6 mm) seam allowance. Press the seam open.

14. Hem the elbow edge of the mitts ¼ inch (6 mm) (8 to 10 stitches per inch [2.5 cm]).

1740S
Simple Straw Hat

The ever-popular straw hat was a staple of Georgian dress throughout the entire century. A simple straw hat, like the one we're demonstrating here, is a great example of a working-class piece. However, there are many ways to skin a hat! Just a quick look at period images will show you myriad design options. Be creative and have fun!

MATERIALS

- *1 straw hat blank—a fine straw with a shallow crown, approximately 15" (38 cm) in diameter, natural or black*
- *3–4 yards (3–4 m) of silk ribbon, 1–2" (2.5–5 cm) wide*
- *Silk thread (#30)*

ASSEMBLY

1. Measure a length of ribbon long enough to carry over the top of the hat, down the sides, and tie under the chin (about 60 inches [1.5 m]). Fold this ribbon in half to find the center point, and pin it to the center top of the crown.

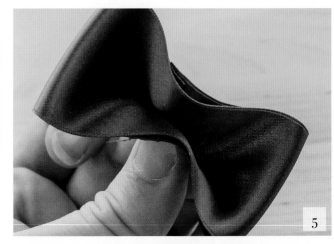

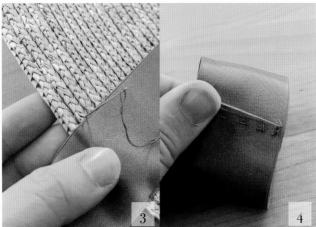

2. Smooth the ribbon down the sides of the crown and stitch in place on each side.

3. Smooth the ribbon along the brim to the edges and finely tack stitch each side of the ribbon.

4. To make the bows, cut two short lengths of ribbon, approximately 6-inches (15-cm) long. Lap the ends of the ribbon to make a loop. Stitch to hold.

5. With the join at the back, pinch the bow in the middle. Pass a few stitches through the back of the pinched portion to hold in place, then press the bow flat with the iron. Repeat for the second bow.

6. Place the two bows atop one another at right angles to form the rosette. Stitch through all layers to secure the bows together.

7. Stitch the finished rosette to the hat at the base of the crown. Repeat for the opposite side.

Done!

How to Get Dressed
and Wear Your English Gown

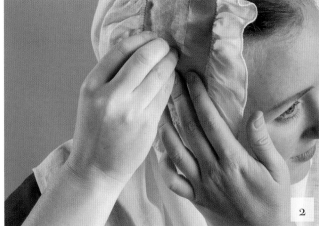

ASSEMBLY

1. Start with your shift, stockings and shoes on. Put on your under-petticoat and tie it around your waist. Next come the stays, laced on over the under-petticoat. If you have a pocket, tie it on. Hook the bow under one of your stay tabs.

2. Put on your cap and pin into place with two straight pins on either side.

3. Next is the petticoat. Put the petticoat on over your head, then tie the back tapes to the front of the body with the bow off to one side. Then tie the front of the petticoat to the back of the body.

4. Put on your gown and lace up the hidden lacing strips to secure the gown to your body. Pull your shift sleeves down and out so they are visible at your elbow.

5. Pin your stomacher over the top of your gown laces but beneath the front edges and robings of the gown itself.

6. Pin two lovely pieces of ribbon to each side of the gown front edges, just below the top of the stomacher. These ribbons may also be stitched to the gown permanently.

7. Tie the ribbons together in a bow at the center front of your stomacher.

8. Now pin the gown closed with strong straight pins. Pin underneath the robings, through the hidden front edges of the gown and to the stomacher. The pinning doesn't have to be perfect, just secure. Pin all the way down to the waist on both sides. If needed, pin the top of the robings in place at the waist edge to keep them smooth and secure.

9. Tie on your apron by hooking the front "dip" under the robings and allowing this area to be a little loose. Cross the apron ties in back and bring back around to the front, tying in a bow and hooking it under the robings and stomacher.

10. Put the kerchief on with the long edge around the back of your neck and tuck the tails through the ribbon at the top of your stomacher.

11. Lastly, for outdoor activities, tie and pin the hat over your cap. For the 1740s, the hat ties may be worn either at the back of the head or under the chin. We recommend tying to the back of the head; under the chin can look unintentionally dorky.

12. And if it happens to be cold that day, pull on your mitts. These take a little tugging if the fit is right, so don't despair should they feel too small at first—the bias cut allows them to stretch.

Now you're ready for the market!

CHAPTER THREE

The Sacque Gown 1760s-1770s

INSPIRED BY FRANCIS COTES'S *A PORTRAIT OF A LADY*, 1768 & *PATTERNS OF FASHION*, PG 25.[1,2]

Often when new costumers think of their 1700s "dream dress," they immediately envision the robe a la française, or what was contemporarily known in English as the sacque gown.

The stacked box pleats falling from the shoulders to the floor create some of the most elegant lines in the history of women's fashion. The beautiful silhouette and peculiar construction of the sacque gown does make it tricky, even for the skilled costumer, but we hope to bring clarity to the quirks of this beautiful style.

Our sacque gown comes from the late 1760s, and while it is not extreme in its proportions, we aren't skimping on the ruffles. Oh, there will be ruffles!

The most popular fiber for the sacque is silk: silk taffeta, silk damask or silk satin. Pretty, expensive printed cottons were used too, as well as the occasional embroidered linen.

This design also lends itself to the short form, known as the short sacque or *pet en l'air*. It's all in the name—the short sacque is cut jacket-length, longer earlier in the century and shorter later on. Now, if you know French or you're a wiz at Google Translate, then you'll know that *pet en l'air* means "fart in the air." This saucy name is indeed historically accurate! As it turns out, Madame Pompadour invented this style of short dress, and on the first day she debuted the outfit, one of her maids "gave vent to some confined air." Apparently Madame Pompadour thought this was *hilarious* and decided to name her new outfit after this happy little accident.[3]

Robe à la Française (Detail), c. 1760, The Metropolitan Museum of Art, 1996.374a-c

Robe à la Française (Detail), c. 1775, The Los Angeles County Museum of Art, www.lacma.org, M.2007.211.720a-b

Robe à la Française, c. 1775, The Metropolitan Museum of Art, 2005.61a,b

OUR CHOICES FOR THE SACQUE GOWN

Let's be honest. Our main motivation and goal for our late 1760s sacque was to look like a cake covered in delicious frosting. It was the motivation of many a Georgian lady as well! When looking at portraits from the 1760s and early 1770s, we see that women loved using matching trim for their gowns. While trim could be hemmed or pinked, gathered or pleated, even sacque gowns that were not "formal" were still heavily trimmed, often with passementerie trimming the trim of the gown! We have used pinked self-fabric trim for the gown and petticoat, with careful attention to the proportion of the trim to achieve that flattering and historically accurate effect.

Our gown is designed to go over moderately sized hoops. Their construction is such that they should be easy and quick to make and to store or travel with. We don't recommend wearing a full sacque gown *without* hoops. Having that additional width is important to successfully show off the trim on the front of the gown and the pleats in the back while giving the illusion of a smaller waist. Bonus!

In this chapter, we will demonstrate a number of sacque-specific fitting techniques along with trimming tips and tricks for tight-woven silk and tutorials for working with lighter-than-air organza. Onward!

A NOTE ON HAIR STYLING FOR YOUR SACQUE GOWN

Before we move on to the projects, we want to address some potential styling issues. Ninety-five percent of ladies who want to make and wear a sacque gown ensemble also want to rock the very large, super tall hairstyles because "that's so eighteenth century!" But that's not always the case. Hairstyles changed constantly throughout the century, and there are distinct shifts in hairstyles every couple of years in the last half of the 1700s.

The tall Georgian hairstyle was actually only in fashion for a short time: 1772 to 1775. Before 1772 at the earliest, English women wore their hair much lower, and usually unpowdered or very lightly powdered. Post 1776, while hair is still tall, the style starts to widen out at the top creating a more heart-shaped style and eventually morphs into the "hedgehog" hairstyle of the 1780s, wider than it was tall.

As always, return to research. Collect primary-source images from the year you are portraying and study the hairstyles closely. Compare and contrast with other years, particularly in the same decade, to develop your Georgian style sense.[4]

OH, SWEET, SWEET SILK

Working with and wearing real silk is magical. While there were many different types of silk fabric used in the eighteenth century, silk taffeta is a go-to choice today. An incredibly common fabric in the eighteenth century, silk taffeta is crisp, lightweight and makes the best swooshy noises when you walk. When you're working with real silk, it doesn't slip and slide like faux polyester silk. It's easy to pleat a lot of fabric into a tiny space, allowing those super full, super pretty skirts. It really can make you feel luxurious and glamorous. However, there are some drawbacks and tricks to silk that we need to address.

Did you know that silk is the hottest fabric to wear? It is the least breathable of the four natural fibers (yes, even wool!). You will probably regret wearing it to an outdoor summer event, unless becoming a walking sauna is your plan. Silk also doesn't do water, so avoid a rainy day. There are not enough tissues in the world to soak up those tears of devastation.

The biggest problem with silks today is the loom widths. You see, eighteenth-century silk was woven at half an ell wide, which equates to anywhere between 18 and 24 inches (20.3 to 60.9 cm) wide, significantly narrower than the up-to-60-inch (152.4-cm)-wide fabric we have today.[5] The width of silk affected the way a mantua maker cut a gown, how it hung, how they achieved the fullness in some places, etc. While cutting silk up into panels is sometimes a smart option, there are some cases where this might not be necessary, opting instead for a false seam. Why create more work for yourself? The eighteenth-century mantua maker certainly wouldn't have!

Silk came in different qualities and weights in the eighteenth century. Not all silks were, or are, created equal. Here's a quick guide for shopping eighteenth-century-style silk taffetas.

1. Plain woven and changeable (different colors for warp and weft). These are always acceptable and a good choice, but avoid slubby plain weaves such as duppioni, raw or Thai silk. Slubs in silk are considered faults in the eighteenth century, and so the bigger the slubs, the lower the quality. While a modern machine woven duppioni with very small and minimal slubbing could work for a "cheap" eighteenth-century silk gown, give it a pass for a ball gown or any sort of formal dress.

2. Stripes. Popular throughout most of the eighteenth century. Be sure to make note of stripe width and design repeat in relation to the decade you're re-creating. Not all stripes will do.

3. Plaids or "cross-barred." Popular for sacques during the 1760s and 1770s. Be mindful of colors, density and scale and choose wisely. Eighteenth-century cross-barred silks are not tartans!

4. Embroidered. Most modern silks are machine embroidered in too-modern designs. Be careful when choosing one of these, or consider hand-embroidering plain-weave taffeta yourself.

5. Brocade/jacquard/damask. A gorgeous choice for early-to-mid-eighteenth-century sacques. Be careful of the fabric weight, scale and colors used. Avoid the home decor section like the plague, and steer away from Victorianesque motifs.

6. Painted. Original painted silk was commonly done in China or India and is impossible to find today. This is one you'll have to do yourself with readily available silk paints on plain-weave taffeta.

Whichever type of silk you decide on, be sure to *really study* the scale, color and layout of fabric designs on original garments before spending money on the wrong fabric!

1760s Undies
Side Hoops

Eighteenth-century gowns are well known for their "hippy" silhouettes. These shapes were achieved with various types of hooped petticoats, from the full-length grand panniers to hip pads to pocket hoops like these. These hoops can be made smaller or larger for different effects.

MATERIALS

- *1–1½ yards (1–1.5 m) of linen or cotton*
- *15–17 yards (15–17 m) of ¾" (2-cm) cotton or linen tape*
- *4 yards (4 m) of ½" (1.3-cm)-wide cane boning*
- *Linen thread (60/2)*

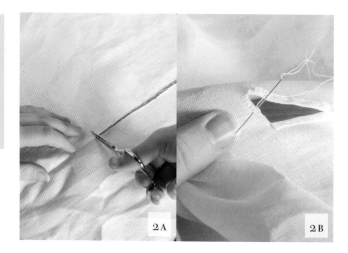

ASSEMBLY

1. Cut out the pattern according to the diagram (page 76).

2. Cut the pocket opening and a small T at the bottom, turn and hem both edges. Whip over the bottom cut.

1760s Side Hoops

This simple pattern makes up two medium-sized hoops. Scale up or down for earlier or later silhouettes.

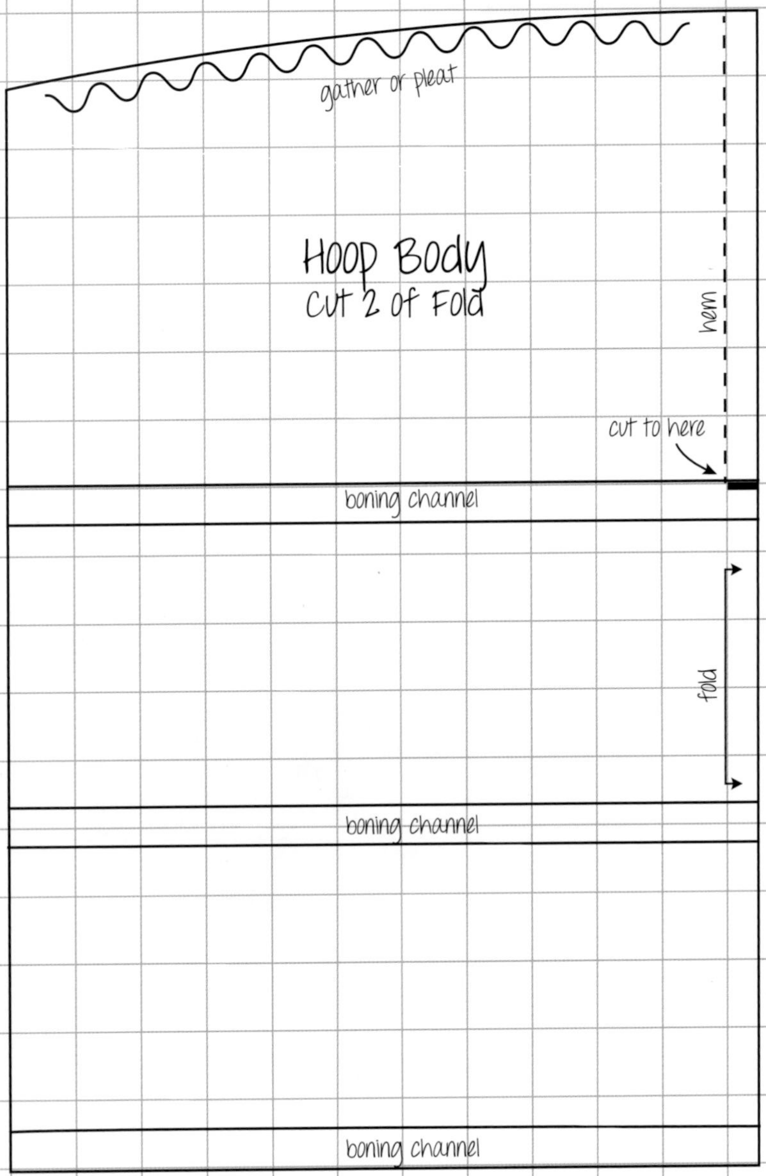

gather or pleat

Hoop Body
Cut 2 of Fold

hem

cut to here

boning channel

fold

boning channel

boning channel

Ties

Hoop Interior - 19 in (48.3cm). Cut 8

Bottom Hoop - 39 in (99.1 cm). Cut 4

Waist Tape - 36 in (91.4 cm).* Cut 2
* Adjust the waist tape length for your waist measurement.

Boning Channels - 23 in (58.4 cm). Cut 6

1 in / 2.5 cm

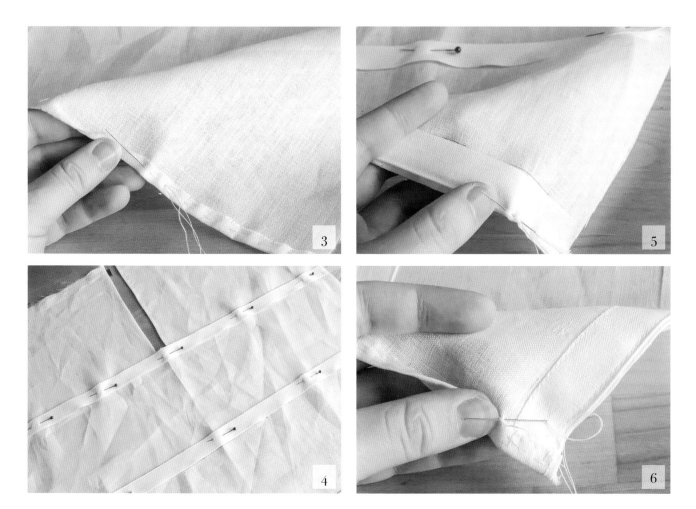

3. Turn up and baste the bottom edge ½ inch (1.3 cm).

4. Mark channels for ¾-inch (2-cm) tape at the bottom, across the bottom of the pocket opening and halfway between the two (see pattern). Line up the bottom tape over the basted edge and the top tape along the whipped bottom of the pocket slit.

5. Pin the tape and running backstitch (6 to 8 stitches per inch [2.5 cm]) both edges in place, leaving the ends open. (If you want to save time, you can use a machine for sewing your channels.)

6. Turn, baste and hem one side of the hoop, closing one end of the boning channels.

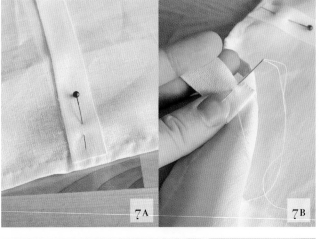

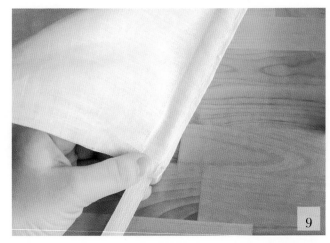

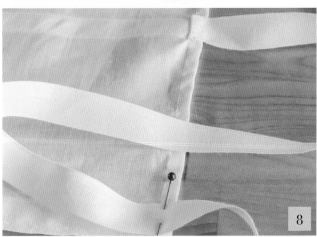

7. Add the ties—these need to be strongly stitched on. On the wrong side of the hoop, place the tie with the raw edge just in from the hemmed edge of the hoop. Stitch across the end. Do not cut your thread. Fold the tape to the outside, over the raw edge. Hem stitch the side, backstitch across the end, hem stitch the opposite short side, then hem stitch the other long end to secure it all in place (10 to 12 stitches per inch [2.5 cm]).

8. On the bottom tie, fold the long tape in half, mark the center and match this point to the hemmed edge at the bottom hoop channel. Backstitch securely in place (8 to 10 stitches per inch [2.5 cm]).

9. Insert the boning. Clip the ends about ½ to ¾ inch (1.3 to 2 cm) short of the ends of the boning channels to allow turning the edges.

Your boning may be a bit too curly. To flatten it, spritz lightly with water and weigh it down with books until dry and flatter.

10. Hem the remaining side over the boning channels and add the ties as before.

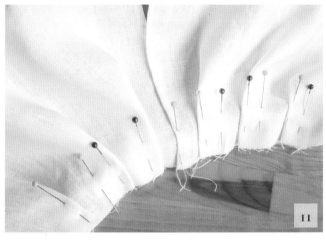

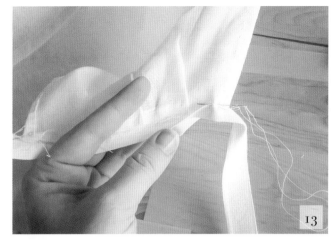

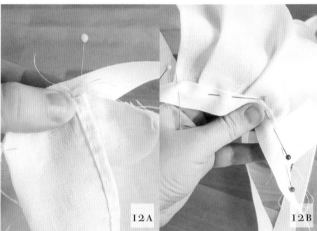

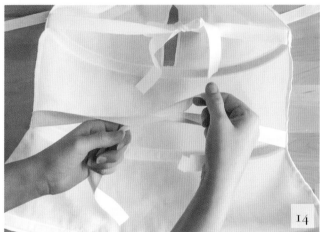

11. For a trim waist, pleat the top edge down to about 10 to 11 inches (25 to 28 cm) with several knife pleats. This is not an exact science. We took 3 pleats on each side toward the pocket slit. Match the edges of the pocket slit together and tack stitch to hold.

12. Find the center of the waist tape and match this point to the pocket slit. Apply the tape to the outside of the hoop, overlapping the raw edge by half the width of the tape. Hem stitch (10 to 12 stitches per inch [2.5 cm]).

13. Fold the tape over the raw edge to encase it, and hem stitch on the inside.

14. On the inside of the hoops, pull the ties on each hoop to about the same arc and tie in a bow. You can adjust the spring of the hoops by tying these tapes tighter or looser.

15. Now you get to do this all again for the second hoop!

1760s
The Sacque Petticoat

Petticoats made to fit over understructures are a little different than your average all-one-length petticoat. This petticoat features a shaped top and straight hem and is measured over the side hoops created in this chapter. Remember the measuring for the petticoat must be done on the body or dress form over all underpinnings and with the intended shoes on.

MATERIALS

- *3 yards (3 m) of 60" (153.4-cm)-wide fabric (Your yardage will vary depending on fabric width, model's height and size of understructures.)*
- *2 yards (2 m) of fabric for petticoat trim (optional)*
- *Silk thread (#30 for seams, gathers and topstitching and #50 for hemming)*
- *3.5+ yards (3.5+ m) ¾–1" (2–2.5-cm)-wide cotton or linen tape*

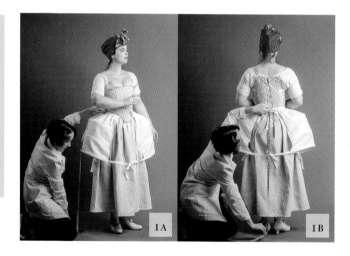

ASSEMBLY

1. From waist to floor, measure the center front, center back and side length over the hoops. Your side measurement will be longer than your front and back.

2. Determine how high your hem will be from the floor and subtract this measurement from the center front, center back and side numbers. Add seam allowance for the hem.

1760s Petticoat Over Side Hoops

Petticoats made to go over hoops are shaped at the top while the hem remains on the straight.

Measure from Waist to Floor at:
A. Center Front
B. Side Over Hoop
C. Center Back

Petticoat Top is
cut in this shape - angle may be
shallower or deeper depending on the size
of your hoops.
Petticoat Front and Back may also have
different angles.

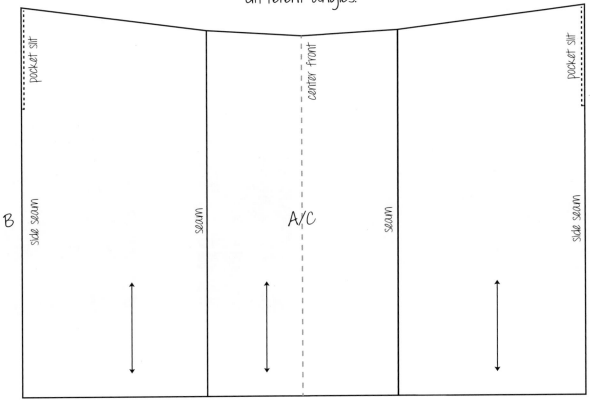

pocket slit

center front

pocket slit

B

side seam

seam

A/C

seam

side seam

Hem - total hem circumference bewteen 100 - 130 in (254 cm - 330.2 cm)

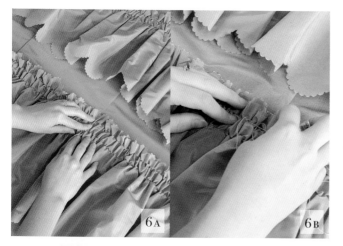

3. Cut all of your panels by length according to the side measurement, and by width to create a total hem measurement between 100 and 130 inches (2.4 to 3.3 m).

Depending on your fabric width, you may need to cut and seam your panels together or create faux seams. For our petticoat, our fabric was 60 inches (153.4 cm) wide, so we have used one full panel for the back and one for the front, trisecting each and stitching ¼-inch (6.35-mm)-narrow false seams to give the look of a 6-paneled petticoat.

4. Mark the center point at the top waist edge of the petticoat front. Subtract the center front measurement from the side measurement, and measure down this amount from the center point. Mark.

5. Draw a line from the top side edge of the petticoat panel to the center mark you just made, and back up to the opposite side of the top edge of the petticoat, creating a V. You can smooth this into a soft curve. Repeat steps 4 and 5 for the back and cut this V shape out.

6. Apply all trim to the front of your petticoat before making up.

7. Stitch one side seam of the petticoat using a running backstitch for selvage edges or a mantua maker's seam for raw edges (6 to 8 stitches per inch [2.5 cm]). Leave 10 to 12 inches (25.4 to 30.5 cm) open at the top for the pocket slit and hem these edges to finish them.

8. Pleat the front and back of the petticoat at the waist. You are pleating along the curves you cut earlier, but be sure to line the pleats up as if they were cut on the straight. Leave ½ inch (1.3 cm) seam allowance on the unsewn side seam.

9. For the front, begin knife pleats 2 inches (5 cm) from center, working the pleats toward the side seams.

10. For the back, box pleat inward at the center back, then continue knife pleats toward center back on both sides, working out to the side seams. Baste across the front and back waist pleats to hold them.

11. Stitch the second side seam, using a running backstitch for selvage edges or a mantua maker's seam for raw edges. Leave 10 to 12 inches (25.4 to 30.5 cm) open at the top for the pocket slit. Turn and hem the edges of the pocket slit.

12. On the right side of the pleated petticoat waist apply the cotton tape right sides together, matching the raw edge at the top. Hem stitch the bottom edge of the tape in place (10 to 12 stitches per inch [2.5 cm]).

13. Turn the tape fully to the inside and hem stitch the free edge in place. Repeat for the back.

14. Hem the bottom of the petticoat (6 to 8 stitches per inch [2.5 cm]).

Done! The final result will be a petticoat that fits over your pocket hoops with a perfectly level hem.

1760s
Pinked Trim!

One of the most fun and iconic types of eighteenth-century decoration is pinked trimmings. Pinking became extremely popular in the sixteenth century and went in and out of fashion up through the nineteenth century. Originally, pinking was done with sharp, shaped punches rather than shears or scissors. These punches are difficult to find and tricky to use today, but scalloped pinking shears are available and can be used to create a convincing look.

Pinked edges were most commonly scalloped, often with small scallops within larger scallops. While zigzag pinking punches existed, it is best to wield your zigzag pinking shears with caution to avoid a too-modern look.

Tightly woven silk fabric is the best fabric for pinking. The dense weave and stiff hand allowed the pinked edge to fray very little. We *do not* see pinking on cotton or linen garments. These materials fray too easily, resulting in a messy look, and so cotton or linen trims feature hemmed edges.

Finally, while we've shown the method for whip-gathering pinked trim, there are other treatments too. Try box pleats, knife pleats, stuffed pleats, undulating serpentine ruffles, flipped ruffles, offset gathers, applied fly-fringe on top of the gathered ruffles, loops, puffs and bows. Your options are truly limitless!

MATERIALS

- *1–3 yards (1–3 m) fabric (gathering ratio 1:2)*
- *Silk thread #30*

READY, SET, PINK!

1. Fold your fabric yardage in half selvage to selvage and trace the template onto your fabric, moving it along to repeat the pattern. When tracing out multiple lines of trim, give yourself space between the scalloped edges to be able to work the shears later.

Pinking Templates

Trace these templates onto silk taffeta as a guide for pinking, either with a punch or pinking shears. Play with scale for different effects.

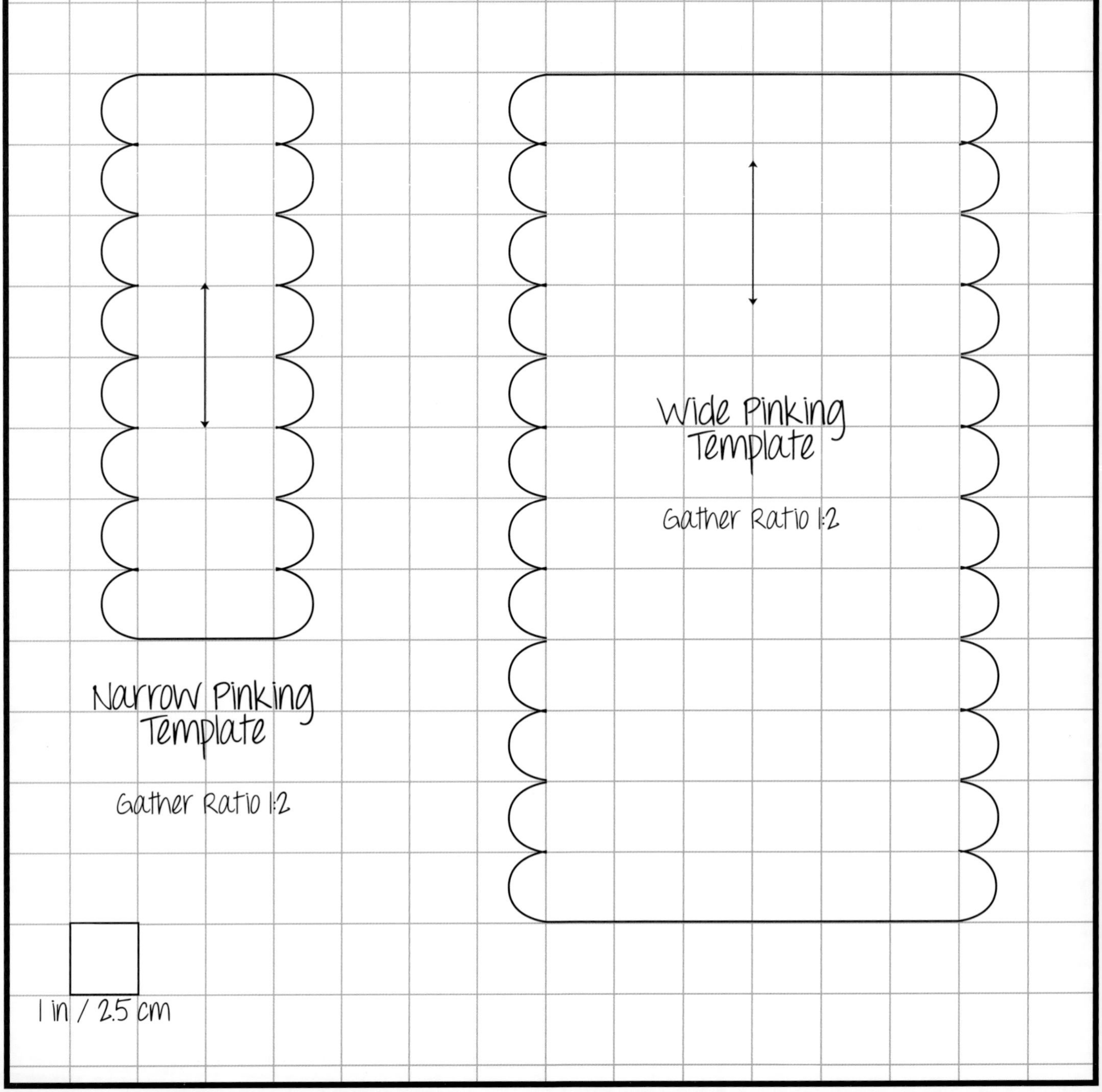

Wide Pinking
Template

Gather Ratio 1:2

Narrow Pinking
Template

Gather Ratio 1:2

1 in / 2.5 cm

2. Pin through the center of the fabric strips to hold the two layers together, then cut the scallops with your scalloped shears. This is a pain, but the result is worth it.

3. For single row gathered trim: fold the strip in half lengthwise and run a whip gathering stitch along the folded edge.

4. If your trim ratio is 2 to 1, whip gather stitch 12 inches (30.5 cm) and pull up the stitch to gather the trim down to 6 inches (15.2 cm), then tack stitch to hold in place. Carry on with the same thread, 12 inches (30.5 cm) at a time. If you are doing a ratio of 1.5 to 1 this equals 12 inches (30.5 cm) gathered down to 8 inches (20.3 cm).

5. For double row gathered trim: draw out both fold lines on cut trim pieces.

   • Fold the first row and whipstitch over the fold, but do not gather up.

   • Fold the second row and whipstitch over the fold, stopping at the same point as the first row.

   • Gather up both threads simultaneously to fit your desired ratio.

   • Individually lock stitch both rows in place, and continue on in this manner until complete.

6. After gathering up the trim, press the ruffles open with your iron.

7. Pin the gathered trim where you like on the gown or petticoat and prick stitch in the gutter of the whip gathers with small running stitches. For double-gathered trim, stitch both lines.

1760s
The Sacque Stomacher

The stomacher of a gown was at once a method of closure and a vehicle for more trim. We have chosen to mimic trim designs seen in portraiture for our sacque, but you have an endless array of options when it comes to how you wish to trim your own. Just remember that you do need to be able to pin it into place—you don't want your bows to be in the way! Finally, while we've included a gridded pattern for the stomacher (page 94), we do recommend that you take your own measurements to ensure a proper fit.

Materials
- *1 yard (1 m) fashion fabric*
- *½ yard (0.5 m) linen buckram*
- *½ yard (0.5 m) linen or cotton*
- *Silk thread (#30 for construction and #50 for hemming bows)*

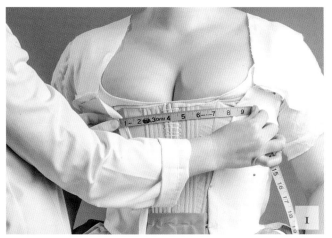

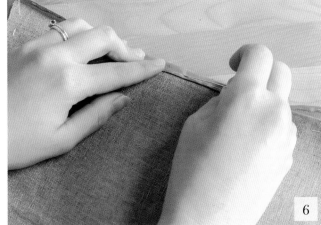

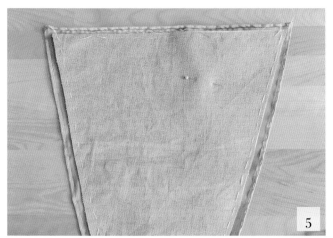

ASSEMBLY

1. Measure the length and width needed for the stomacher or follow our pattern on page 94. The length should be from the top edge of the stays to just below the "points" of the bodice front edges. The width should be across the bust and across the waist with an additional 1 inch (2.5 cm) added on both sides for the gown front edges to overlap. Add ½ inch (1.3 cm) seam allowance.

2. Cut 1 layer of linen, 1 layer of linen buckram and 1 layer of the fashion fabric.

3. To make linen buckram, liberally paint medium-weight linen with gum tragacanth and allow to dry in the sun. Do it outside. This stuff stinks.

4. Cut off the seam allowance of the linen buckram pieces and pin or baste both layers together. Turn in half of the seam allowance on the fashion fabric and baste.

5. Center the linen pieces on the fashion fabric with even seam allowance on all edges. Pin to hold.

6. Fold the straight top edge of the fashion fabric over the raw edge of the linen buckram and hem stitch. Continue working the sides and bottom edge. Fold in the remaining seam allowance, covering the raw edge of the linen buckram.

7. At the bottom curve, with a loose running stitch, gather and ease the fashion fabric around the bottom. Pin as you go, then hem stitch in place (6 to 8 stitches per inch [2.5 cm]), catching just the linen buckram. Make sure to keep the stomacher absolutely flat to avoid weird tension issues with the fashion fabric.

8. Decorate! There are so many different ways to decorate your sacque stomacher. Bows, lace, embroidery, ruffles, fly fringe, you name it. We used 5-Loop Bows (page 90) and pinked ruffles (page 85) for ours, but don't be afraid to experiment and really stack those trims on.

1760s
5-Loop Bows

This bow configuration is copied from *Portrait of a Lady* by Francis Cotes. Five-loop bows are constructed, not tied. For this tutorial, each bow will use two pieces of ribbon stitched together. Use your 5-Loop Bows to decorate your gown stomacher and sleeves.

MATERIALS

- *1 yard (1 m) of 3" (7.6-cm)-wide ribbon (hemmed taffeta or silk ribbon) per bow*
- *Silk thread (#30 gathers and #50 for hemming)*

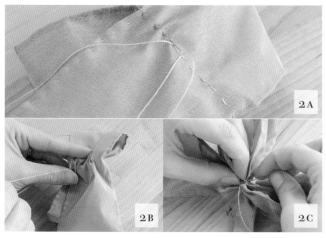

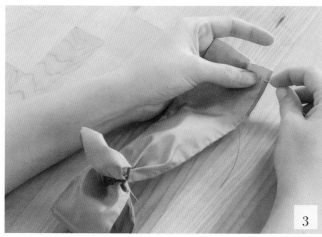

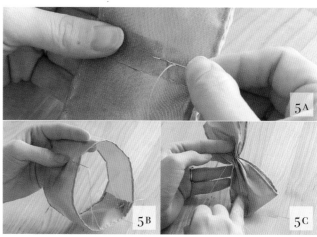

Assembly

1. Cut two pieces of ribbon approximately 19 inches (48.3 cm) long and 12 inches (30.5 cm) long. The length and width of your ribbon will determine the size of your bow—for smaller bows, use a shorter length of ribbon; for larger, use longer ribbon.

2. With the longer length of ribbon, roll the first loop over matching the raw end to about one third of the way down the ribbon. Do a fine running stitch through both layers halfway between the raw edge and fold. Draw up the thread and tack stitch in place. Do not cut the thread.

3. Find the length of the second loop by rolling it up toward what will be the center of your bow. Just mark this length with your fingers or a pin, then open flat again.

4. Do a fine running stitch at this point, draw up the thread, roll the loop back up to the base of the first loop and tack stitch in place. On the opposite end, run a fine gathering stitch, draw up the ribbon and roll the loop to the base of the other two bows. Tack stitch in place.

5. For the remaining 2 loops, roll the short length of ribbon into a loop, lapping the ends. Run a fine gathering stitch across this join then, without cutting the thread, use a gathering stitch on the opposite side, stitching in the opposite direction. Pull the thread to gather up both sides together and tack stitch the center in place.

6. Place the 2-loop bow behind the 3-loop bow and tack stitch the bows together from inside the loops.

1760s
The Sacque Gown

As with all of our gowns, the sacque bodice lining is fitted on the body and the gown is constructed on top. The lining for the sacque plays an important role for the look, fit and wearability of the gown, forming a structural foundation for the free-hanging back pleats while controlling fullness and fit at the sides.

MATERIALS

- 6–8 yards (6–8 m) silk (taffeta, satin, damask, jacquard) or floral printed cotton
- 1–2 yards (1–2 m) linen
- Silk thread (#30 for seams, gathers and prick stitching and #50 for hemming)
- Linen thread (60/2)—optional

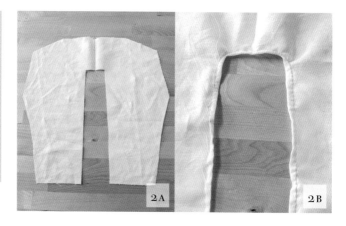

2A   2B

BODICE AND FIRST FITTING

The sacque bodice lining (page 94) forms the foundation upon which the flowing, "loose"-looking gown is built. Though similar to the lining pieces of the other gowns in this book, the sacque lining features adjustable ties in back and two shoulder strap fitting seams.

1. On the back lining pieces, measure down 4 to 4½ inches (10 to 11.4 cm) at the center back and mark. This measurement determines how deep the stitched back pleats will be later.

2. Fold the lining in half and cut in about 1 inch (2.5 cm) from the fold up to the mark. Open the lining back up and hem back all 3 sides of the resulting rectangular cutout (6 to 8 stitches per inch [2.5 cm]).

1760s Sacque Gown Bodice Lining + Stomacher

Use this pattern for the lining pieces upon which to build your sacque.

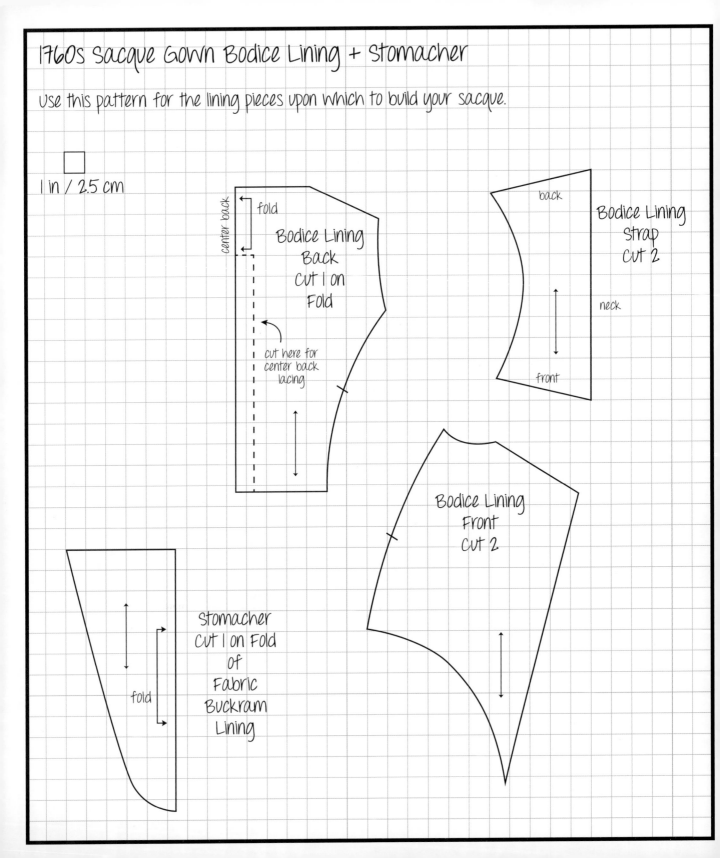

1 in / 2.5 cm

center back

fold

Bodice Lining
Back
Cut 1 on
Fold

cut here for
center back
lacing

back

Bodice Lining
Strap
Cut 2

neck

front

Bodice Lining
Front
Cut 2

Stomacher
Cut 1 on Fold
of
Fabric
Buckram
Lining

fold

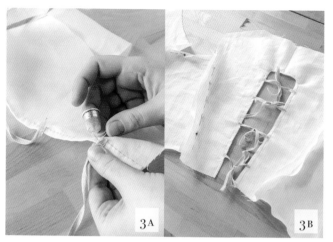

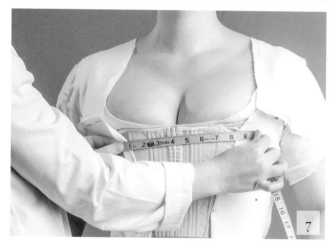

3. Attach 3 to 4 laces evenly down the back opening and stitch into place. Tie the back laces in loose bows so the back lining lies even and smooth.

4. Roughly pin the lining pieces together at the front and back shoulder seams and the side seams. Then put the bodice on the model over all the underpinnings.

5. Pin the front edges of the bodice to the stays in their intended placement and begin working around the body, pinning and adjusting the front edges and shoulder straps until the bodice lining is correctly placed at the waist, front and center back.

6. Now pinch up the side back seams and pin, alternating between both sides of the body. Smooth and pin until the bodice lining fits snugly, then mark along the waistline with a pencil, chalk or pins.

7. Measure for the stomacher across the bust and waist at the front for the width and length of the stomacher.

8. Unpin the shoulder straps and bodice front edges and carefully remove the lining from the model. Do not remove the pins in the side back seams or any marking the waist.

9. Turn up and baste the seam allowance on the bodice front edges, neckline and waist. At the waist, turn up the excess along the waist markings you made earlier.

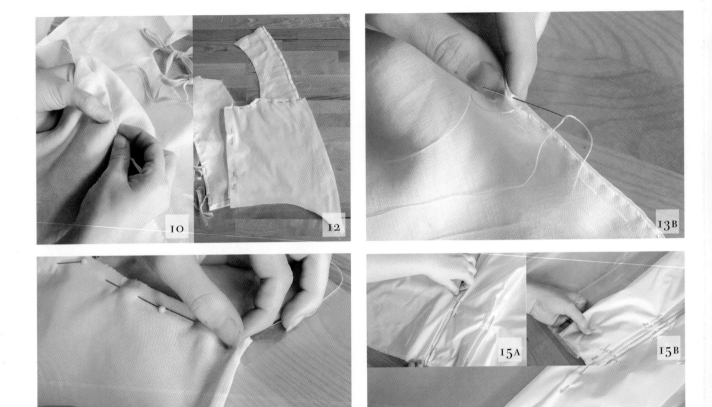

10. With the bodice lining flat, stitch the side back seams from the inside with a fine hem or whipstitch (10 to 12 stitches per inch [2.5 cm]).

11. Press the seam allowance open and trim the excess, leaving a good ½ inch (1.3 cm) allowance.

12. Working flat, align the raw edges of the bodice front fashion fabric and lining along the shoulder strap edge and armscye. Pin to hold.

13. Smooth the fashion fabric over the lining working out toward the front edge. Turn under the seam allowance along the bodice front, neckline and waist edges and stitch to the lining using a small running stitch or hem stitch (8 to 10 stitches per inch [2.5 cm]). Leave the waist fabric and lining free about 4 to 5 inches (10 to 12.7 cm) from the side back seam.

14. Next, we need to make the beautiful box pleats for the back. We used 4 panels of 20-inch (50-cm)-wide fabric to create the back of the gown, each seamed together with a mantua maker's seam for raw cut edges and a running backstitch for selvage edges. The overall width needs to be quite wide—at least 80 inches (2 m) wide or more for broader backs.

15. Working flat on your table and over the bodice back lining, make the back box pleats as shown on page 97, making sure that all pleats are on the straight of grain. The interior pleats at the center back are not as deep as the pleats to the side. In earlier gowns the pleats are wider across the shoulders and in later gowns they are narrower. Keep this in mind when you're making and designing your gown.

1760s Sacque Back Pleats

Half

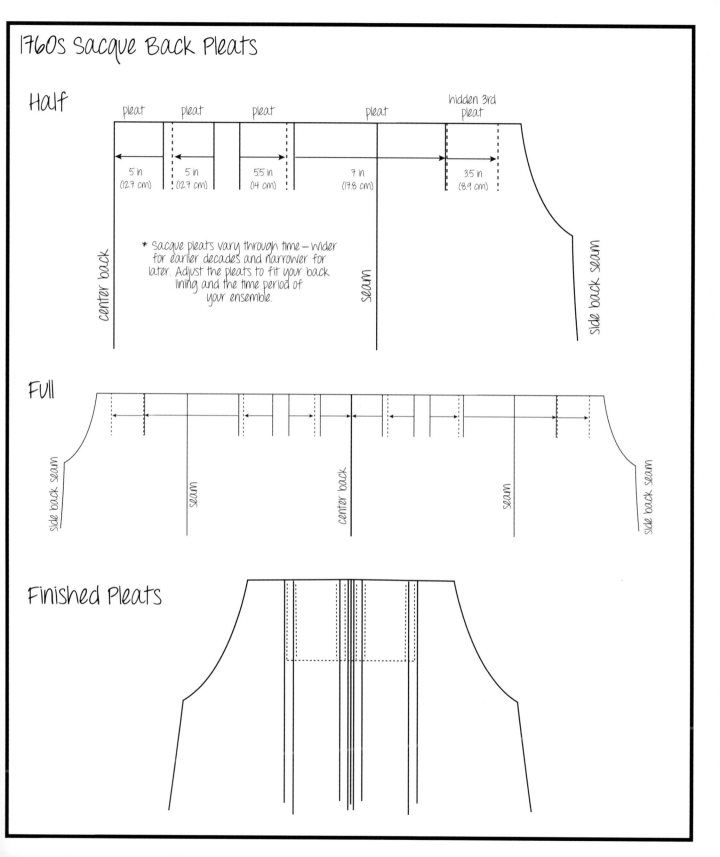

pleat   pleat   pleat   pleat   hidden 3rd pleat

5 in (12.7 cm)   5 in (12.7 cm)   5.5 in (14 cm)   7 in (17.8 cm)   3.5 in (8.9 cm)

center back

seam

side back seam

* Sacque pleats vary through time — wider for earlier decades and narrower for later. Adjust the pleats to fit your back lining and the time period of your ensemble.

Full

side back seam   seam   center back   seam   side back seam

Finished Pleats

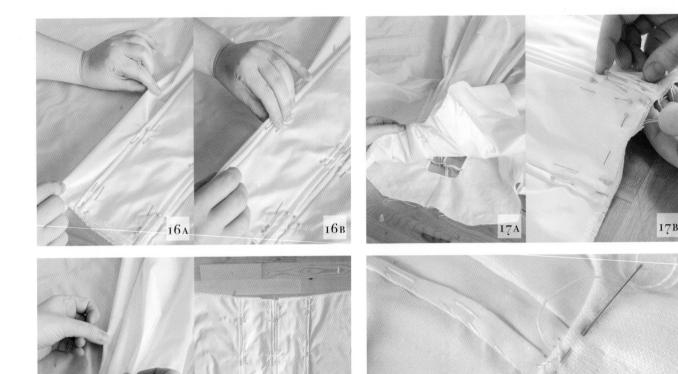

16A   16B   17A   17B   16C   16D   18

16. After you create the box pleats, at each side make a third hidden pleat that will lie underneath the second pleat. It will not be visible at the top of the box pleats, but you will see it at the side when the pleats flow away from the body. This third pleat is extremely common in sacque gowns and is there to kick out the pleats from the body and give that pretty line. Don't skip it lest you run the risk of droopy pleats!

17. Place the pleated fashion fabric centered over the bodice lining, wrong sides together. Pin, then prick stitch the pleats through all layers at either ⅛ inch or ¼ inch (3 or 6 mm) square and down to that 4- to 4½-inch (10- to 11.4-cm) mark you made in step 1.

18. Once complete, flip the bodice lining-side up. Herringbone stitch the pleats from the back from edge to edge, using the top of the open panel back as a guide.

19. With the back laid out right side up and all layers smooth and straight, pin beneath the back pleats just to the side of the center back opening in the bodice lining. Prick stitch the fashion fabric to the lining parallel to the center back opening. This creates a smooth, fitted back while allowing the pleats to flow out from the body. Make sure you keep this on the straight and it doesn't pull or twist or you'll have to pick the stitches out and do it again.

20. You'll notice you have a lot of excess fabric to the sides of the back. Smooth the back of the gown over the side back seam on the lining and pin. Cut out the excess fabric at the bodice side seam edge, then square it off about 1 to 2 inches (2.5 to 5 cm) above the waistline, leaving the lower portion of the extra fabric for your skirt.

21. At the side back seam, turn under the raw edge of the front bodice fashion fabric, lap it over the bodice back raw edge and pin it into a gentle curve. Repeat on the other side and make sure that both seams are curving symmetrically and are the same distance from the center back. These outer seams do not need to line up with the bodice lining side back seams.

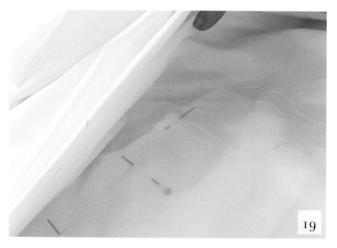

22. Prick stitch the side back seams down using either ⅛ or ¼ inch (3 or 6 mm) square. When you reach about 1½ inches (3.8 cm) from the waist, continue prick stitching but do not catch the lining. You will later slide your skirt pleats into this pocket.

Skirt Panels and Second Fitting

Now comes the trickiest part of the sacque gown—fitting the skirts. Because of the large shape of the hoops, sacque gowns were extended, arranged, pleated and smoothed to gracefully fit over them while also creating a canvas for the trimmings. These techniques *must* be done on the body or dress form over the underpinnings.

1. Cut your front skirt panels. We used the historic width for silk of 20 inches (50.8 cm) and the waist-to-floor measurement taken for the petticoat previously (page 81).

2. The gore is cut from the front skirt panel, then flipped and seamed (see page 100). At the top edge of the skirt panel, mark approximately 6 inches (15.2 cm) in from one side and 2 inches (5 cm) at the opposite end. Connect these two marks with a straight line to draw the gore. This small-but-mighty gore added to the side of the sacque skirts creates extra length in the hem that allows the train to lay properly. Don't skip it, darlings!

3. Cut along the line, then flip the gore so the 6-inch (15.2-cm) width is now at the bottom of the skirt panel, matching angled cut to angled cut. Using a mantua maker's seam, stitch the gore to the front skirt panel (6 to 8 stitches per inch [2.5 cm]). Leave 10 to 12 inches (25.4 to 30.5 cm) free at the top for the pocket slit.

4. Finish the pocket slit edges with a narrow hem stitch (6 to 8 stitches per inch [2.5 cm]). This will be a little tricky where the mantua maker's seam begins. Take your time. Press the seams and pocket slit hems.

5. With a mantua maker's seam, stitch the front skirt panel and gore to the back skirt and press.

6. Turn and baste the front long edge of the front skirt panels ¼ inch (6 mm) to prepare the skirt for the fitting.

7. Now we're going to explain the second gown fitting. Start with putting the gown on the model over all underpinnings, and pin in place. With the shoulder straps roughly pinned at the front, pull the straps over the shoulder to meet the shoulder seam at back. Pinch the two edges together and pin.

8. Adjust the shoulder strap seam on the front, pinching and pinning as needed to get a perfectly smooth, tight fit. Don't worry about keeping the raw edges even here—work out any gapping, excess or looseness at this front seam.

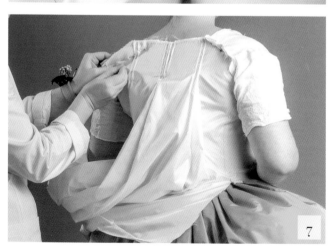

1760s Sacque - Skirt Gore

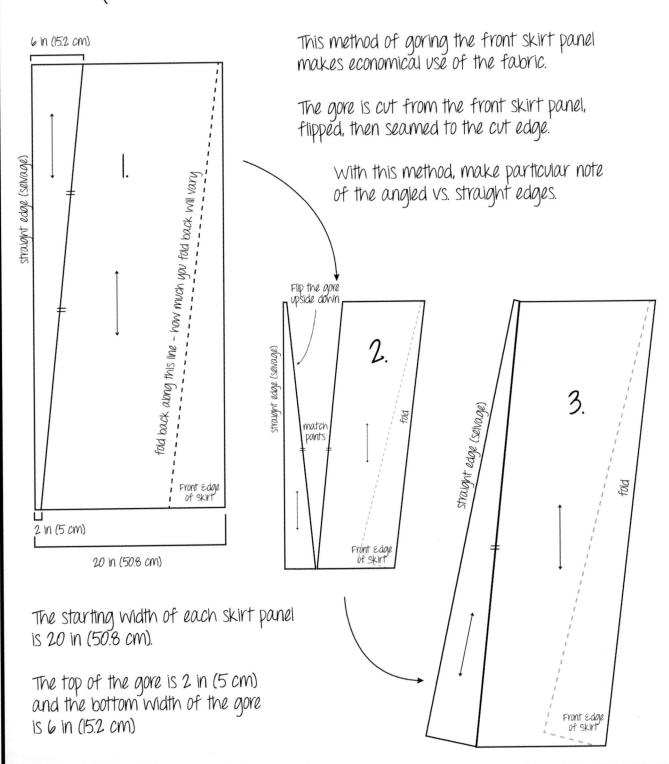

6 in (15.2 cm)

straight edge (selvage)

1.

fold back along this line - how much you fold back will vary

Front Edge of Skirt

2 in (5 cm)

20 in (50.8 cm)

This method of goring the front skirt panel makes economical use of the fabric.

The gore is cut from the front skirt panel, flipped, then seamed to the cut edge.

With this method, make particular note of the angled vs. straight edges.

Flip the gore upside down

straight edge (selvage)

match points

2.

fold

Front Edge of Skirt

straight edge (selvage)

3.

fold

Front Edge of Skirt

The starting width of each skirt panel is 20 in (50.8 cm).

The top of the gore is 2 in (5 cm) and the bottom width of the gore is 6 in (15.2 cm)

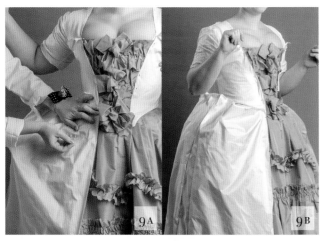

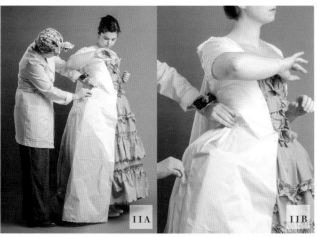

9. Hold the front edge of the skirt up to the waist so the front edges hang mostly straight down to the floor. You will not match the top edge of the skirt panel to the curved waist seam of the bodice; it will overlap. Pull the skirt up from the top and pin at the bodice waist seam until the skirt panel hangs smoothly over the petticoat. This will create an excess wedge of skirt at the waist seam, but don't worry about it yet.

10. Pin the pocket slit together at the top edge and place it 1 to 2 inches (2.5 to 5 cm) behind the petticoat pocket slit. This seems counterintuitive, but this placement is important for the volume over the pocket hoops.

11. Pleat the excess of the front skirt panel at the waist back toward the pocket slit with 2 to 3 pleats. Place these pleats far enough back so as not to interfere with any trim you plan for the front of the skirt. The idea is to create a smooth, flat-ish canvas on the skirt front panels for your trim.

12. The top of the front skirt panel will now have an obvious wedge shape. Pin along the waist edge of the bodice to mark. You will later fold down this excess and applique stitch it to the bodice, so don't cut it off! With your preferred marking method, mark the bodice waist edge on the skirt panels.

13. Turn the front edge of the front skirt panel back to create the inverted V opening. Turn it back as much or as little as you like—this is personal taste. The front skirt panels on sacques are often angled open at the front edges to show off the trimmed petticoat. This cutaway is vital to the drape of the sacque skirts and in achieving the right silhouette. Don't worry about your stitches being visible from the turn back, this part of the gown will be covered with trim later.

14. Once satisfied, carefully remove the gown from the model, keeping the skirt pleats, edge pins and shoulder strap pins in place.

15. Securely stitch the shoulder straps at the back and front seams on the inside with a fine hem or backstitch (10 to 12 stitches per inch [2.5 cm]).

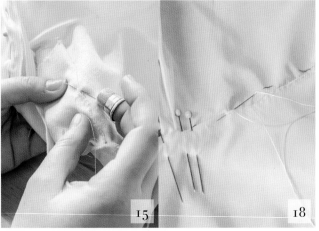

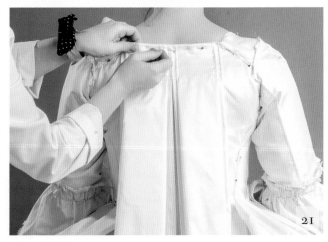

16. Working flat, running stitch the folded front skirt panel edges into place, keeping the visible stitch small (6 to 8 stitches per inch [2.5 cm]).

17. Mark the pocket slit placement on the bodice with a pin, then unpin the skirts from the bodice completely but leave the skirt pleats pinned in place.

18. Lap the bodice waist edge over the skirt, following the waist marking on the skirt as closely as possible. It may not be exact, but take the average line. Pin the skirts in place and adjust the pleats if necessary to avoid bubbling. From the outside, applique stitch the bodice waistline to the skirts, stopping at the pocket slit (10 to 12 stitches per inch [2.5 cm]).

19. Pleat the remaining back skirt panel in 3 to 4 pleats toward the center back, matching the remaining space between the pocket slit and the side back seam.

20. Tuck the raw edge of the back skirt panel pleats up between the bodice fashion fabric and lining. Applique stitch from the outside (10 to 12 stitches per inch [2.5 cm]) and hem stitch the lining on the inside (6 to 8 stitches per inch [2.5 cm]).

21. There are a number of ways to finish the back of a sacque gown, from binding the top pleats in the same manner as the English Gown (page 29), to simply turning to the inside and stitching in place. Both are accurate for sacques, so feel free to use whichever method you prefer. Here, we have folded the back top neckline to the inside about ½ inch (1.3 cm) and loosely basted down.

22. Cut a strip of fashion fabric on the straight a bit more than the length of the turned edge and a little more than the width needed to fully cover the raw edge. Add seam allowance.

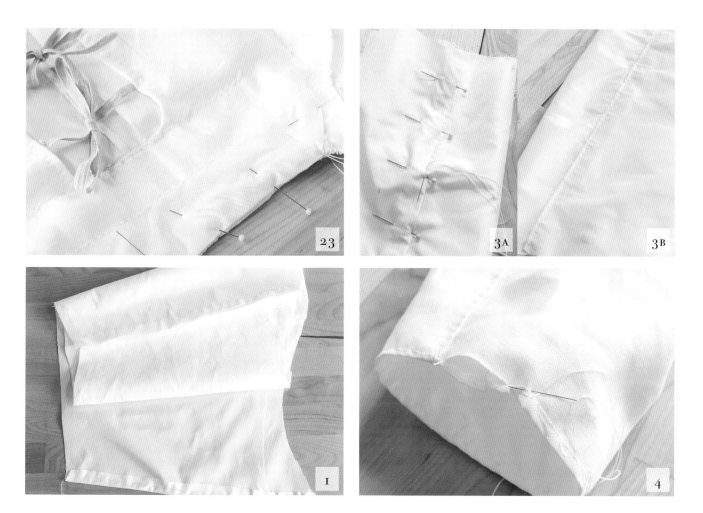

23. Turn up and baste the seam allowance on all edges of this strip, then apply the strip over the raw neckline edge, hem stitching it to just the lining (6 stitches per inch [2.5 cm]). It doesn't have to be pretty; it just needs to cover the raw edges of the neckline.

SLEEVES, THIRD FITTING, HEM AND TRIM

Throughout the eighteenth century, sleeve widths evolve. Broad and full in the earlier decades and narrow and tight in the later, 1760s sacque sleeves were right between—not too full and not too tight. Here you will learn a second method for sleeve construction, along with the eighteenth-century sleeve-setting technique on the body. Lastly, we will finish up the gown with trim application and a faced hem.

1. Lay out the sleeves with left and right sleeves wrong sides together. Cut off the seam allowance of the bottom edge/cuff of the sleeve lining to reduce bulk in later finishing.

2. With the lining atop the fashion fabric, fold just the lining over to match the raw edges and pin. Mark the seam allowance on the lining, then baste the three layers together.

3. Now turn up and baste the seam allowance on the opposite edge of the fashion fabric. Lap this edge over the other three, pin and prick stitch through all layers ⅛ x ⅛ inch or ¼ x ¼ inch (3 x 3 mm or 6 x 6 mm). Place your hand inside the sleeve as you stitch to avoid sewing through the other side.

4. Turn the sleeve inside out and finish the elbow/cuff by basting up the seam allowance of the fashion fabric, then folding it up again over the raw edge of the lining and hemming in place (6 to 8 stitches per inch [2.5 cm]). It's okay if you go through all the layers. The ruffle will hide the stitching.

1760s Sacque Gown Sleeve + Sleeve Ruffles

The sleeve ruffles for this style can be single, double or treble. Here we have a rough guide for pinking the edges of your ruffles for a silk gown, but these ruffles may also be cut without the scallops, hemmed and other trims applied.

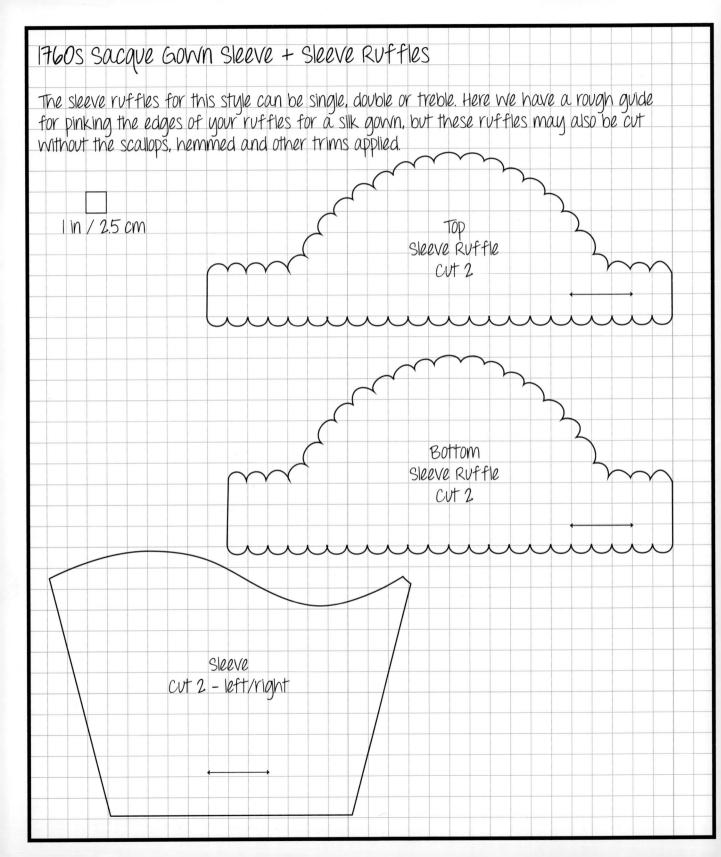

1 in / 2.5 cm

TOP
Sleeve Ruffle
Cut 2

Bottom
Sleeve Ruffle
Cut 2

Sleeve
Cut 2 – left/right

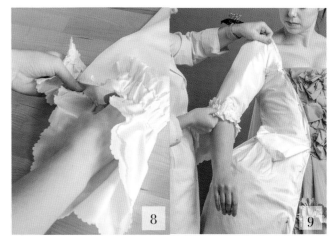

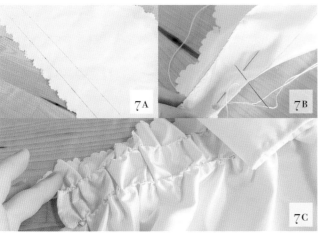

5. Sleeve ruffles were another facet of the extravagance of eighteenth-century sacque gowns and could be single, double or treble ruffles. We've chosen a double ruffle, pinked and whip gathered, but let your creativity guide you in your choice of fluff. For pinked taffeta ruffles, see page 85.

6. If you are creating double or treble ruffles, lay them all together with the smallest as the outer ruffle. Center the stacked ruffles upon one another so that each end has an extra ½ inch [1.3 cm] offset. Match the top edges. Pin or baste to hold the layers together, then turn up twice and hem both short ends with the two ruffles as one, enclosing the shorter raw edge.

7. From the wrong side, fold along the gathering lines and run two lines of whip gathering stitches over the fold. Stitch both folds as on page 87. Gather up the ruffles by drawing up both threads together. Adjust to fit the sleeves and pin into place.

8. Pin, then prick stitch to the sleeve through both gathering lines, and carefully connect the sleeve ruffle at the short ends with a fine applique stitch (6 stitches per inch [2.5 cm]).

9. Now it's time for the final fitting. Start by putting on the gown with all its underpinnings. Then pull the sleeve over the arm and pin it to the top of the shoulder to anchor it.

10. Starting at the front armpit crease, work your way under the arm, folding in the sleeve seam allowance and pinning in place. You might be tempted to not "get up in there" but remember: the higher the armscye, the greater the mobility. Just be careful with your pinning if you're fitting the gown on a real person. Continue pinning to the back of the arm and around the top of the armpit crease.

11. On the front, smooth and pin the sleeve over top of the shoulder, working toward the back. There is no need to turn the seam allowance on the sleeve head—it will be covered by the fashion fabric shoulder strap later. Any excess fabric left in the sleeve head should be pleated or tucked toward the back, between the shoulder point and armpit crease.

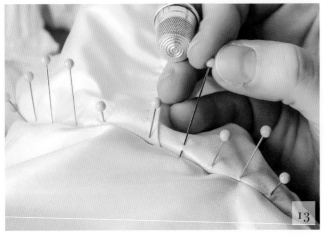

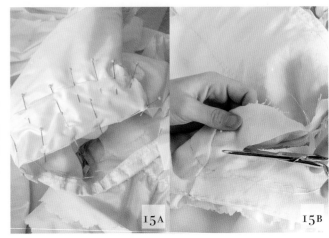

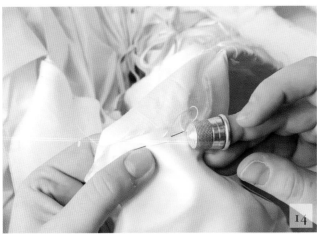

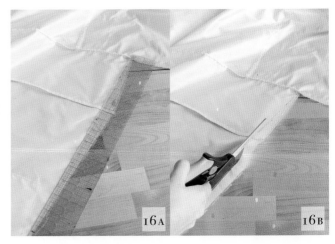

12. Check that both sleeves are even, that the back seams are symmetrical and that both sleeves lie smoothly with no rucking, twisting or weirdness. Got weirdness? Refer to Troubleshooting on page 230 to identify and correct any sleeve fitting issues. Once you're finished with the fitting, remove the gown from the model.

13. Now to stitch the sleeves. First, very carefully convert the underarm pins into the vertical pinning method shown. Mark the stitch line with a pencil, making sure both arms match.

14. Once completed, backstitch the underarm into place (10 to 12 stitches per inch [2.5 cm]). On the exterior, with big backstitches, stitch the top of the sleeve to the lining, including the pleats. These stitches don't have to be pretty.

15. Next lay the fashion fabric shoulder strap in place with enough seam allowance overlapping the shoulder strap seams, neck edges and sleeve edge. Pin in place. Turn under the seam allowance on all four sides. Applique stitch the short edge at the front shoulder strap seam (10 to 12 stitches per inch [2.5 cm]), then prick stitch ⅛ x ⅛ inch

(3 x 3 mm) the shoulder edge. Applique stitch the back of the strap in place over the back shoulder strap seam. Finally, with a hem or fine running stitch, attach the strap around the neckline (10 to 12 stitches per inch [2.5 cm]). Finally, cut away the excess fabric in the armscye underarm.

16. Now it's time to finish the skirt of the gown with a faced hem. With the gown skirts laid out flat, draw a straight line from the edge of the front skirt panel to the side back skirt seam. Add seam allowance and cut. This creates a gentle slope from the front of the gown to the train. If your sacque does not have a train, you can skip this step.

17. Determine the width of your hem facing—this should be a bit wider than the length of skirt that drags on the floor, so the top edge does not make contact with the ground. Add seam allowance to both edges.

18. On the straight of grain, cut your hem facing the width from the previous step by the length of the entire gown hem. You may need to piece fabric together to get the full length needed. There is no need to cut shaped facings even though the hem of the gown is angled.

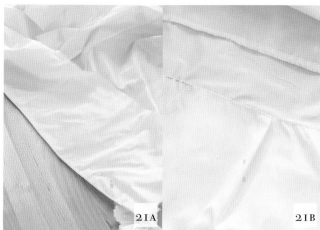

19. Turn and baste up the seam allowance on all edges of the facing. Turn up and baste the bottom edge of the gown skirt according to your seam allowance too.

20. Apply the facing to the bottom of the gown skirt, wrong side to wrong side, matching the bottom edges and skirt front edges with the facing set ⅛ inch (3 mm) in from the gown skirt edge. Stitch these two layers together with a very fine running stitch (10 to 12 stitches per inch [2.5 cm]).

21. Smooth the facing and gown skirt upward, pinning at intervals. Tuck the excess along the top edge of the facing, pinning in place. It's better to take a couple of tucks in each panel than one large tuck. Just be sure everything looks smooth and lovely on the outside. Once pinned into place, stitch the top edge of the facing into place with a fine running or hem stitch (6 to 8 stitches per inch [2.5 cm]). Press.

22. Now it's time to apply the trim to your gown. Our gown trims were created using the pinking and gathering method detailed on pages 85, using a single-gathered, narrower trim for the neckline and a double-gathered, wider trim for the gown skirt.

23. Start with the narrow trim. Since ours was one width, we started it at the beginning of the shoulders and pinned it down the front of the bodice to the edge of the skirt. Stitch it down using a largely spaced out prick stitch.

24. With the serpentine trim, make sure the trim is symmetrical on both skirt panels. It's easier to place these large-scale trims with the gown laid out flat. Measure, adjust and pin as you go. Be careful not to pin through to the back of the gown. When placing your trim on the skirt, be aware of where the trim is sitting on the skirt panels. Make sure that the trim doesn't wander off toward the back of the gown! Once satisfied, prick stitch the trim into place in the groove of both whip gathers. Trim off any excess on the ends, fold and applique stitch into place to prevent fraying.

25. Last of all, make and stitch a lovely bow to add to the sleeve ruffles at the crook of the elbow. For the 4-Loop Bow and 5-Loop Bow, see page 65 and 90.

Hey, guess what? You're done!

1760s
Ribbon Choker Necklace

This easy choker was a classic addition to women's ensembles in the 1760s and early 1770s. They're easy to make and super cute! This is just one way to make a choker, but your options are endless: pinked silk, lace, bows, etc. Find an example in a portrait you like and be creative!

The silk ribbon in this tutorial was generously provided by Britex Fabrics, San Francisco.

MATERIALS
- ½–1 yard (0.5–1 m) 2" (5-cm)-wide silk satin ribbon
- Silk thread (#30)
- ½" (1.3-cm)-wide linen or cotton tape the circumference of your neck
- ⅛–¼" (3–6 mm)-wide silk ribbon for ties in the back—enough to tie a bow plus a little extra

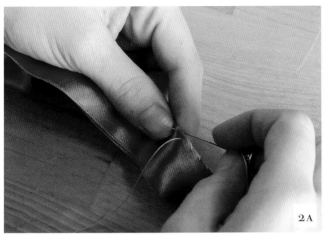

ASSEMBLY

1. Baste and hem the ends of the ribbon and cotton tape.

2. Fold the ribbon in half lengthwise and right sides together, then whip over the fold with heavyweight silk thread. Pull up the thread, gathering the ribbon to fit the length of the cotton tape and secure the thread, then open up the ribbon and gently press flat with the iron.

3. Prick stitch the gathered ribbon to the cotton tape through the middle of the gathers so the stitches are not visible from the outside (6 stitches per inch [2.5 cm]).

4. Fold the edge of the ribbon and securely whip it to the edge of the linen tape.

5. Cut your ribbon ties with enough length to tie in a bow, plus a little extra. Stitch each tie securely to each end of the choker.

1760s

Organza and Lace Apron

Aprons were more than functional garments throughout most of the eighteenth century. Women wore them as a way to finish the look of their ensemble, further adorning themselves in more silk, lace and embroidery.

The drawn waist on this apron is uniquely suited to silk organza. We do not recommend this method for linen or cotton aprons, as it will appear bulky and unflattering, but the delicate lace paired with lighter-than-air organza makes for an attractive and textural accessory.

MATERIALS

- ½ yard (0.5 m) silk organza
- 4 yards (4 m) lace for decorating the edge of the apron
- 1.5 yards (1.5 m) Jacob's Ladder Beading Lace for the top
- Silk thread (#50)
- 2 yards (2 m) of ¼" (6-mm)-wide silk ribbon for waist ties

ASSEMBLY

1. Cut out the silk organza according to diagram (page 112).

1760s Organza & Lace Apron

This apron is made of fine, transparent organza edged with lace. The waist edge is gathered on lace rather than stroke gathered to a waist tape, but both methods are accurate and create beautiful results.

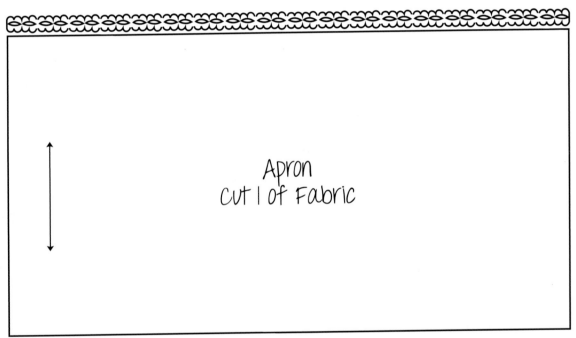

Apron
Cut 1 of Fabric

23 in
(58.4 cm)

45 in (114.3 cm)

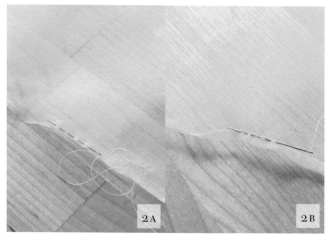

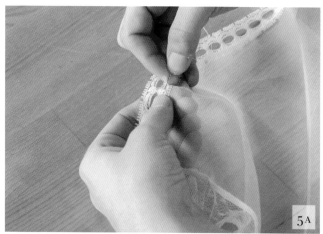

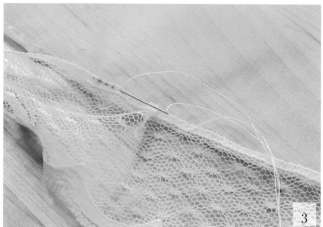

2. Baste up and hem all four sides using fine running stitches (8 to 10 stitches per inch [2.5 cm]). Do not roll hem this organza, as you are applying lace over the top and need a flat surface to work with.

3. Lay the lace over the top of the hemmed edge and attach with fine running stitches (8 to 10 stitches per inch [2.5 cm]). Take small tucks at intervals when applying the lace to prevent it from buckling and hanging funny.

4. When you reach the corner, ease the lace around it by taking tiny tucks. Don't skimp on the lace when turning the corner. There needs to be enough for the corner to lie flat.

5. Apply the Jacob's Ladder Beading Lace along the top edge of the apron using fine running stitches. Thread with the narrow silk ribbon and gather the apron to suit your preferences when worn.

1760s–1770s
Organza and Lace Cap

This cap is inspired by images from the early 1770s.[6,7] It's a good transitional design linking the 1760s and 1770s, and is well-suited to the moderate hair styles of these years. The cap's small size will also accommodate modern short hairstyles, too.

Materials

- *½–1 yard (0.5–1 m) silk organza*
- *2 yards (2 m) of ¼" or ½" (6-mm or 1.3-cm) lace*
- *18" (45.7 cm) cording or candlewicking*
- *Silk thread (#30 gathering and seams and #50 hemming)*

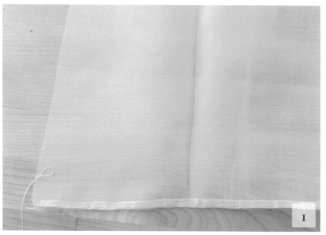

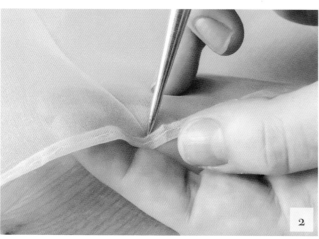

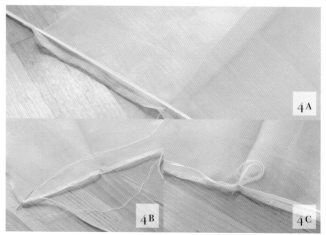

ASSEMBLY

1. Cut the fabric according to the pattern (page 116). Baste the caul edges ⅛ to ¼ inch (3 to 6 mm) on all sides.

2. Fold the caul in half lengthwise, and using an awl poke a hole just above the bottom basted edge.

3. With silk thread #30, whip the eyelet open, and poke the hole with the awl again to round it out.

4. On the wrong side of the caul, backstitch the cord or candlewicking to each side of the straight bottom just above the basted edge. Pull the tails through the hole.

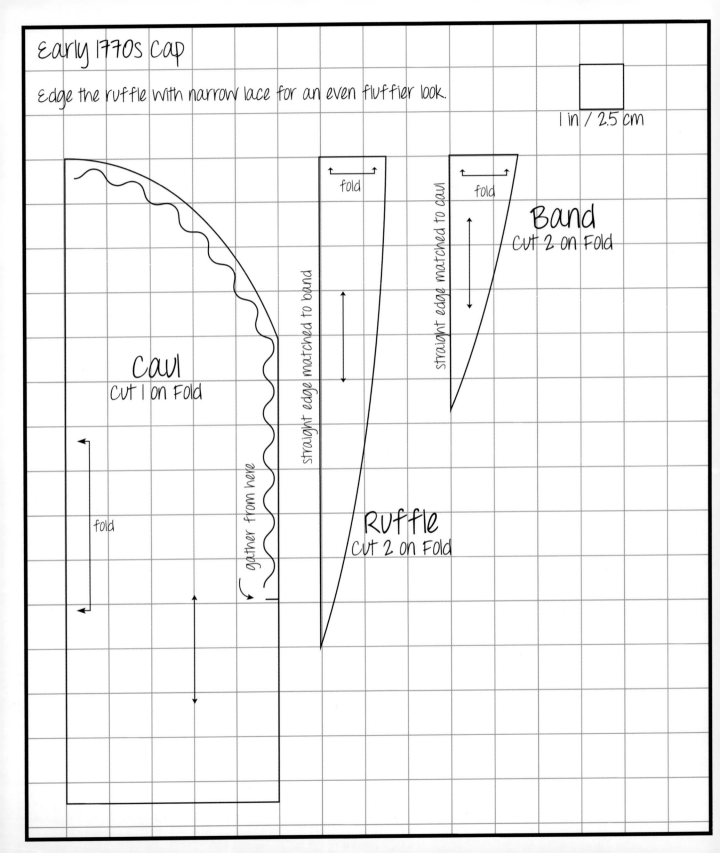

Early 1770s Cap

Edge the ruffle with narrow lace for an even fluffier look.

1 in / 2.5 cm

Caul
Cut 1 on Fold

fold

gather from here

straight edge matched to band

fold

Ruffle
Cut 2 on Fold

straight edge matched to caul

fold

Band
Cut 2 on Fold

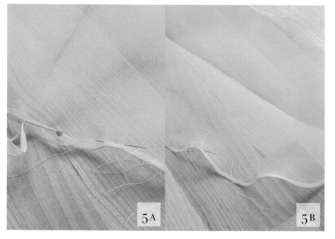

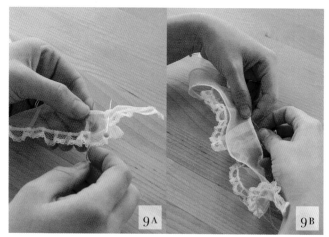

5. Turn up the bottom edge of the caul again over the cord and finely hem, making sure not to catch the cord. Turn the remaining basted edges of the caul up again and finely hem with a fine running or hem stitch (10 to 12 stitches per inch [2.5 cm]).

6. Baste and finely hem all sides of the band with narrow turnings about ⅛ to ¼ inch (3 to 6 mm) wide.

7. Baste and finely hem all sides of the ruffles with narrow turnings about ⅛ to ¼ inch (3 to 6 mm) wide.

8. Hem the short ends of the lace, then attach it to the face side of the ruffle with fine running stitches, taking small tucks as you go to ease the lace around the curved edge.

9. Once the lace is attached, pleat and pin the ruffles to fit the band. Next, whipstitch the ruffle to the band, catching all layers of the pleats from the wrong side of the cap.

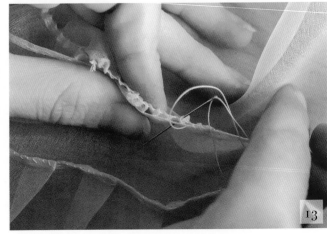

10. Match the center point of the band and ruffle together and stitch to form one length.

11. Referencing the pattern, mark the straight sides of the caul just where the sides begin to curve into the top of the caul. Fold the caul in half lengthwise and pin to mark the halfway point at the top.

12. Whipstitch over the hemmed edge of the caul between the markings from step 10. Pin the ungathered, straight side of the caul to the band and then gather up the rest of the caul to fit the rest of that half of the band.

13. With right sides together, whipstitch the caul to the band, making sure to catch every bump of the gathers. Repeat for the other side of the caul.

14. Trim the cap with a silk ribbon or bow, using some tacking stitches to hold the trim in place. You can find instructions for the standard 4-Loop Bow on page 65 and the 5-Loop Bow on page 90.

1760s
Organza and Lace Treble Stacked Sleeve Flounces

These three delicate layers add to the fluffy, frothy goodness that is such a hallmark of Georgian dress. Our method here uses layers of silk organza trimmed in lace, but the pattern may also be used as a guide for all-lace flounces or finely hemmed cotton or linen ruffles.

MATERIALS

- *2 yards (2 m) silk organza*
- *10 yards (10 m) lace*
- *Silk thread (#30 gathers and seaming and #50 hemming)*
- *1–1.5 yards (1–1.5 m) linen or cotton tape*

1760s Treble Stacked Sleeve Ruffles

These ruffles may be made of organza and hemmed or trimmed with lace. They may also be made of just lace, stacked and joined together at the straight edge.

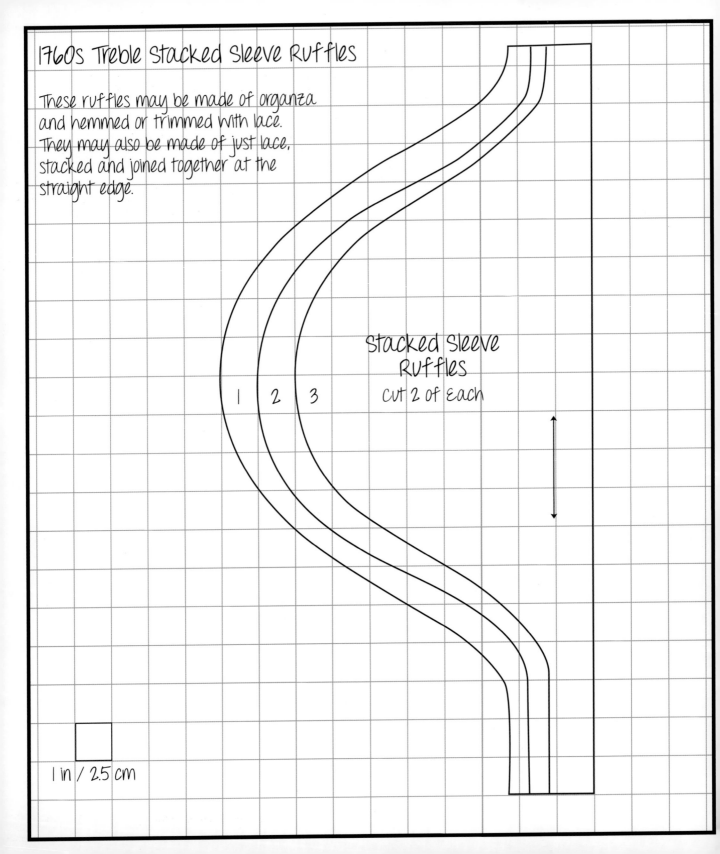

1   2   3

Stacked Sleeve
Ruffles

Cut 2 of Each

1 in / 2.5 cm

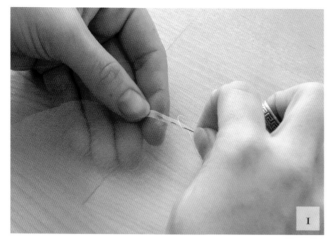

Assembly

1. Cut out the pieces according to the pattern and baste and hem all 6 flounces with fine running stitches (10 to 12 stitches per inch [2.5 cm]). Also hem the ends of the tape that you will attach the flounces to.

2. Apply the lace with a fine running stitch (10 stitches per inch [2.5 cm]), taking small tucks at intervals to ease the lace around the curves of the flounces. Hem the edges of the lace ruffles at each end.

3. Line up the flounces so you have a left side and a right side with the opening angled toward the inside of your arm, closest to the body. Pin the flounces so that the shortest flounce is on the outside and the longest flounce is the closest to the arm. Whipstitch the three layers together, and gather them up to fit the linen tape.

4. With right sides together, whip the flounces to the tape, making sure to catch every bump of the gathers. Finally, tack the ruffles into the gown sleeve lining using large hem stitches.

1760s
Lace Tucker

During the 1760s, women had many choices for decorating the necklines of their gowns. Even though their gowns were trimmed, they would still wear a kerchief or a tucker around their necklines. Here we've chosen a simple tucker of gathered lace to match the apron and treble elbow flounces. Simple, quick and darling, this tucker is the final step in achieving the "stepped out of a portrait" look.

MATERIALS
- *2 yards (2 m) lace*
- *1½–2 yards (1.5–2 m) linen/cotton tape*
- *Silk thread (#30)*

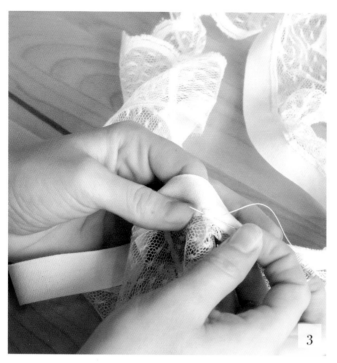

ASSEMBLY

1. Measure the neckline of your gown and the entire top width of the stomacher. Cut the linen tape to fit with an additional 1-inch (2.5-cm) overlap.

2. Finely hem the short ends of the lace and the tape.

3. Attach the lace to the linen tape using a fine running stitch (8 to 10 stitches per inch [2.5 cm]). Take small tucks as you go to give dimension and allow the tucker to curve around the neckline.

4. Lay the tucker into the neckline of the gown and attach using big hem stitches. Make sure you sew through only the lining of the gown. With stomacher-front gowns, attach the tucker along the sides and back of the neckline on the gown only, leaving a length of the tucker free on one side. This length should approximately match the width of your stomacher top edge. Once dressed, pull this loose end across the top of the stomacher to the opposite side of the gown, tucking the tape edge to the inside and pinning lightly to hold the piece in place.

How to Get Dressed and
Wear Your Sacque with Style

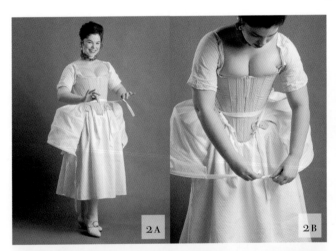

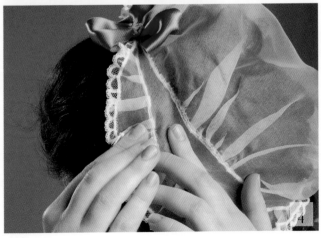

Assembly

1. Start with your shift, stockings and shoes on. Put on your under-petticoat, lace up your stays and if you have a pocket, tie it on around your waist.

2. Put on your hoops: tie the back tapes at center back and the front tapes off center with the bow hooked under your stays. Adjust as needed until the hoops are positioned correctly on your hips. Tie the tapes at the knees across the back and front loosely—these shouldn't be pulling, but don't skip them, as they are vital to keeping the hoops from folding up when you sit.

3. Put on the petticoat over your head. Tie the back tapes to the front and off to the side, then tie the front tapes to the center back.

4. If you have chosen to wear a cap this fine day, put it on now, pinning it into place on each side.

5. Next, pin your stomacher to the stays, matching the top edge of the stomacher to the top of your stays.

6. Put on your gown, overlapping the front edges of the gown over the sides of the stomacher. Pin the front edges of the gown to the edges of the stomacher under the ruffles so the pins are hidden. If your gown is a bit loose or tight after pinning the front edges, adjust the ties in the bodice back lining for a smooth fit.

7. Pull the tail of the lace tucker across the bust, tucking under the top edge of the stomacher. Pin at the center and opposite side to secure the tucker.

8. If you're wearing an apron, put it on now. You may choose to tuck the center front of the apron beneath the bottom edge of the stomacher, but over the stomacher is also accurate. Pull the ties through the pocket slits and tie behind your back, under the back pleats of the gown. You may need an extra set of hands for this.

Time to turn heads at court!

CHAPTER FOUR

The Italian Gown, 1770s-1790s

INSPIRED BY CUT OF WOMEN'S CLOTHES DIAGRAM XXII

The Italian gown, or Italian night-gown, is the English name for the fitted gown with two to four pieces in the back and the separate skirt attached at the waist.[1] Remember the English Gown (page 15)? Though long tagged with just one label, these gowns *are not the same*. While the English gown evolves early on from the mantua, the Italian gown appears to have made its debut around 1776.

From the number of extant Italian gowns that survive today, it appears that the Italian gown completely overtook the English gown in popularity. Even books like *The New Bath Guide* and period newspapers implicate that the Italian gown is equal to, and eventually replaced, the sacque gown for full dress in the 1780s and spawned many a 1790s gown too.[2] Even though early references to this gown involve the upper social class, the Italian gown is suitable for every social level, and can be made out of every type of fabric, from worsted wool to silk satin.[3]

Finally, there were two major aesthetic shifts coinciding with the Italian gown in the late 1770s and early 1780s that affected women's fashion for the rest of the century. First, we have the shift from wide side hoops to large and full false rumps. While early Italian gowns could be worn with hoops, they are best suited for a fashionable false rump, as both style trends seem to appear around the same time.[4] Next, sleeve styles and lengths for women's gowns diversified. In this chapter, we demonstrate the "split" sleeve at a fashionable forearm length, while instructions for full-length, two-piece sleeves can be found on pg 143.

Gown, c. 1780, The Metropolitan Museum of Art, 1976.146a,b

Robe à la Française (Fabric Detail), c. 1770, The Los Angeles County Museum of Art, www.lacma.org, M.2007.211.718

Robe à l'Anglaise (Detail), 1770–1780, The Los Angeles County Museum of Art, www.lacma.org, M.57.24.8a-b

OUR CHOICES FOR THE ITALIAN GOWN

Printed cottons were all the rage throughout most of the eighteenth century, including the early 1780s, when this style of Italian gown was trendy. For our third historic fiber we've chosen a lightweight printed cotton that is close in style to examples from the 1780s.

In this chapter, you will also see a silk petticoat leveled over a split bum paired with our printed cotton gown. Though it might seem odd to our modern eyes, colorful printed cottons were *expensive* in the eighteenth century, and these two fibers were commonly paired. While matching printed cotton petticoats are an expected choice, a colorful, contrasting silk petticoat is an excellent way to pick up the color in the flowers of your cotton gown and to encourage that full-skirted silhouette. However, pairing a printed cotton petticoat with a silk gown or jacket doesn't quite fit the dominant eighteenth-century aesthetic. Avoid this combination *unless* you have solid documentation to back up your choices.

With the rise of large false rumps, we see a lot of fabric in the skirts of Italian gowns, often up to a 120-inch (3-m) hem. Focusing all of that fabric in the back creates the fashionable fullness over the false rump and makes tying up the skirts even more fluffy. However, thicker fabrics may want for less volume—both looks are accurate.

Lastly, on our Italian gown you will see no trim. Yep, no trim! Though not a hard-and-fast rule, many primary references depict this popular dress with minimal or no trim, and the fluff comes in other forms—the apron, the cap, the tucker and sleeve ruffles, each included in this chapter. Gown trims, of course, are up to you, but whatever you do—and we cannot stress this enough—do *not* pink your cotton! Don't do it! Cottons, historic and modern, are not woven tightly enough to pink without the fabrics raveling terribly, and extant cotton gowns simply don't show pinked self-fabric trim. If you want to add trim to your cotton gown, we strongly encourage you to hem the edges.

PRINTED COTTON DO'S AND DON'TS[5,6]

A beautiful floral-printed cotton is one of the most beloved and recognizable textiles of the eighteenth century. We all lust after that perfect printed chintz, but the pursuit of an accurate eighteenth-century print can be a murky flower swamp of confusion. Not all modern floral cottons are created equal. The vast majority of printed cottons available are *totally wrong* for this period. It takes skill and knowledge to spot an eighteenth-century-appropriate printed cotton, so study, study, study those original gowns to train your eye.

Here are our guidelines for hunting that perfect printed floral cotton.

Colors = Cash. The more colors in a printed cotton, the more expensive it was. Each color required a different mordant and a special application, which meant serious cash for enough yardage for a gown. Some printed cottons were more expensive than silk!

Block Printing. Most eighteenth-century prints were block printed rather than roller printed, which was not invented until the 1790s. Block printing creates a unique look, sometimes appearing quite sloppy.

Scale. Printed cottons were manufactured for various uses. Large-scale prints are often earlier, intended for large, early eighteenth-century hooped gowns or furniture. Smaller prints became popular after 1750 with the changing silhouette.

Keep It Natural. While white grounds were arguably the most common for printed cottons, and the safest choice for costumers today, you do see dark brown, Turkey red and blue grounds too. Pastel backgrounds are uncommon. Generally, look for colors that can be achieved with natural dyes. Reds, blues, purples and yellows were common for flowers. Stems and leaves were achieved with green, black and brown. Note that colors like purple were caustic in the eighteenth century and turned brown very quickly—what might appear to be a brown flower could have originally been purple.

What to avoid at the fabric store:

1. If it looks Victorian, walk away. Cabbage roses have no place in the eighteenth century.
2. Avoid toile. That "toile" fabric that we all think of as "classically Georgian" comes from copper plate printing invented in the 1750s. It was most commonly used for home interiors, not clothing.
3. Technology. If the print looks like it is inspired by silk or wool damask or jacquard, leave it behind. What worked for weaving did not always work for printed cottons.
4. Exercise caution with a certain amount of forgiveness. That carefully reproduced printed cotton from a museum is a safe bet, but that does not mean it's perfect. Be aware of what might not be correct.

Overwhelmed? Fear not! Printed cotton stripes, polka dots and some basic geometric shapes are also accurate for the eighteenth century and are easily found in your local fabric stores!

1780s Undies
The False Rump

The first references to false rumps, or cork rumps, seem to begin around 1776, which interestingly coincides with the rise in popularity of the Italian gown.[7] These false rumps came in a variety of shapes and designs. We've chosen to create a split rump, which cleverly allows the long center back point of the Italian gown to lie flat to the body and creates that beautiful and suggestive silhouette that was so popular in this decade.

Our false rump is stuffed with feather down from an old pillow, a readily available material today, but ground cork appears to be the stuffing of choice in the eighteenth century. Both are accurate options.

As with all historic silhouettes, proportion is key. For this particularly tricky understructure, we've analyzed original fashion prints and portraiture versus satirical prints. We found the normal proportion for the bum to be roughly double the size of the waist while satirical prints like "The Bum Shop"[8] show the hips at almost triple the waist. This has resulted in a simple formula that should create the perfect, flattering and accurate size for your false rump.

MATERIALS
- *1–2 yards (1–2 m) tightly woven linen or cotton*
- *1½–2 yards (1.5–2 m) cotton or linen tape*
- *Thread*
- *1 old feather throw pillow*

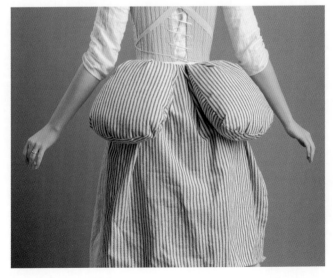

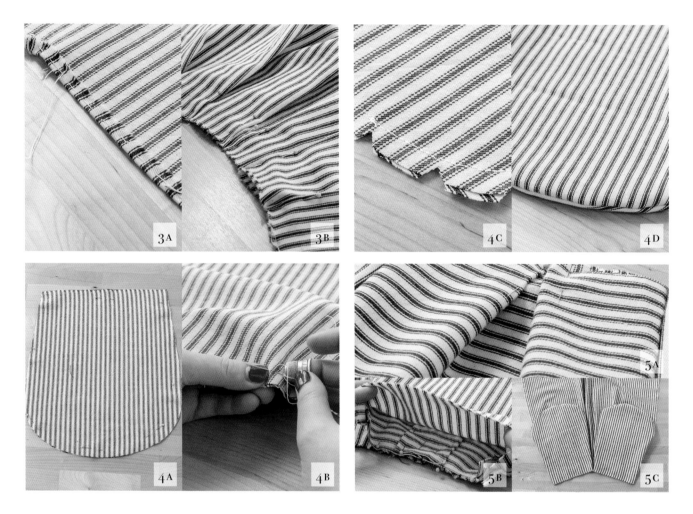

ASSEMBLY

1. Before constructing your false rump, determine your waist-to-bum size. Here's our example:

   Waist—28 inches (71.1 cm)

   Hip (Full)—40 inches (101.6 cm)

   28 x 2 = 56; 56 – 40 = 16

2. Your false rump needs to add 16 inches (40.6 cm) of fullness to your hips. Use the gridded pattern (page 132) as a guide and adjust as needed.

3. Hem (6 to 8 stitches per inch [2.5 cm]) the bottom and sides of the skirt with a ½-inch (1.3-cm) hem. If there is a good selvage on the sides you can skip it. Pleat the skirt to half of the waist measurement (e.g., 14 inches [35.6 cm]), and baste into place. These do not need to be pretty or even. No one will see them.

4. With right sides together, backstitch (6 to 8 stitches per inch [2.5 cm]) the rump pillows together, leaving the top open. Clip, turn and press the seams smooth. You should now have 2 rump pillows.

5. Pleat the under part of each rump pillow to fit half the width of the skirt. Keep the pillows flush to the sides of the skirts and do not worry if there is a bit of a gap (¼ to ½ inch [6 mm to 1.3 cm]) between the bum pillows at the center back. Pin the pillows in place, leaving the upper part of the pillow open and free so you can stuff the rump later.

1780s False Rump

Waist - 28 in (71.1 cm)
Hip - 40 in (101.6 cm)

Determine your false rump size based on your waist to
hip ratio and adjust the pattern as needed.

To determine rump size:

Waist Circumference X 2 = X
X - Hip Circumference = Y (amount to add to your rump)

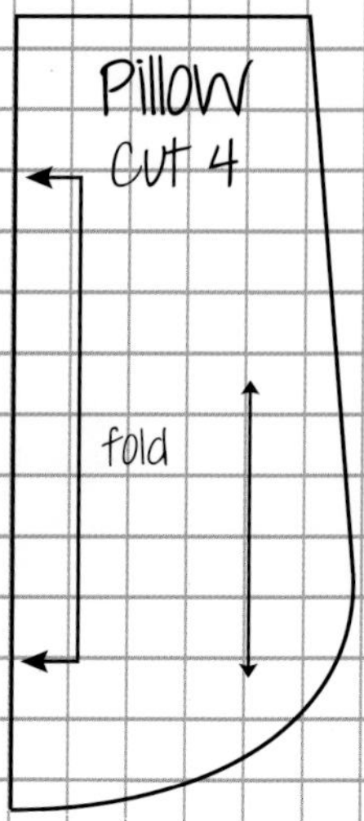

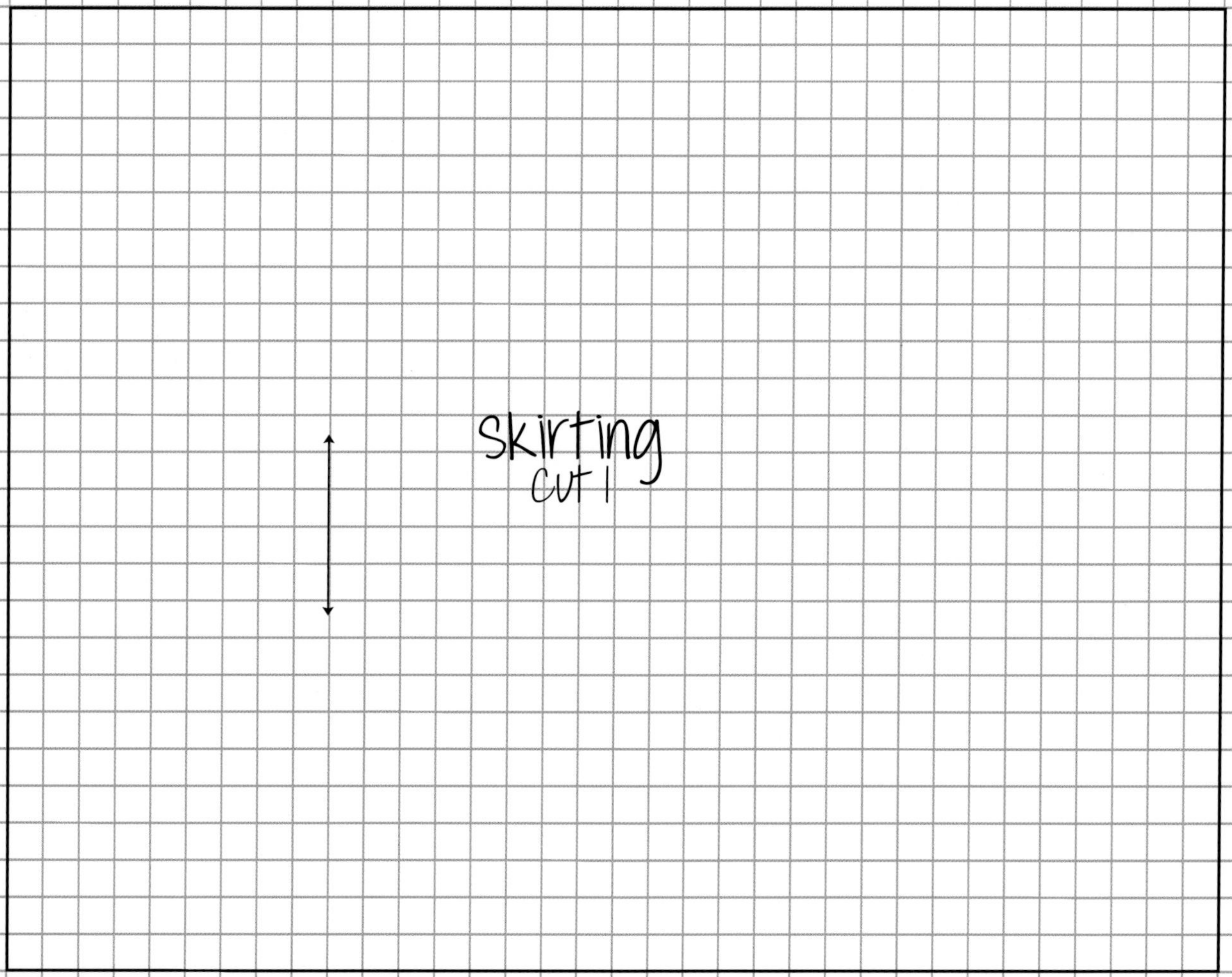

1 in / 2.5 cm

Pillow
Cut 4

fold

Skirting
Cut 1

6. Hem stitch the skirt and under rump pillows to the bottom half of the waist tape (10 to 12 stitches per inch [2.5 cm]). Do not secure the upper part of the pillows.

7. Now it's time to stuff the bum. On your model or dress form, stuff the bum pillows, measuring the new hip circumference as you go. Remember that petticoats and gown skirts will add more girth, so don't overstuff your pillows.

8. Pleat the open edge of the bum pillows to match the underside and tack to the skirt. Fold the waistband over the top of the false rump and hem stitch the waistband through all layers (10 to 12 stitches per inch [2.5 cm]).

Done!

1780s
Silk Petticoat over the False Rump

Petticoats made to fit over understructures are a little different from your average all-one-length petticoat. While you can pattern out this petticoat with a shaped top to accommodate the curve of the false rump, we demonstrate how you can fit and level petticoats on the body, too.

ASSEMBLY

1. Determine the petticoat length according to the fullness of your backside. Over the middle of one of the false rump pillows, measure down to just below your ankle. Cut all your petticoat panels according to this length.

2. Stitch one side seam of the petticoat using a running backstitch (6 to 8 stitches per inch [2.5 cm]) for selvage edges or a mantua maker's seam for raw edges. Leave 10 to 12 inches (25.4 to 30.5 cm) open at the top for the pocket slit and hem these edges to finish them.

3. Pleat the front and back of the petticoat at the waist. For the front, begin with a box pleat about 4 inches (10.1 cm) wide, and continue knife pleating toward the side seams. For the back, make an inverted box pleat at the center back, then continue the knife pleats facing the center back on both sides, while working out toward the side seams. Leave ½ inch (1.3 cm) seam allowance on the unsewn side.

4. Baste across the front and back waist pleats to hold them. Leave your pins in place to help with the fitting.

5. Stitch the second side seam, using a running backstitch for selvage edges or a mantua maker's seam for raw edges. Leave 10 to 12 inches (25.4 to 30.5 cm) open at the top for the pocket slit. Turn and hem the edges of the pocket slit.

6. Hem the petticoat with either a ¼- or ½-inch (6-mm or 1.3-cm) hem (8 to 10 stitches per inch [2.5 cm]).

7. With your model or dress form in all underpinnings and shoes, pull the petticoat over her head and situate it around her waist. Tie the back waist tape securely around the model's waist to the front, over the pleats, then pull the pleated edge of the petticoat upward to create an even hem. Check the hem with your yardstick as you go, measuring from hem to floor. When the petticoat is level, pin it to the waist tape. Repeat this on the front petticoat panel. This sounds easy, but it's not. It takes time and patience but the results are lovely.

8. On the outside of the pleated petticoat waist, hem stitch (10 to 12 stitches per inch [2.5 cm]) the bottom edge of the tape in place, sewing through all layers of the petticoat pleats. Then, turn the tape fully to the inside and hem stitch the free edge in place. Repeat for the back panel.

1780s
The Italian Gown

Italian gowns were first identified with four back pieces sewn in curves to create a flattering line for the waist. This style can be made with just two back pieces as well. It is important that your mock-up be well-fitted through the back before cutting and sewing the gown pieces.

MATERIALS

- *6–7 yards (6–7 m) fashion fabric*
- *1–2 yards (1–2 m) linen lining*
- *Silk or linen thread (#30 for gown construction and #50 for skirt hem only, or 60/2 and 80/2)*
- *1 piece of ¼" (6-mm)-wide boning, the length of the center back bodice*
- *5 yards (5 m) ¼" (6-mm)-wide twill tape*

BODICE AND FIRST FITTING

By the mid-1770s, the seamed back of the Italian gown overtakes the pleated back of the English gown in popularity. This seaming made use of a specific stitching technique called the English stitch (page 13), a clever and efficient way to stitch four edges together in one go, resulting in a very fine and easily alterable seam. Read on to learn more about this ingenious mantua maker's technique.

1780s Italian Gown

For this pattern, the bodice fashion fabric and lining match up exactly. There is an option for variation in the back seams—add additional side back seams or leave the back in two parts. Pay particular attention to the grain lines on the bodice pieces, as these are essential to a smooth fit. The bodice is constructed, then applied over the pleated skirt and stitched from the outside.

Clean finishing between bodice and skirt is not necessary for this style of gown—the top edge of the skirt and turned-under waist edge of the bodice are left raw. Additionally, the excess at the top of the pleated skirt is often left uncut and is instead simply split at the center back and the excess folded down to reduce bulk at the waist and pad the skirt top.

The split sleeve was a popular design in the 1780s, but not exclusive. A single-piece straight sleeve is also accurate, as is a two-piece shaped sleeve. Lengths may vary from elbow to wrist.

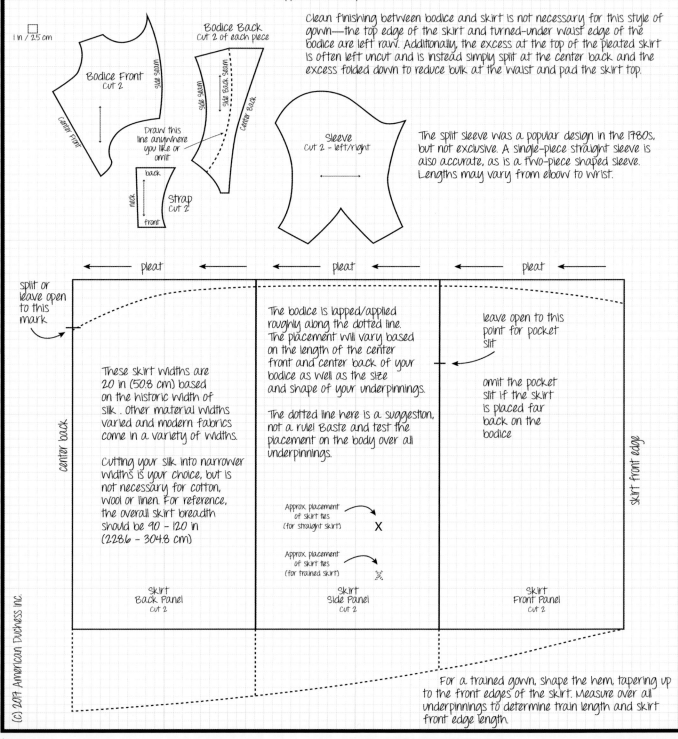

1 in / 2.5 cm

Bodice Front
Cut 2

Center Front

Side Seam

Bodice Back
Cut 2 of each piece

Side Seam

Side Back Seam

Center Back

Draw this line anywhere you like or omit

Sleeve
Cut 2 - left/right

back
neck
front

Strap
Cut 2

pleat   pleat   pleat

split or leave open to this mark

center back

These skirt widths are 20 in (50.8 cm) based on the historic width of silk. Other material widths varied and modern fabrics come in a variety of widths.

Cutting your silk into narrower widths is your choice, but is not necessary for cotton, wool or linen. For reference, the overall skirt breadth should be 90 - 120 in (228.6 - 304.8 cm)

The bodice is lapped/applied roughly along the dotted line. The placement will vary based on the length of the center front and center back of your bodice as well as the size and shape of your underpinnings.

The dotted line here is a suggestion, not a rule! Baste and test the placement on the body over all underpinnings.

Approx. placement of skirt ties (for straight skirt)   X

Approx. placement of skirt ties (for trained skirt)   X

Skirt Back Panel
Cut 2

Skirt Side Panel
Cut 2

leave open to this point for pocket slit

omit the pocket slit if the skirt is placed far back on the bodice

skirt front edge

Skirt Front Panel
Cut 2

For a trained gown, shape the hem, tapering up to the front edges of the skirt. Measure over all underpinnings to determine train length and skirt front edge length.

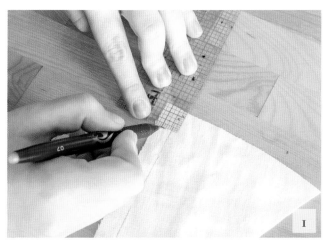

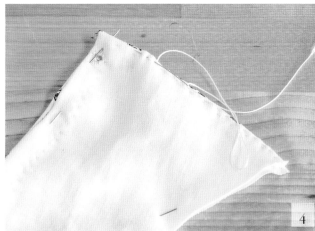

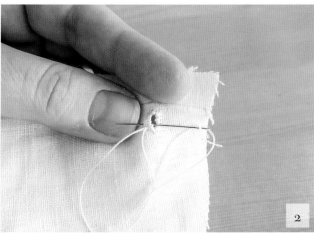

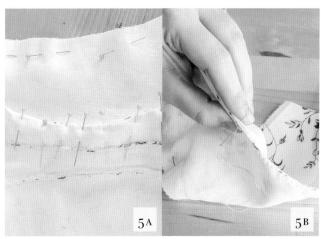

1. Mark the seam allowance on the lining for the center back seam.

2. Measure down ¾ to 1 inch (1.9 to 2.5 cm) from the top of the neckline and mark where the eyelet for the boning needs to go. The finished eyelet must face the body when the pieces are made up so that you can remove the boning later to clean the gown. With an awl, make the hole for the eyelet and whip it open using thick or doubled thread.

3. Turn back the seam allowance and stitch with a fine running stitch to create the boning channel (8 to 10 stitches per inch [2.5 cm]).

4. On the two center back pieces, match the raw edges of the fashion fabric to the lining, wrong sides together, at the side back edges and smooth. Fold in and baste the center back seam allowances of the fashion fabric. Wrong sides together, lay the lining in to sit just inside the fashion fabric and baste the two layers together. Also fold and match the fashion fabric and seam allowance for the top neckline edges.

5. Right sides together, match the two center back pieces at the center back seam. Pin through all layers—two linings and two fashion fabrics—starting at the top and working downward. English stitch the pieces together in the same direction as you pinned (12 to 14 stitches per inch [2.5 cm]). Once stitched, open the back pieces out flat and press the seam.

6. The same method is used to attach the side back pieces to the center back pieces. Follow steps 4 and 5 until the entire back is constructed. Do not baste the remaining side seams on the back. They are important for fitting the bodice. Now place the boning into the channels at the center back seam.

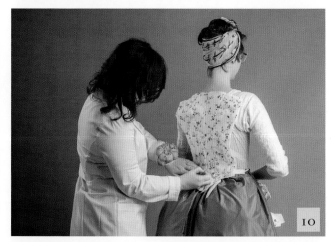

7. On the bodice front pieces, baste up the seam allowance at the waist, center front edges and neckline on your fashion fabric, starting where you plan to place the front edges of the skirt and ending just below the shoulder strap seam.

8. With wrong sides together, match the bodice front lining to the raw bodice front side seam and armscye. Smooth and pin the fabrics together. Along the basted edges, fold in the seam allowance of the lining to just inside the fashion fabric, pin and baste. Finely running stitch the two layers together along the edge. Repeat on other bodice piece.

Triple-check that the length of the center fronts match. Lay one side over top of the other and smooth it down to confirm their length. You might find that even though you basted them the same, one side came out longer than the other. It's that weird magic of dressmaking—stuff gets funky when on the bias.

9. Turn in and baste the seam allowance on the neck edge of the shoulder strap pieces.

10. Now it's time to fit the bodice. With the model in all of her underpinnings, pin the back of the bodice in place, making sure that the center back line is straight and even.

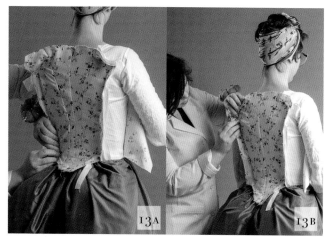

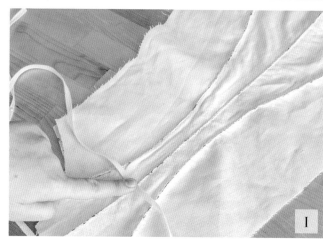

11. Pin the front bodice pieces into place with the desired overlap at center front, making sure the center front line is straight on the body.

12. Pin the shoulder straps in place at the front, then pull over the shoulder and pin to the back shoulder seams to hold the bodice in place. Check that the waist is still in place—don't pull it up when fitting the shoulder straps!

13. Smooth the front bodice lining toward the back. At the side seams, pinch and pin the three layers together, leaving the fashion fabric on the bodice free. Pinch and pin the side seams for a smooth, tight fit, working both sides of the bodice simultaneously and ensuring that nothing is pulled askew.

14. Adjust the fit at the front if needed and continually check the waist length and neckline fit. Refer to the troubleshooting guide on page 230 to work out any issues.

I. *If you find that the back of your gown is standing away from the body, add a waist tie. Mark the waist on the center back seam on the inside of the bodice and stitch a narrow tape at just this point. This can be done at any time.*

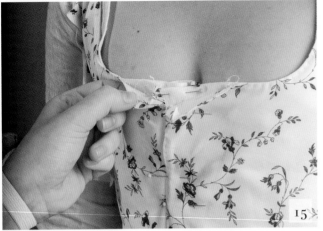

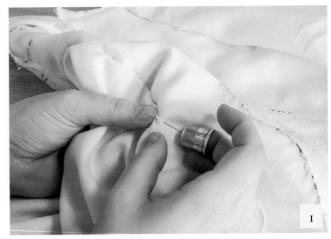

15. If the neckline is too high or wibbly, you can easily adjust it on the body. Pick out the basting stitches and roll the seam allowance down until you get the shape you want.

16. In the back, turn under the waist edge, curving down into the center back point. Pin.

17. Carefully unpin the front closure of the gown, leaving the shoulder straps and side back seams pinned, and remove the gown from the model.

FINISHING THE BODICE AND ATTACHING THE SKIRTS

Again departing from its older sister the English gown, the skirts of the Italian gown were very full, finely pleated and surprisingly roughly finished. The skirts of many extant Italian gowns show raw edges on the inside, merely folded down and split at the center back. In this section, we demonstrate the how and why of this technique.

1. At the side seams, hem stitch (10 to 12 stitches per inch [2.5 cm]) the lining through all 3 layers. Press the seam open and trim out any excess seam allowance leaving about ½ inch (1.3 cm).

2. Now smooth the bodice front fashion fabric over the lining, folding under and pinning the edge of the fashion fabric over the side seam to create an elegant curve that mirrors the back seams. Repeat for the opposite side, matching the curves and placement so both seams are symmetrical. Prick stitch the side back seams through all layers using a ⅛-inch (3-mm) square stitch.

3. Inside the bodice, hem stitch (12 to 14 stitches per inch [2.5 cm]) the front shoulder strap lining to the bodice. Do not stitch the back seam yet.

4. At the waist edge, turn under the seam allowance of fashion fabric and lining together and baste. While raw edges on the waist seam are period accurate, you may instead wish to finish this edge. To do so, turn under and baste the fashion fabric and lining separately, matching the edges, and hem stitch or running stitch together.

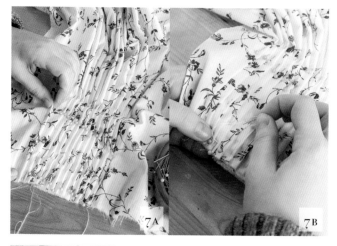

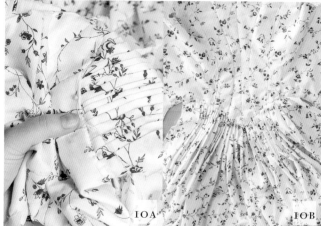

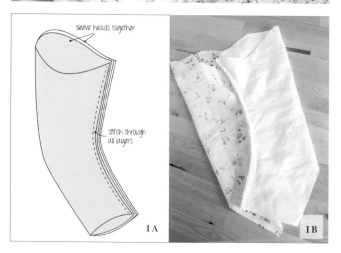

5. Seam all the skirt panels together with a mantua maker's seam for raw edges or a running backstitch for selvage edges. Hem the front edges of the skirt (8 to 10 stitches per inch [2.5 cm]).

6. With the bodice laid open flat, measure straight across the waist from the mark on the side front of the bodice where the skirt will attach to its corresponding point on the opposite side of the bodice. This is the measurement you will be pleating the skirt into. Divide by two and work each side of the skirt in sections.

7. Find the center of the skirt—usually a seam, but not always—and knife pleat the skirts on both sides toward the center back. Keep the visible part of the pleat small, around ¼ to ½ inch (6 mm to 1.3 cm). Pin as you go and continually check pleats against the waist measurement. Vertically baste the pleated skirts together at the top to hold.

8. Lay the waist edge of the bodice over top of the skirt, wrong side to right side, and pin. Slice or open the center back seam of the skirt at the top where the bodice point overlaps it. This helps the pleats flare out correctly and can make the fitting process easier.

Because of the how the bodice is constructed, skirts on Italian gowns are commonly mounted to the bodice with the interior raw edges folded down toward the hem. This prevents bulk at the waist while the uncut fullness adds volume to the top of the skirts. Additionally, this method allows the gown to easily be picked apart and remade later without any loss of yardage.

9. Double-check the seam allowance of the skirt on both sides. If you have a trained skirt, you might need to pull the skirt up higher at the sides to accommodate for the length.

10. Applique stitch the bodice to the skirt from the outside (8 to 12 stitches per inch [2.5 cm]). Catch all the layers and all the pleats. This will be slow and a bit tedious, but stick with it. Once sewn, fold and press the edge of the skirt down toward the hem.

THE SLEEVES AND FINAL FITTING

For most of the eighteenth century, the standard three-quarter-length sleeve dominated women's fashion. In the 1780s, though, sleeve options come alive. While the three-quarter sleeve would never lose popularity, full-length and forearm-length sleeves rose to meet them. Sleeve construction diversified as well, with single-piece, split and two-piece sleeves appearing. In this section, we will construct a forearm-length "split" sleeve, shaped at the elbow, using an ingenious seaming method, and demonstrate fitting the sleeves in the eighteenth-century manner.

1. Here is a third method of sleeve construction that we are really fond of: fold both the lining and fashion fabric in half lengthwise, right sides together. Lay them atop each other, sandwiching the sleeve heads together and matching the raw edges. Backstitch all four layers together (10 to 12 stitches per inch [2.5 cm]). Leave the elbow dart free.

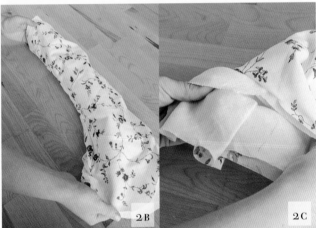

2. Stick your arm through the two fashion fabric layers and pull the sleeve right-side out. This cleverly leaves the seam allowance sandwiched in the other layers of the fabric, seaming both layers with just one line of stitching.

3. Put the gown on the model over all underpinnings. Pin the bodice closed at center front. Double check the fit of the bodice and gown skirts and make note of any adjustments needed.

4. Fit the shoulder straps in the back. Pull them tight over the shoulder and pin securely at the back shoulder seam, keeping their angle and placement on the back as symmetrical as possible. You may need to set them farther in or out to achieve a well-fit neckline both in front and back. If you feel a need to stitch the shoulder straps before fitting the sleeves, remove the gown from the model and hem-stitch the shoulder strap lining in place from the inside, then put the gown back on the model for the sleeve fitting.

5. Slide the sleeve up the arm and pin at the shoulder point. Starting at the front and working around the underarm toward the back, pin the sleeve into place trying your best to catch the gown but not the shift, stays or person.

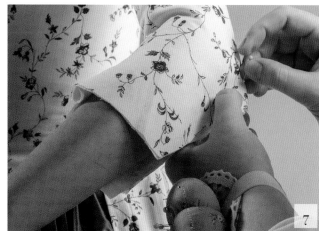

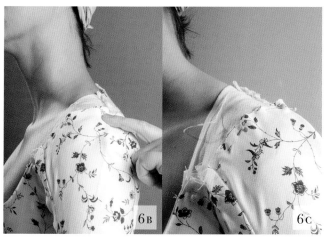

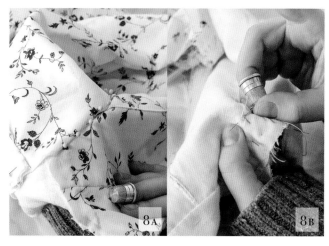

6. At the front underarm crease, smooth the sleeve up over the shoulder, working toward the back. If you have any excess fabric, take a tuck on the back side of the sleeve, right behind the top of the shoulder.

7. Pinch up the raw edges of the sleeve dart to fit the model's elbow. Don't fall victim to the "sexy but too tight sleeve." Make sure the model can bend her arm to take a drink of water. If one sleeve is a bit longer than the other, mark where it needs to be shortened and make that adjustment off the body. This sometimes happens in the fitting process. Once finished, remove the gown from the model, leaving the sleeve and shoulder strap pins in place.

8. On the sleeve underarm, very carefully adjust the pins to vertical pinning. On the inside, mark the stitch line in pencil, making sure both arms match. Backstitch the underarm in place (10 to 12 stitches per inch [2.5 cm]) through all layers.

9. On the outside, stitch the top of the sleeve in place over the shoulder strap with large backstitches. Lay the fashion fabric shoulder strap in place, lining up the seam allowance on the neck edge of the strap, and pinning and smoothing over toward the shoulder. Carefully turn under each edge and pin in place to completely cover all the raw edges. Take your time with this.

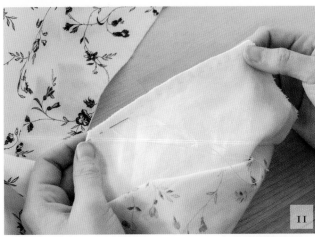

10. On the outside, applique stitch the short edge of the strap at the front shoulder strap seam. Then prick stitch ⅛ x ⅛ inch (3 x 3 mm) over the top of the shoulder. On the outside, applique stitch the back of the shoulder strap in place. Finally, edge hem or finely running stitch the shoulder strap around the neckline. Once satisfied with the sleeve, trim out the excess underarm fabric inside the bodice, leaving ¼ to ½ inch (6 mm to 1.3 cm) seam allowance.

11. Release just the fashion fabric from the pinned elbow dart. Keep the lining pinned and backstitch along this seam line. Trim and press the seam allowance open or to one side.

12. On the outside of the sleeve, smooth one side of the fashion fabric over the lining dart and pin. Turn under the seam allowance on the remaining fashion fabric edge, lap it over the dart seam, covering all raw edges, and prick stitch (⅛ x ⅛ inch [3 x 3 mm]) to finish the dart.

13. Fold up the sleeve cuff hem to the inside, baste, then hem stitch in place (8 stitches per inch [2.5 cm]).

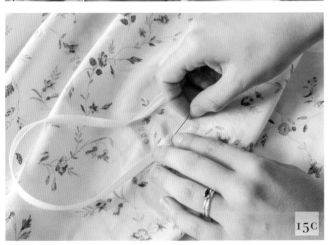

14. It's time to finish the gown. Mark the skirt front length. This is easily done on the model, but an approximate length will do. Aim for a couple of inches off the floor to just above the ankle, depending on your preference. With the skirt laid out open and flat, draw a straight line from this mark down to the raw hem at the side back of your skirt. If your skirt has pocket slits, use these as a reference, if you don't have pocket slits, it's okay to eyeball it using your skirt panels and reference. Just make sure that the lines are symmetrical. Cut along this line to create a train. If you don't want a train, you can skip this part by just making sure your skirts are even when you set the skirt to the bodice. Once satisfied, baste and hem the skirt with about 8 to 10 stitches per inch [2.5 cm].

15. On the inside where the side seams of the bodice lining meet the waist edge, stitch a narrow tape on each side about 12 to 16 inches (35 to 41 cm) long. With the skirt laid out open and flat, determine the placement of your skirt ties. This will vary depending on the fullness and length of your skirt. Our ties were placed 27 inches (69 cm) from the skirt front edges and 13 inches (33 cm) up from the hem. Experiment with placement to find the sweet spot. To tie the skirt up, match the waist tie and skirt tie on each side and tie in a bow. The ties may be pulled up high or left looser for different looks. This is just one way that you can attach tapes to your skirts to gather them up. There were many different ways to achieve this look in the eighteenth century, including applying buttons on the exterior waist and using ribbons to gather up the skirt.

An Italian gown with the skirt pulled up is not a robe à la polonaise. The robe à la polonaise is an entirely different style exhibiting a cutaway bodice often cut all-in-one like a man's frock coat. They were worn loose at the front and drawn up at the back, in long or short form. [9]

Done! Congratulations! You are now the proud owner of a fabulous Italian gown!

Early 1780s Cap

This cap is based on several prints published in the early 1780s and is typical of the large, decorative styles in this decade. Proportion is important with caps and hair, which means you have to take the hairstyle into consideration when making a cap. Finding the balance can be difficult, but we think this cap is just right. It's a cute cap that is big and fluffy but not overwhelming.[10,11]

MATERIALS

- *2 yards (2 m) cotton voile/muslin, silk organza or fine Irish linen*
- *Silk or cotton thread (#30 for gathers and seams and #50 for hems)*
- *20" (50.8 cm) of ¼" (6-mm)-wide fine cotton tape or candlewicking*

ASSEMBLY

1. Use the pattern on page 150 and cut the fabric. Lightly spray starch and iron all the cap pieces. Turn up ¼ inch (6 mm) on all sides of the band and ruffles of the cap and baste. Fold this ¼ inch (6 mm) in half again to create a ⅛-inch (3-mm)-wide narrow hem. Hem stitch in place with a minimum of 12 stitches per inch (2.5 cm).

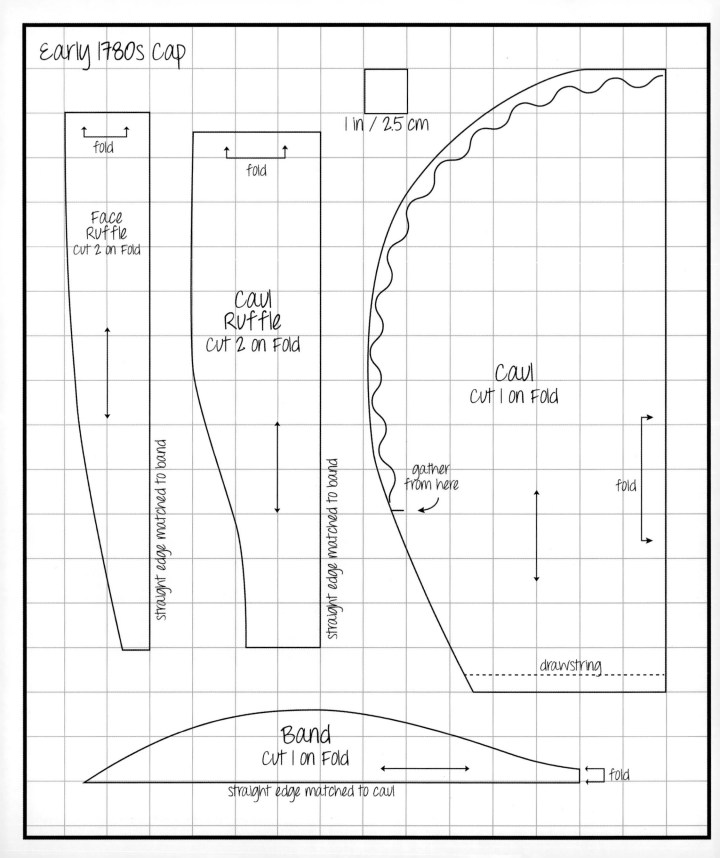

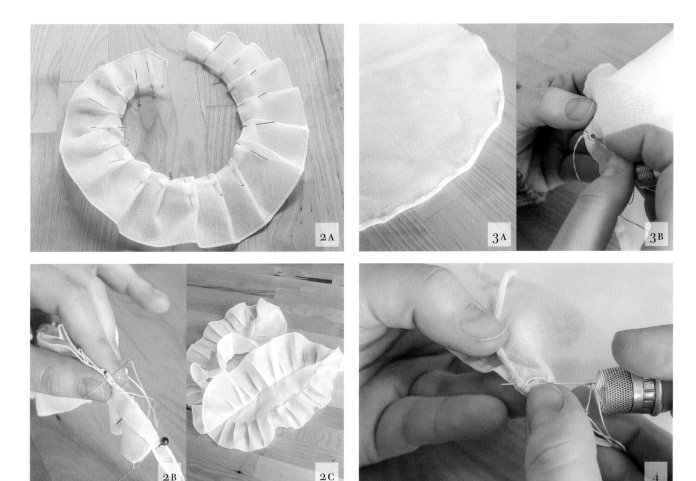

2. Pleat up the first ruffle to fit half of the band, and pin into place. With right sides together, whipstitch the ruffle to the band, catching in all the layers of the pleats. Repeat this for the other side and the caul ruffles. Once all the ruffles are attached, starch and press the seams open, and then fold the band in half to find the center and mark with a pin.

3. Turn up ¼ inch (6 mm) on all of the edges of the caul and baste. Fold the caul piece in half lengthwise to find the center and mark just above the basted seam at the bottom of the caul. Pierce the fabric with an awl at this mark, then stitch the eyelet open with #30 thread. When complete, poke with the awl again to further open and shape the eyelet.

4. Atop the turned and basted seam allowance, secure the candlewicking to the base of the caul piece on each end using a few strong backstitches. Pull the excess candlewicking through the eyelet, using an awl or pin to push the wicking through.

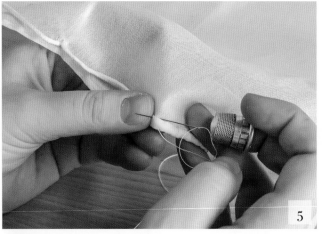

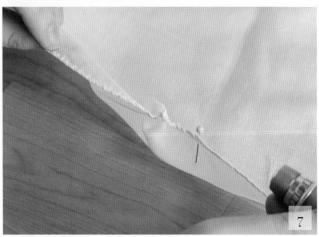

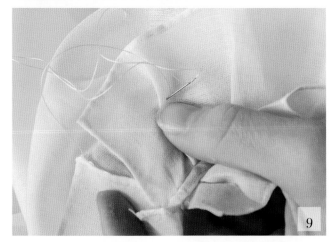

5. Fold up the straight bottom edge of the caul piece over the candlewicking. Hem, making sure not to catch the wicking in the stitches. Continue to hem the rest of the caul using the narrow hem method shown on page 11.

6. Following the pattern, mark where the gathering should start on each side of the caul of the cap with a pin.

7. Fold the caul in half lengthwise to find the top center point and mark with a pin. Loosely whip over the curved hemmed edge of the caul from one side to the center point, about 4 to 6 stitches per inch (2.5 cm). Pull up this thread to gather half of the caul to approximately half the length of the band. Repeat for the other side of the caul.

8. Pin the caul to the band with right sides together, matching the center marks. Whipstitch the two pieces together, catching every bump of the gathers. When complete, open up the seam and press.

9. Smooth the caul ruffle over the caul and loosely tack it down at every pleat to keep the ruffle from flopping over. Iron the seams so everything lies smoothly and starch as needed.

10. Attach your decoration to your cap with small tacking stitches. In the next project you will learn how to make poufs and bows to go on this cap.

Done! Now let's work on decorating your new cap!

1780s

Poufs and Bows

We've decorated our 1780s cap with a row of prestitched poufs with a bow at the center. This type of cap decoration can be used throughout much of the century, and the skills learned here can be applied in numerous ways. Try these techniques on caps, hats, gown trims and wherever else you fancy some poufs and bows.

The silk ribbon in this tutorial was graciously provided by Britex Fabrics, San Francisco.

MATERIALS
- 1–3 yards (1–3 m) silk ribbon
- Silk thread (#30 or #50)

ASSEMBLY

1. Let's start with the poufs. First hem the starting end of the ribbon.

2. Mark your ribbon at even intervals, then stitch along these marks across the width of the ribbon with a loose running stitch. Pull the thread to gather the ribbon, tack stitch and knot off your thread.

3. Repeat until you have a row of poufs that fit the band of your cap. Before you make your last pouf, quickly hem the remaining end of the ribbon.

4. While we only add one 4-loop bow at the center of the cap, you can add more. To learn how to make a 4-loop bow, refer to the 1740s Simple Straw Hat on page 65.

5. Lay the decoration on the cap and secure it in place with a couple of tacking stitches.

Done!

1780s
Silk-Covered "Brain" Hat

Fluffy, puffy and never stuffy. The silk-covered hat in this tutorial was highly fashionable for the 1770s and 1780s. Depicted in black, white or even multicolored, this hat presents almost limitless variations and options for creative expression. Have fun and don't be scared to experiment with size, color, texture and trimmings.

MATERIALS

- *Shallow crown straw hat (approximately 15" [38 cm] diameter or less)*
- *2 yards (2 m) silk taffeta*
- *2 yards (2 m) silk organza*
- *Silk thread (#30 for construction and #50 for hemming)*
- *Assorted feathers, ribbons and trims*
- *Hatpin (optional)*

ASSEMBLY

1. Measure the diameter of the straw hat crown interior and cut two squares of the silk taffeta approximately 4 inches (10.2 cm) larger. Center one square piece over the crown interior and work it into the concave shape, smoothing, stretching and pinning as you go. Stitch in place with large basting stitches. Cut away the excess, leaving some seam allowance for later.

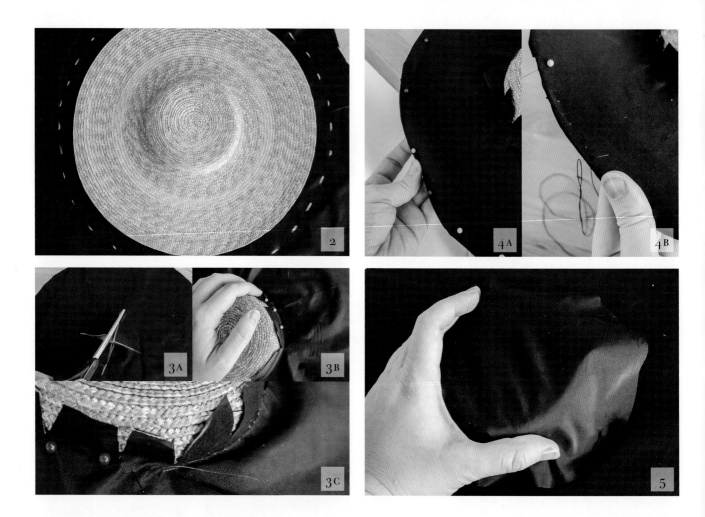

2. Place the straw hat base on a double layer of the silk taffeta and trace around the edge of the brim. Add 1 inch (2.5 cm) seam allowance and cut out the circles. You will have two circles.

3. Roughly mark the center crown with an X. Cut open the X, then continue to clip outwards from center while working the silk piece over the crown. Clip as needed, a little at a time, to release any wrinkles or tension so that the silk piece smoothly fits down over the crown. Pin as you go, and baste the silk to the hat around the base of the crown. Once the silk is smooth, trim off excess fabric that might flap over the crown, and cut any extra notches you might need for that smooth fit.

4. Next smooth the silk over the straw base toward the outer edge of the brim. Turn the seam allowance of the silk over the edge of the straw base. Do not overstretch this—it helps to roll the brim over the edge of a table while pinning to keep the silk from pulling the brim up. Once pinned into place, baste the silk in place around the edge of the brim.

5. This next step was done because our straw base was a light color and we did not want it to show through the black silk gauze. If you are using a hat base that is close to the color of the silk, you can skip this part. Place the second square of silk taffeta from step 1 over the crown and roughly pin down around the base. Mark the silk around the base of the crown, adding ½ to 1 inch (1.3 to 2.5 cm) seam allowance. Remove the taffeta from the crown, lay flat, then cut out the circle you marked.

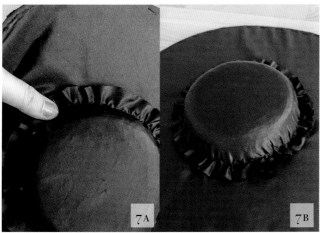

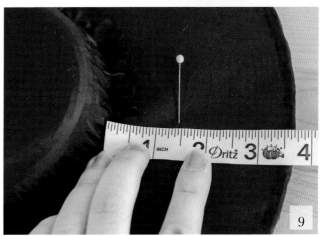

6. Reapply this taffeta circle to the crown, pinning at the center, then smoothing the fabric over the sides of the crown and pinning at the base. Work around the circle, pinning until it is totally smooth across the top. Don't worry about the raw edges on this piece, as they will be covered by the silk gauze "brain" bit.

7. Stitch around the base of the crown to secure the silk covering to the hat.

8. Now the fun part: it's time to make the brain! Measure and cut your silk organza about 24 to 30 inches (61 to 76.2 cm) long and selvage to selvage. Fold this organza piece in half, matching raw edges, so it is about 12 to 16 inches (30.5 to 40.7 cm) high. Baste the layers together, creating a long tube. Do not press the folded edge!

9. On the folded organza, quarter the length and mark with chalk or pins. Repeat this step on the brim of the hat, marking about 1½ to 2 inches (3.8 to 5 cm) out from the base of the crown.

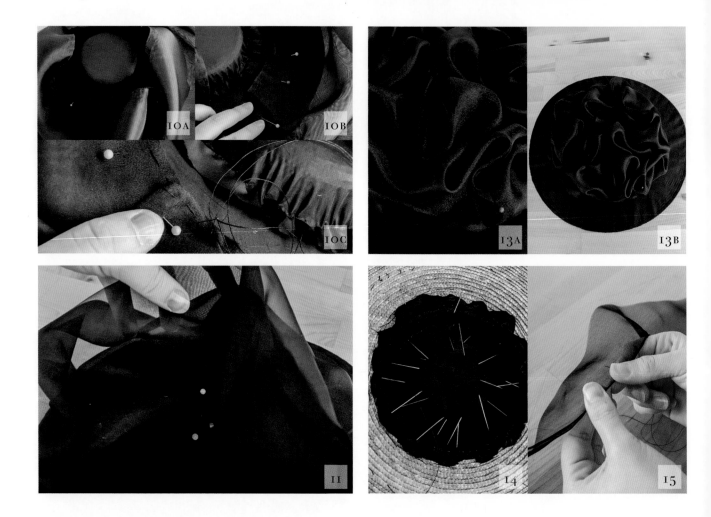

10. Apply the organza to the hat, with the raw edge facing the crown, matching up the quarter points, and secure with pins. There will be lots of excess fabric between the pinned quarters. Pleat this excess down and pin to the brim roughly along that 1½- to 2-inch (3.8- to 5-cm) circle away from the base of the crown. These pleats don't have to be fancy—just a few between each quarter will do the job. Make sure you catch all layers of the pleat as you pin. Stitch the organza to the brim with running stitches.

11. Pull the organza tube upward toward the middle of the crown. Finely running stitch the selvage edges of the tube together to close it off.

12. Begin the "brain" puffs by pulling the two layers of organza apart at the top, folded over edge. At intervals—quarters or fifths—pull the inner layer of organza down to the center top of the crown and pin.

13. Work from the top of the crown outward, pushing the organza down to the crown and pinning at any point that feels too puffy. Futz as needed, but avoid being too particular with the placement. There's no

right way to do this—pin and adjust until you feel the brain is well-balanced and brainy enough to suit your taste. The desire to make this bit symmetrical is human nature, but strive for a natural, uncontrived look. Take as much time as you need to brain through this.

14. Now you get to sew those 30-some-odd pins you just stabbed into the crown in place. With a long, well-waxed thread, tack-stitch at each pin. There is no need to knot and cut the thread—move from one point to the next on the inside until complete. This is tedious as heck and you will stab yourself. If you don't bleed during this project, it's not done yet.

15. Time to trim the hat. An organza ribbon looks jolly good around the brim of a brain hat. You may use premade organza ribbon about 2 inches (5 cm) wide, or make your own. Do this by doubling the circumference of your hat brim to find the length for your organza ribbon—our hat was 37.5 inches (95.3 cm) around, so we cut our organza strip 75 inches (190.5 cm) long by 2 inches (5 cm) wide. Finely roll hem your organza (see page 11).

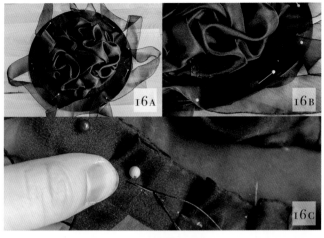

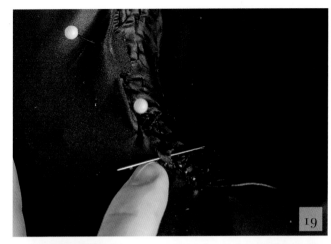

16. Pin the organza ribbon around the hat brim by quarters. Then pleat or gather one quarter at a time, working around the brim and pinning the pleats or gathers in place along the edge. Prick stitch the organza ribbon trim in place, making sure to catch every pleat.

17. Once your trim is attached, it is time to add the under-brim lining. Lay the second large circle of taffeta cut in step 2 atop the underside of the brim, pinning it in place.

18. Around the silk brim, clip into the seam allowance, then turn to the inside and pin around the brim edge. Applique stitch (6 to 8 stitches per inch [2.5 cm]) the edge of the under-brim silk to the edge of the silk rolled over the brim. Do not go through the entire hat, you just need to catch the silk along the edge.

19. On the interior circle, clip into the seam allowance, turn under and pin to the crown lining. Applique stitch (6 to 8 stitches per inch [2.5 cm]) the turned edge of the under-brim lining to the crown lining.

20. For the hat ties, choose prefinished ribbon or hem the edges of silk taffeta to make your own. The ties should be long enough to easily tie in a bow at the nape of your neck. Ours are about 26 inches (66 cm) long and 2 inches (5 cm) wide. Applique stitch (8 to 10 stitches per inch [2.5 cm]) the ribbon ties to the underside edge of the hat brim.

21. You may now choose to decorate the hat even more! Try bows, feathers, flowers or cockades to finish off your fashionable new hat!

Early 1780s
Ruffled Apron

The fluffy, ruffly aprons of the early 1780s are truly pieces of joy. They are so fun to wear, with great texture, movement and whimsy that really take an ensemble to the next level. Add this apron to your outfit with the matching cap, neck tucker or handkerchief and elbow ruffles and you will look like you just walked out of an eighteenth-century portrait.

Materials

- *2 yards (2 m) cotton voile*
- *2 yards (2 m) ½" (1.3-cm)-wide cotton or linen tape*
- *Silk thread (#30 for gathers and topstitching and #50 for hemming)*

Assembly

1. Cut out the pieces according to the pattern (page 162).

2. Hem three edges of the apron with a fine running stitch. Leave the top of the apron unsewn. Set aside.

3. Next, connect and hem the ruffles on all sides. Seam the edges selvage to selvage with fine running stitches (8 to 10 stitches per inch [2.5 cm]) and press open. For the hem, you can either use the narrow hem (page 11) or roll hem (page 11) technique on cotton voile.

Early 1780s Ruffled Apron

This apron's glamour is in the wide ruffle around all three sides, paired with delicate stroked gathers at the waist.

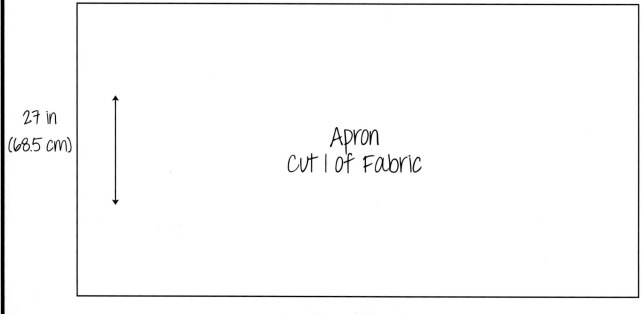

27 in
(68.5 cm)

Apron
Cut 1 of Fabric

54 in (137 cm)

Ruffle

The Ruffle for this apron is double the length of the three edges of the apron. Join the fabric as needed to make the width.

6 in
(15.2 cm)

Ruffle

6 yards
(5.4 meters)

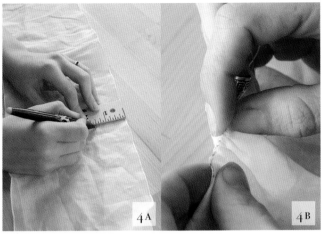

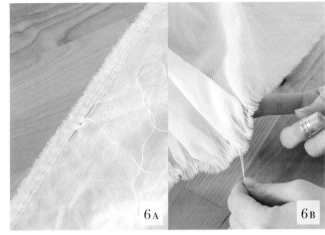

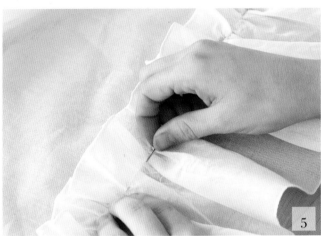

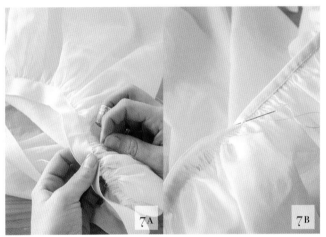

4. After all the ruffle edges are hemmed and seamed, fold over the top of the ruffle 1 to 1½ inch (2.5 to 6.4 cm), and whipstitch over the fold, working in sections of 12 inches (30.5 cm) at a time and gathering them down to 6 inches (15.2 cm). Tack stitch at each interval and carry on to the next. Continue whip gathering until you've gathered up the entire ruffle, then steam and finger press the ruffle open.

5. Pin the gathered line of the ruffle over the hemmed edge of the apron, easing it around the curves and leaving about ¼ to ½ inch (6 mm to 1.3 cm) unruffled at the top. Prick stitch into place through the gathered line to hide the stitches.

6. Mark the center of the waist edge with a pin. Using #30 thread, stitch 3 lines of even running stitches for stroke gathers, stopping at the center of the apron. Then start new lines at the center and work toward the other end of the apron. Gather up to the desired width between 13 and 16 inches (33 and 40.6 cm), anchor the tails to a pin and "stroke" the gathers to even them out.

7. Apply half the width of the waist tape over the stroke-gathered waist edge. Hem stitch along the tape edge, catching every bump of the stroked gathers. Fold over the remaining half of the tape to the inside and repeat the step. Check and adjust the gathers as you go. You want to keep them as evenly spaced as possible. Do not rush this; it is worth it to take your time.

8. Once finished, starch and iron the apron and ruffles to keep their shape and volume.

1780S
Neck Tucker
and Elbow Ruffles

For the Georgian woman, having something around the neckline of her gown was just as important as putting on her shift. While you can wear this style of gown with a large and full neck handkerchief (and it looks fabulous when you do!), having a cotton voile set of apron, tucker and ruffles is not only easy but extremely fashionable. Whether you choose the kerchief or the tucker, *do not go out without one or the other*. It's a cardinal rule of being a gorgeous Georgian lady!

MATERIALS

- ¼–½ yard (0.25–0.5 m) cotton muslin or voile, silk organza or fine linen cut into strips about 1½" (3.8-cm) wide
- Silk thread (#30 for attaching pieces and #50 for hemming)
- 2–3 yards (2–3 m) ½" (1.3-cm)-wide cotton or linen tape

1. Cut the tape to fit the neckline of your gown. Hem the raw ends of the tape.

2. Join your strips of voile to make one length double the length of your gown's neckline measurement. Join pieces selvage to selvage with a fine whipstitch, or fine hem each end before whipping the seams.

3. Next, narrow hem or roll hem the long and short edges of the tucker.

4. Whip over one long edge of the tucker and gather up to fit the tape. With right sides together, pin the ruffle to the tape and whipstitch it to the edge, making sure to catch every bump. Open the ruffle and tape out flat and press just the seam if needed.

5. Lay the tucker into the interior neckline of the gown, pin and tack it into place using large hem stitches. Make sure to sew the tucker to only the lining of the gown!

6. Repeat these exact steps for your elbow ruffles, just in smaller lengths.

How to Get Dressed and
Wear Your Italian Gown with Style

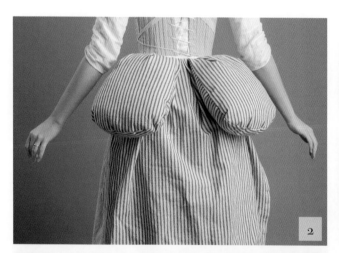

ASSEMBLY

1. Start by putting on your shift, under-petticoat, shoes, stays and pocket.

2. Put on your false rump, tying the bow off to the side of your center front and making sure you can still reach your pocket.

3. Next, put your petticoat on over your head and arrange the skirt over the false rump. Tie the back tapes to the front with the bow tied off to one side, then lap the front of the petticoat over the back tape and tie in back.

4. Pin your cap on both sides of your head with small pins, catching your hair.

5. Put on your gown and tie the waist tape around your waist with the bow off to one side. Don't pin your gown yet!

6. If you want to have your gown point over your apron, put your apron on now and tie it at your center back, underneath the gown.

7. Now you can pin your gown closed. If you're right handed, lay the right side of the bodice down first and overlap with the left side so you can push your pins in at the seam of the left piece (this helps hide them). Do the opposite if you're a lefty. Start at the bottom edges of the bodice and pin up toward the neckline until the gown is secure and smooth. Bury the edges of the pins into your stays. Pinning your garments takes patience and practice, and you will also develop your own preferences and techniques for starting point and pin orientation.

8. You may wish to add a bow or other ornament to your neckline—pin this on last, hiding the head of the pin in the loops of the bow.

9. If you are wearing your hat, place it on over your cap at a forward angle. Carefully pass a hatpin through one side of the hat, into your hair, and back out the opposite side of the hat. Then tie the hat ties in a bow in back at the base of your skull.

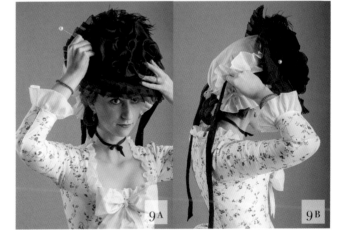

You are now ready for a fashionable jaunt to the milliner's shop!

CHAPTER FIVE

The Round Gown, 1790s

INSPIRED BY TIDENS TØJ, WHITE WEDDING DRESS, C. 1797
#426-1923 & CUT OF WOMEN'S CLOTHING DIAGRAM XXXIII
FABRIC & THREAD PROVIDED BY BRITEX FABRICS, SAN FRANCISCO

The 1790s is such an incredible decade for clothing. The massive political and social changes during this decade, coupled with the popularity of Classical Greece, Rome and the Orient, resulted in fashion that was unlike anything prior. The rising waistlines, preferences for sheer, gauzy fabrics and the growing emphasis on a more natural body shape for women were all meant to reference Classical art, a departure from the artificially enhanced Georgian silhouette.[1] Though it may seem sudden, there was actually a gradual progression of the silhouette beginning in the 1780s and slowly, subtly shifting until the waist was well and truly under the bust in the mid-1790s.[2]

Gowns from the mid- to late-1790s are also quite different from the dresses seen in the early 1800s. The 1790s silhouette is full and round, transitioning toward the later columnar Regency shape. Almost all of the gowns in our book use between 5 and 7 yards (5 and 7 m) of fabric. This gown is no different, with over 4 yards (4 m) of fabric in the skirt and 1 yard (1 m) of fabric in the two-piece shaped sleeves alone. Though it may seem excessive, these gowns need this much fabric to give that beautiful ethereal look that is necessary to step back into the 1790s.

Finally, stays started losing their rigid, primarily conical shape by the early 1780s, continuing to get softer and "thrustier" into the 1790s. A full bosom that sits in a well-supported natural position on the body is crucial for a successful 1790s look. However, the bustline of the 1790s is still *nothing* like the "lift and separate" of early 1800s corsets. We encourage you to make or purchase a dedicated pair of 1790s stays or a corset to achieve the natural shape of this unique period of dress.

Woman's Dress (Round Gown), c. 1795, The Los Angeles County Museum of Art, www.lacma.org, M.57.24.12

Collection of English Original Watercolour Drawings: Morning Dress 1795, Ann Frankland Lewis, 1795, The Los Angeles County Museum of Art, www.lacma.org, AC1999.154.21

OUR CHOICES FOR THE ROUND GOWN

The fabric for this gown is a creamy open weave linen with embroidered spots. The drape and sheerness of this linen helps create that beautiful, flowing, elegant and classical look. When stiffer fabric such as silk taffeta is used, it is important to adapt the skirt widths for the additional fullness. Since our linen is so sheer and open, we were able to make our skirt hem circumference about 150 inches (3.8 m). However, if this gown were made of silk taffeta, it would need to be closer to 90 to 100 inches (2.3 to 2.5 m) skirt hem circumference to accommodate the difference in fabric drape.

You will notice there are many additional millinery projects for this chapter. This is because the 1790s is all about accessories! It's easy to change your whole look with just your choice of chemisette, sash, turban, cap, etc. A white or ivory linen or cotton gown provides the perfect backdrop to display all the fun millinery that really makes the 1790s pop with personality.

We encourage you to try various colors and textures throughout your accessories. The late eighteenth century did *not* abide by modern matchy-matchy rules. Complementary colors were popular in the late eighteenth century, which may seem bold and garish to a modern eye, but when you start putting these various pieces together, you'll see what a difference it makes in gaining that "fashion-plate perfect" look. If you're nervous, experiment with colorful shoes, gloves or reticules and expand your color combinations from there!

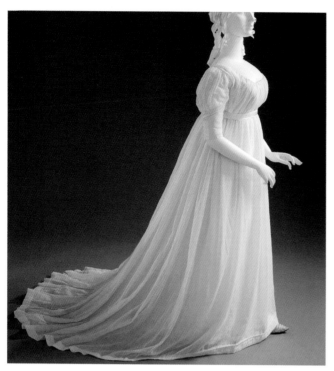

Woman's Dress, c. 1800, The Los Angeles County Museum of Art, www.lacma.org, M.2007.211.868

Women 1790–1799, Plate 034, N. Heideloff, February 1, 1795, Thomas J. Watson Library, The Metropolitan Museum of Art, b17509853

LEARNING TO LOVE LINEN[3,4]

Linen, oh, darling linen, you are a well-loved pain in the backside. Linen is wrinkly, wonky and wackadoodle to work with. Naturally, we want to use it for a cool and comfortable summer gown, but when you actually get to working with it, you end up just wanting to set the gown on fire. While we adore linen for structural gown linings, shifts, caps and kerchiefs, using modern linen to make a gown can be a real struggle.

Here's the deal: most linen isn't made today like it was in the eighteenth or nineteenth century. There has been a shift in the way linen is treated before manufacturing that causes it to be all wibbly-wobbly. It is almost *impossible* today to find affordable linen made of long, strong fibers. And so we preach caution when it comes to working with linen for gowns. It's not because the fabric isn't accurate or pretty. It's simply because modernity has made modern linen much more difficult to work with than in the past.

However, linen is a *great* fabric for summer. As a reed plant, it is far superior in wicking away moisture than cotton and is naturally cool to the touch. When linen is starched, it is crisp and easy to finger press and fold, no iron needed. It holds up well to washing (though go easy on it in the dryer), and different weights are available for different purposes. It was the cheap go-to fabric in the eighteenth century and they used it for everything, though ironically today linen can be quite expensive!

To help stabilize modern linen and make it easier to work with, we recommend that you spray starch your fabric before cutting out the pieces. For our 1790s gown, we've used a very loose-woven linen, and we found that using spray starch on the lining and the fashion fabric throughout the construction process really minimized the wonkiness.

Finally, we would like to quickly address solid colored linen. While linen doesn't take dye as well as other fibers, dyed linen *did* exist in the eighteenth century. There are plenty of primary sources that advertise dyed linen for sale, and there are even original garments made out of dyed linen. Now, does this mean you should make a gown out of a brightly colored linen? As always we recommend caution, research and good judgment when it comes to color choices in your linen garments.

1790s Undies

Under-Petticoat and Back Pad

Because there are precious few primary sources for 1790s under-petticoats, we had a difficult time deciding how to pattern one for the book. Ours is based on two extant petticoats: a riding habit petticoat in the Salisbury Museum[5] and a bodiced petticoat that dates to circa 1790s in the Snowshill Collection.[6] It is important to note that the back pad is crucial to the success of your silhouette, because it helps prevent the gown skirts from collapsing onto themselves. Don't skip it! Finally, though we tried to create an under-petticoat pattern "one size fits many," you may need to adjust the pattern and subsequent fabric yardage to best fit you.

MATERIALS

- ½ yard (0.5 m) medium- to heavy-weight linen
- 2½ yards (2.5 m) cotton voile at 54" (137-cm)-wide
- 1 yard (1 m) cotton candlewicking or ¼" (6-mm)-wide cotton tape
- Scrap of cotton fabric large enough for the pad
- Stuffing (feathers, wool or cork)
- Silk thread (#30 for seams and gathering and #50 for hems)
- Linen thread (60/2)

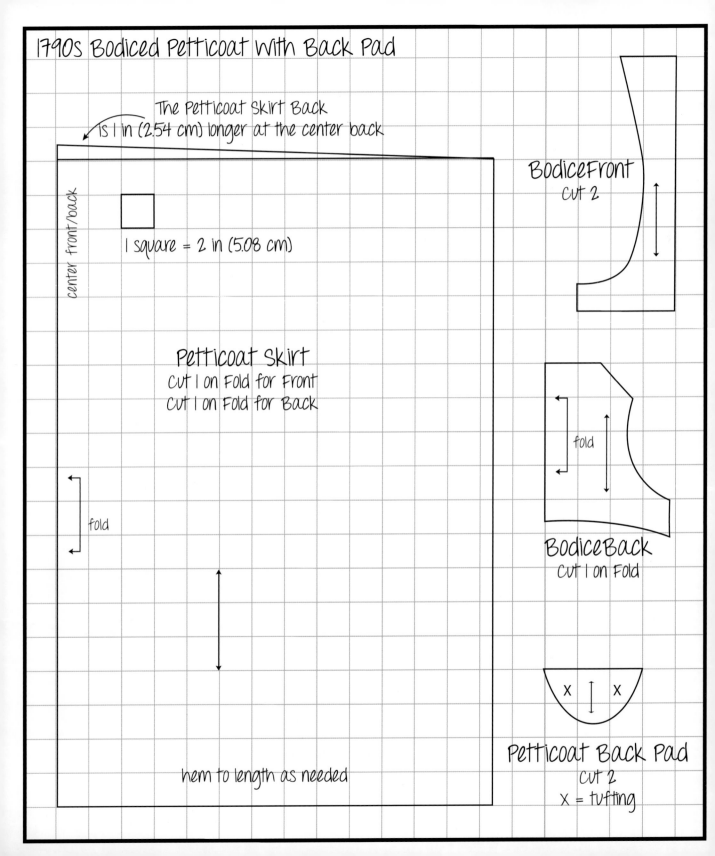

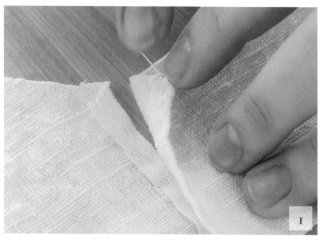

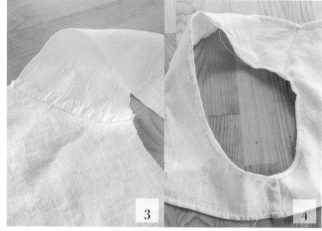

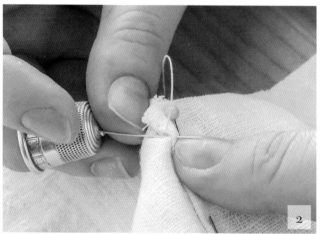

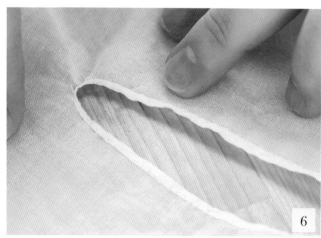

ASSEMBLY

1. Cut out the pieces according to the pattern. Then turn under and baste the seam allowance on the bodice front pieces on the wrong side of the fabric. On the bodice back piece, turn under the seam allowance and baste to the right side.

2. Attach the bodice fronts to the bodice back by pinning the front bodice side seam over top the back bodice side seam, covering the basted edges. Hem stitch down the edges on outside and inside of the side seam. Repeat for the opposite side.

3. Attach the shoulder strap seams using the same method as above.

4. Baste and hem all of the remaining raw edges on the bodice—neckline, center front, waist edge and armscyes.

5. Cut out the skirts according to your measurements.

6. Divide the front skirt panel in half selvage to selvage and mark the center with a pin. From this point, measure down 10 to 12 inches (25.4 to 30.5 cm), mark and cut straight down from the top edge to this mark. Fine hem the edges of this slit open and carefully whipstitch the bottom of the slit to prevent fraying or tearing.

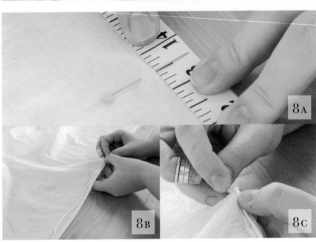

7. Seam the petticoat panels together using a running backstitch for selvage edges or a mantua maker's seam for cut edges. Next, baste ¼ to ½ inch (6 mm to 1.3 cm) around the top of the skirt.

8. Now fold each half of the front panel in half again and mark the quarter points with pins. With the length of the drawstring laid out flat toward the center front slit, backstitch the front drawstring ends in place at both pins.

9. Hem around the entire top of the skirt. When hemming over the drawstring, make sure you don't catch it in the stitches.

10. Starting from the side front skirt marking (where the anchor end of your drawstring is), stitch 3 rows of equal running stitches to the skirt side seam. Do not yet gather up. Fold the back skirt panel in half and mark the center with a pin. Stitch 3 rows of running stitches on each half of the skirt back panel. Now repeat this step on the other front skirt panel. You should now have 4 sections of running stitches to gather up the skirt.

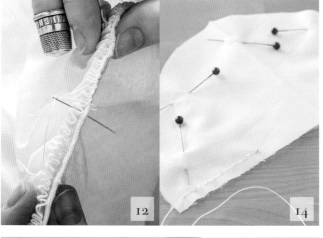
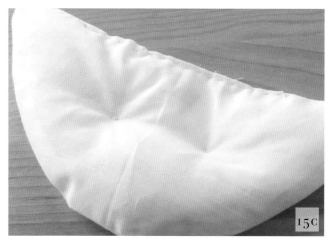
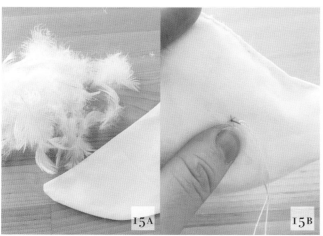
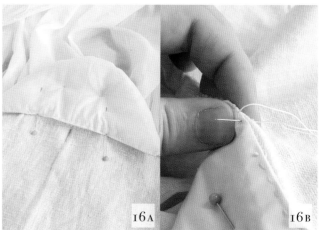

11. Gather up the portions of the skirt in sections to match the side seams and center back of the bodice. Pin the bodice to the petticoat right sides together as you gather up the skirt. There is not a lot of fabric in this under-petticoat, so keep your gathers evenly spaced and anchor the gathering threads by wrapping the excess thread around a pin.

12. Whipstitch the skirt to the bodice, carefully catching every bump in the gathers. Finally, hem your petticoat.

13. Now let's move on to the back pad. Cut out the shape according to the pattern, adding seam allowance.

14. With right sides together, backstitch around the crescent shape, leaving about 3 inches (7.6 cm) open at the top straight edge. Turn the pad right-side out, taking care to push out the corners.

15. Stuff the pad very full of your stuffing of choice (we used feather down). Then turn the seam allowance in and close up the 3-inch (7.6-cm) hole using a whipstitch. If desired, place a few tufting stitches in the pad to hold the stuffing in place.

16. Line up and pin the pad in the middle of the back of your under-petticoat where the bodice and skirt meet, and whipstitch the pad to the petticoat.

1790s
The Round Gown

Bodice construction in the 1790s seemed to follow the "under-bodice plus over-bodice" convention set earlier in the 1780s with the *chemise a la reine* and similar gowns. The purpose of the under-bodice is to keep the back of the gown secure and well-fitted while the over-bodice floated over the top with no structural demands. You can use this design as the foundation for nearly any 1790s gown design. For our gown we have chosen a pleated-front, V-necked over-bodice, but many different bodice front designs are open to you. Round gathered necklines, bibbed fronts, surplice, and square fitted tops will all work with the under-bodice construction too.

We finished nearly all the seams and edges in this project due to the shreddy nature of the fashion fabric. If your gown fabric is a tightly woven silk or cotton, you can leave the top of the skirts and the bottom of the bodice edges unhemmed.

MATERIALS

- *5½–6 yards (5.5–6 m) fashion fabric*
- *1–2 yards (1–2 m) linen for lining*
- *Silk thread (#30 for seams and gathers and #50 for hems)*
- *2 yards (2 m) ¼" (6-mm)-wide woven tape or candlewicking*

THE UNDER-BODICE AND FIRST FITTING

The 1790s gown is truly a transitional garment, drawing on former standards of construction and blending them with new silhouettes and styles. Read on to assemble and fit this structural bodice.

1790s Gown Bodice Lining

Use these pieces to build your gown back and front under-bodice.
This bodice can be combined with any front style treatment for a
variety of 1790s looks, such as a gathered, surplice, or bib front.

1 in / 2.5 cm

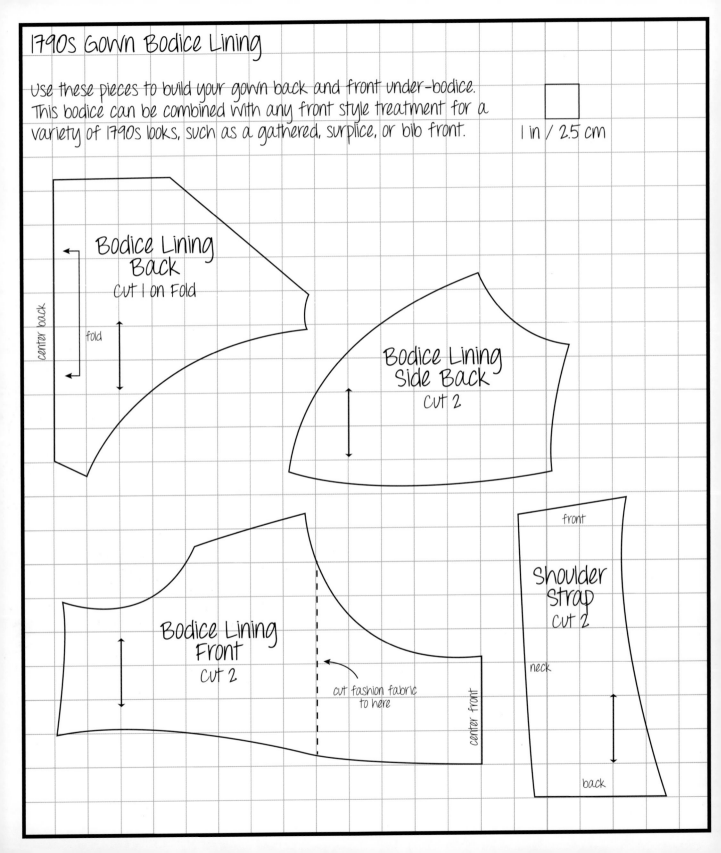

Bodice Lining
Back
Cut 1 on Fold

center back

fold

Bodice Lining
Side Back
Cut 2

Bodice Lining
Front
Cut 2

cut fashion fabric
to here

center front

Shoulder
Strap
Cut 2

front

neck

back

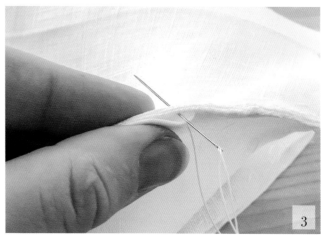

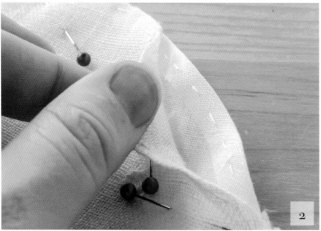

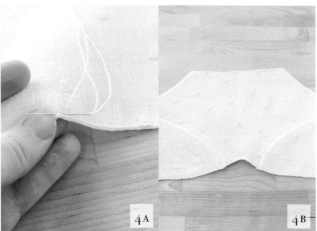

1. Turn under the seam allowance and baste the neck edge, side backseam edges and waist edge of the bodice back lining. Match the bodice back fashion fabric to the raw armscyes and shoulder strap edges of the bodice back lining and pin. Fold under the seam allowance on the gown fabric at the neck edges and stitch the two pieces together with fine running stitches. Fold in the side back seam and waist edges of the gown fabric to match the lining and baste through both layers to secure them together.

2. On the side back lining pieces, turn and baste the side back seams and waist edges. Match the gown fabric to the lining at the armscye and side seam, turn in the seam allowance to match the lining along the side back seams and waist edges and baste the two layers together.

3. With right sides together, pin the back and side back pieces together at the side back seam, working the curve from the waist edge into the armscye. The finished waist edges need to match, but there can be excess in the armscye. English stitch from the waist edge to the armscye, pulling the stitches taught (12 to 14 stitches per inch [2.5 cm]). Open out the pieces and press the seam. Repeat on the other side.

4. Use a fine running stitch to finish the bottom edges of the bodice back. Stop your stitching 1 to 2 inches (2.5 to 5 cm) from the bodice side seams. This will leave room for fitting.

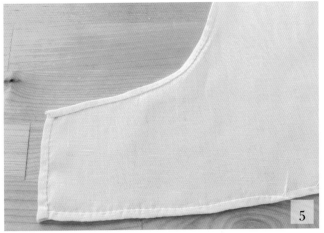

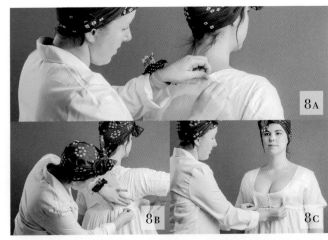

5. On the front bodice lining, turn in the seam allowance, baste, turn up again, then hem the neckline and center front. Also hem the bottom waist edge just to the dotted line where the gown fabric will be applied.

6. Pin the under-bodice front fashion fabric on the lining matching the raw edges at the shoulder strap and armscye. Fold under the fashion fabric along the dotted line and to match the waist edge, then finely running stitch, stopping 1 to 2 inches (2.5 to 5 cm) from the side seam.

7. Turn up the seam allowance on the neck edge and front bodice seam of the shoulder straps and baste. On the inside, lap the basted front shoulder strap edge over the bodice front shoulder strap seam and stitch with a small hem stitch or backstitch (12 to 14 stitches per inch [2.5 cm]). Press and starch the bodice pieces.

8. Now it's time to fit the bodice. Begin with putting on all of your underpinnings. Roughly pin the bodice together at the side seams and back shoulder seam and put on the bodice. Overlap the center front edges and pin closed. Adjust the pins of the shoulder straps in back as needed to achieve the correct high waist placement. If you need bust darts, pinch them up and pin in place now.

Bust darts are normal by the end of the 1790s with the development of the softer, more natural bust shape. It is important to fit the bust darts on the body, as often a lady is not symmetrical.

9. Pin just the fashion fabric out of the way at the side seams, then pinch up and pin the side seams to create a smooth, tight fit. Work both side seams simultaneously for symmetry.

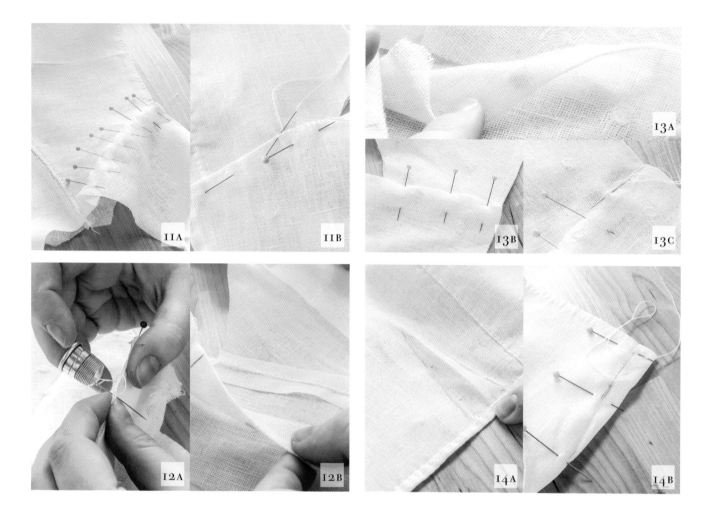

10. Now adjust the back shoulder seams again to create a smooth, symmetrical and secure fit. Once satisfied, remove the bodice from the model, leaving the side seam, shoulder strap and bust dart pins in place.

11. Next, hem stitch (12 to 14 stitches per inch [2.5 cm]) the back shoulder straps to the lining on the inside.

12. For the sides seams, fold the lining open and crease the seam allowance with your fingers along the pin line. Then with right sides together, tightly whipstitch the folded edges from the inside. Remove the pins and press the seam open. Cut off any extra seam allowance, leaving ¼ to ½ inch (6 mm to 1.3 cm).

13. Pin the side back bodice fashion fabric to overlap the lining side seam. Trim away any excess seam allowance. Now pin the bodice front fashion fabric over the layers and fold under the seam allowance to cover the raw edges. Use your lining side seam as a guide for where the fashion fabric seam should go. Prick stitch the fashion fabric side seam from the outside (⅛ x ⅛ inch [3 x 3 mm]).

14. Move on to your bust darts next, and lightly mark with a pencil or erasable ink the dart placement along the base of the pins. Unpin the darts, fold right sides together, carefully matching up the pencil lines and backstitch (6 to 8 stitches per inch [2.5 cm]). Fold the fabric out flat and press the darts toward the side seams.

SKIRTS AND SLEEVES

In this next section, we will make the front and back of the skirt as well as the long, two-piece sleeves. It is at this point that your gown may go on to be a round gown or remain an open robe: just omit the front skirt panel. Those clever Georgian mantua-makers knew the construction was the same! Additionally, we have included a diagram (page 185) for measuring and patterning a two-piece shaped sleeve and how to assemble with the efficient tailor's method.

1. Cut your skirt panels according to the diagram on page 185. Fold the front skirt panel in half lengthwise and mark the center with a pin. Measure down 10 to 12 inches (25.4 to 30.5 cm) and mark. Then cut straight down from the top edge to this mark. Finely hem the slit open, and carefully whipstitch the bottom to secure and strengthen the opening.

2. Seam all the skirt panels together. Use a mantua maker's seam for raw cut edges or a running backstitch for selvage edges. Turn over the seam allowance and baste the entire top edge of the skirt. From the center front of the skirt measure about 16 inches (40.7 cm) toward the side seam and mark with a pin. Repeat for the opposite side. This measurement can be a little longer or shorter, depending on your model's size.

3. Cut two lengths of narrow tape or candlewicking about 18 to 20 inches (45.7 to 50.8 cm) long. This length may also vary if you change the front of the skirt measurement above. Pin the end of the tape to the pin mark and securely stitch it in place. Repeat for the opposite side.

4. Next, turn the edge over again and hem stitch the entire top of the skirt, making sure not to catch the drawstring on the skirt front.

5. If your gown skirt is trained, now is a good time to mark and adjust it. Working on a large flat surface, fold the skirt in half at the center back, matching up each of the skirt panel seams and pin together. With the entire skirt folded and smoothed flat, you will see a "stair step" effect at the hem with the different lengths of each skirt panel. Draw a straight line from the bottom corner of the skirt front panel side seam to the bottom corner of the skirt back panel side seam, creating an angle across the width of the skirt side panel. Continue this line to intersect the bottom edge of the skirt back panel, smoothing into a gentle curve. Cut this angle. Do not hem the skirt yet.

6. On each side, measure straight down from the start of the armscye in the bodice front to find the anchor points for where the skirt is attached to the bodice of the gown and mark with a pin.

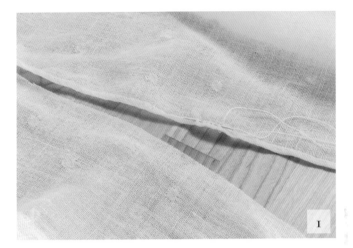

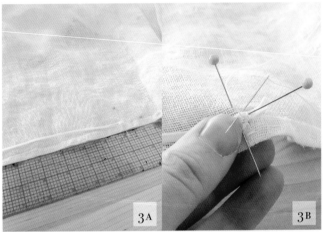

1790s Round Gown Skirt + Train

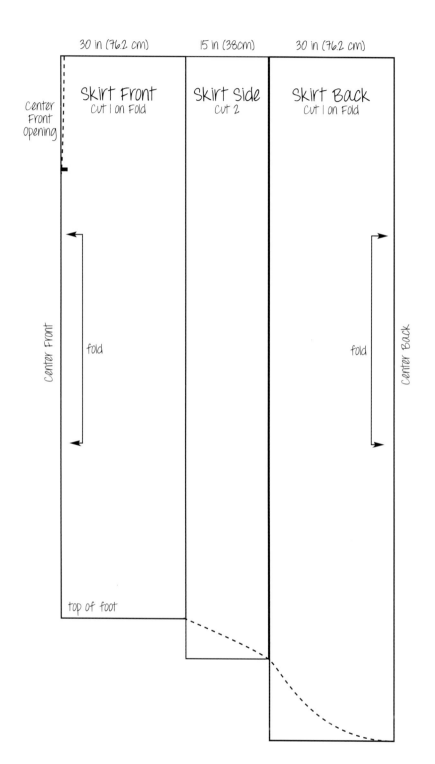

Measure the skirt back from high waist to floor, then add as much extra length as you like for the train.

"Connect the dots" between the skirt front seams, skirt side seams, and skirt center back point.

Draw a shaped line for the train.

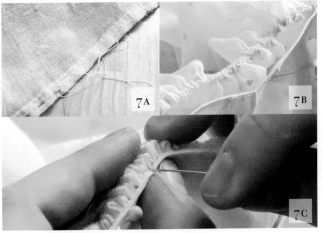

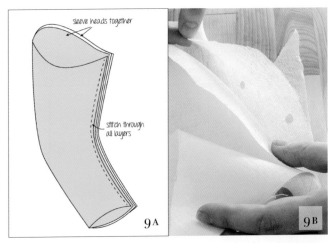

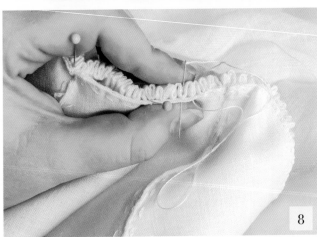

7. Find the center back of your back skirt panel one more time and mark. With #30 thread, make 3 rows of even running stitches at the top of the skirt from the drawstring to the center back, then a separate triple row of running stitches from the center back to the opposite drawstring. Pull the stitches up to gather them to fit the sections marked on the bodice. They will be very tight and full. Pin the skirt to the bodice right sides together as you go and secure the long tails of the gathering threads by winding them around another pin.

8. Whipstitch the skirt to the bodice, catching every bump of the gathers touching the bodice. When complete, open the bodice and skirt out flat and press.

9. Cut out your sleeves using the diagram on page 187 and add 1 inch (2.5 cm) seam allowance on all sides. Pin together, then check the fit of your sleeves and mark any adjustments before you seam them together. Don't make your sleeves too tight—make sure you can bend your arms! Once satisfied, separate the lining from the gown fabric and lay them right sides together. Then stack the lining sleeve on top of the fashion fabric sleeve, sandwiching the sleeve heads. Match up the wrist edge of all 4 pieces and smooth everything out.

10. On the outside seam edge measure up and mark 3 to 4 inches (7.6 to 10.2 cm) from the wrist, which will be the wrist opening. On the inside seam mark ½ inch (1.3 cm) up from the bottom edge. This will give you room to finish your wrist edge once the sleeves are stitched. Backstitch both seams at 8 to 10 stitches per inch (2.5 cm).

Measuring for Shaped Sleeves – 1780s and 1790s

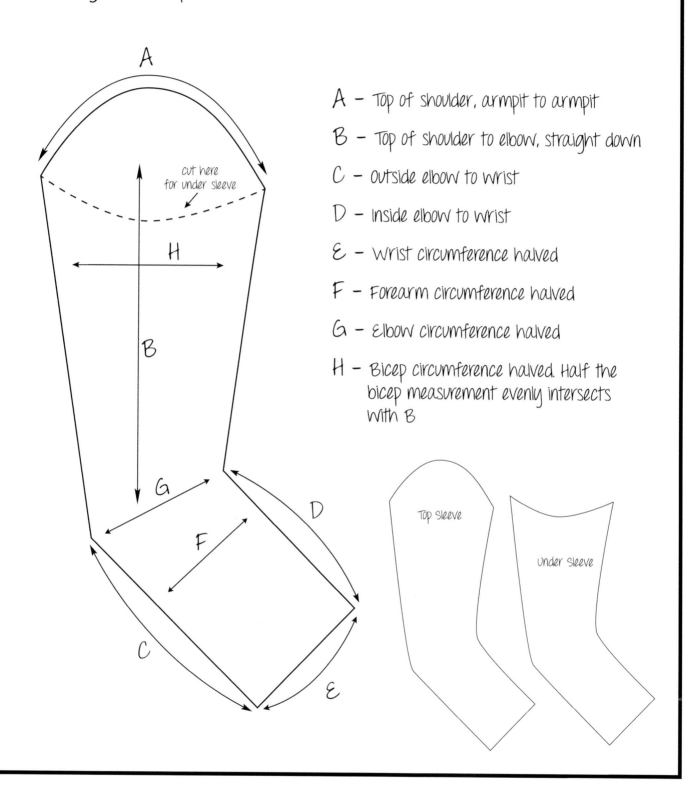

A – Top of shoulder, armpit to armpit

B – Top of shoulder to elbow, straight down

C – Outside elbow to wrist

D – Inside elbow to wrist

E – Wrist circumference halved

F – Forearm circumference halved

G – Elbow circumference halved

H – Bicep circumference halved. Half the bicep measurement evenly intersects with B

cut here for under sleeve

Top Sleeve

Under Sleeve

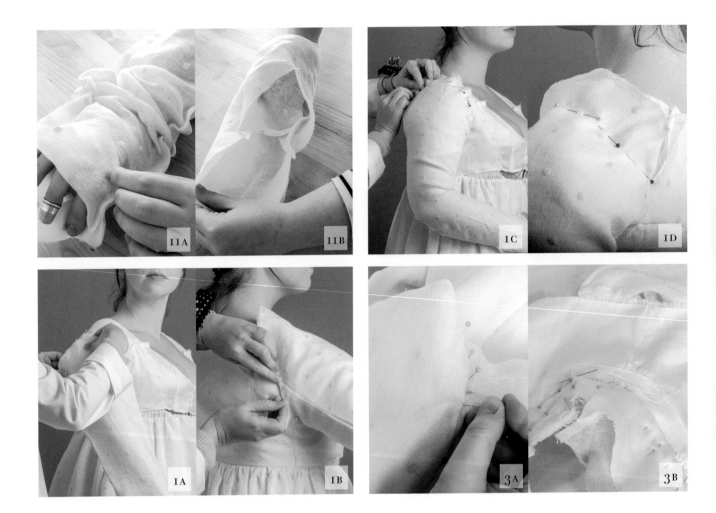

II. Trim the seam allowance to ½ inch (1.3 cm). Stick your arm between the two fashion fabric layers and turn the sleeve right-side out. This will leave your raw edges encased in the layers of the sleeves. Carefully press the seams smooth and shape the sleeve.

SETTING THE SLEEVES AND FINISHING THE BODICE

In the next section, we once again demonstrate the eighteenth century method of setting the sleeves on the body. Additionally, the under-bodice is completed, ready for the final over-bodice treatment.

I. Now it's time to set the sleeves. Begin by putting the gown on the model over all underpinnings. Slide the first sleeve up the arm and pin at the shoulder point. Starting at the front and working around the underarm toward the back, pin the sleeve into place trying your best to catch the gown but not the shift, stays or person. At the front

underarm crease, smooth the sleeve up over the shoulder, working toward the back. If you have any excess fabric, take a tuck on the back side of the sleeve, between the shoulder point and the start of the underarm crease. Check mobility. The model should be able to cross her arms and raise them above her head. Repin as necessary and repeat for the other sleeve.

2. Check the hem of your gown in front and mark a shorter length if it's too long. The hem should just brush the top of your toes and extend gracefully into the train at the back. Carefully remove the gown, keeping all the pins in place.

3. On the sleeve underarm, carefully convert to vertical pinning. Mark the stitch line in pencil, making sure both arms match, then backstitch the underarm portion of the sleeve with about 10 to 12 stitches per inch (2.5 cm).

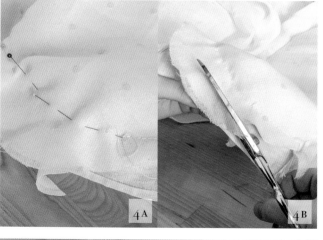

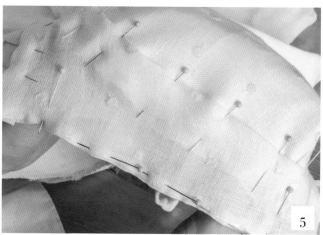

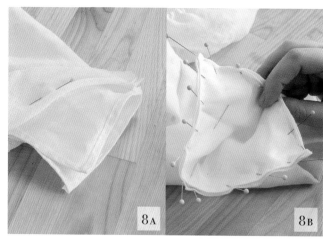

4. With big backstitches, stitch the top of the sleeve in place over the shoulder strap. These stitches don't have to be pretty—they will be covered later. Trim away any excess of just the sleeve head.

5. Now lay the fashion fabric shoulder strap over the lining shoulder strap, matching up the seam allowance at the neck edge. Turn under the seam allowance on all edges and pin the strap in place making sure both sides are symmetrical.

6. Next, applique stitch the short edge of the fashion fabric shoulder strap on the front bodice (10 to 12 stitches per inch [2.5 cm]). Prick stitch ⅛ x ⅛ inch (3 x 3 mm) around the top of the arm. Applique stitch the back of the strap in place over the back shoulder strap seam (10 to 12 stitches per inch [2.5 cm]). At the neckline, finely running stitch to attach the straps.

7. Cut out any excess seam allowance in the armscye, leaving ¼ to ½ inch (6 mm to 1.3 cm). If you have shreddy fabric, or very little seam allowance, do what the Georgians did by roughly whipstitching over the armscye seam allowance.

8. On the sleeve cuffs, turn up and baste the seam allowance on the lining. Then turn under the fashion fabric edges to match, pin and finely running stitch to finish.

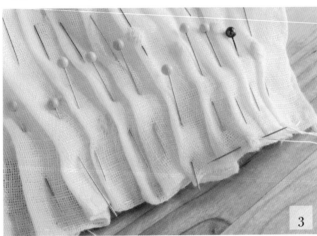

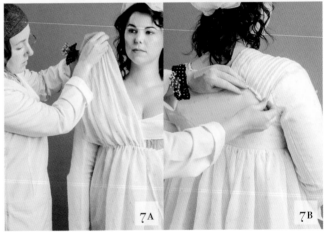

OVER-BODICE AND SKIRT FRONT, THIRD FITTING AND FINISHING

At last it is time for the over-bodice. For our gown we have chosen a pleated, V-neck style, but it is at this point that you may choose nearly any bodice design. The under-bodice construction and purpose remains the same.

1. Hem all four sides of the over-bodice piece. If the over-bodice pieces are ambiguously shaped, be sure to mark the shoulder, bust, left and right edges.

2. At the top of the shoulder, finely knife pleat the fabric to the width of the back shoulder strap. The visible side of the pleat should be between ¼ and ½ inch (6 mm and 1.3 cm) but they will be very deep underneath. Pin and baste in multiple rows across the pleats to hold them in place, then press to set them.

3. Prick stitch the pleats together at the shoulder edge. Be sure to catch all the layers and adjust the pleats to keep them even if necessary.

4. On the underside, backstitch each pleat, only catching the edges, across the width of the piece about 3½ inches (8.9 cm) down from the shoulder edge. Stitch another row a few inches down from the first. These stitches should be loose and invisible on the right side. This keeps the pleats lying correctly over the shoulder.

5. With right sides together, pin and whipstitch the over-bodice waist edge to the drawstring section of the skirt. Be very careful not to catch your drawstring. This is tricky and time consuming, so go slowly and carefully.

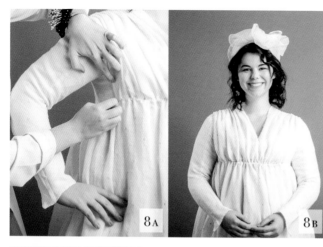

6. Next, put the gown on over all underpinnings and pin the under-bodice closed at center front. Tie the front drawstring under the bust and adjust the gathers. At this point the over-bodice will hang, attached only to the waistline drawstring.

7. Gently pull the pleated top edge of the over-bodice over the shoulder to meet the back shoulder seam. If the shoulder edge of the over-bodice is too long, fold the edge under to lay where you like and pin. Don't overfit this piece—you want it to look graceful.

8. Move to the side of the over-bodice and lay the edge along the side of the bust. Placement may vary—find the natural line. It's important to secure the over-bodice to the under-bodice to control the fullness and drape. Repeat for the opposite side, then remove the gown, leaving the pins in place.

9. Finely applique stitch the over-bodice shoulders into place, making sure to catch all the pleats. Then prick stitch the side of the over-bodice in place from the shoulder to skirt.

10. Hem the skirt of the gown.

Done!

1790s
Sash

While sashes came into fashion in the 1780s (yes, this means you can wear one with your Italian Gown [page 127]!), they were all the rage in the 1790s. Very often women would just use long lengths of wide silk ribbon, but sadly we no longer have access to that quality of silk ribbon, so we have to make our own. However, making your own ribbon from fabric yardage is an excellent way to use up scrap fabric. For our sash, we cut brightly colored striped silk into strips and hemmed the edges. Lastly, there is such a thing as a sash that is too long. Keep this sash between 4 and 6 yards (4 and 6 m) long, *max.*

MATERIALS
- *⅓–½ yard (⅓–½ m) of 54" (137.2-cm)-wide silk fabric or 4–6 yards (4–6 m) of 4–6" (10.2–15.2-cm)-wide silk ribbon*
- *Tassels (optional)*
- *Silk thread (#50 for hemming and #30 for tassels)*

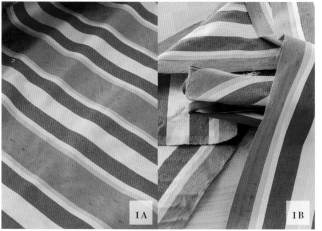

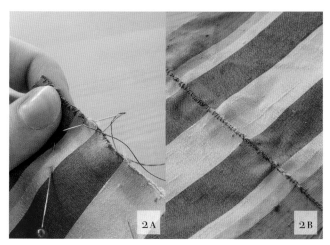

Assembly

1. Cut enough pieces to join for about a 4- to 6-yard (4 to 6-m) length; 54-inch (137.2-cm)-wide fabric means you'll need about 3 to 4 strips at 4 inches (10.2 cm) wide.

2. To join the pieces: place the selvage edges together and whipstitch with small, close stitches. Flatten the pieces out and gently pull at the stitches to abut the edges. Continue adding length with this method.

3. Narrow hem your sash with a ¼-inch (6-mm)-wide finish on the long edges. This will take a while. Put on your favorite movie and you'll be done before you know it.

4. To finish the ends, you have options—a fine hem, a fringed hem or our personal favorite: tassels. With short running stitches, gather the short end tightly. Insert the top loop of the tassel and carefully stitch through the cord to secure it in place, all the way around to cover it. Trim away any remaining looped cord.

1790s
V-Necked Ruffled Chemisette

Chemisettes in the 1790s could be quite integral to the fashionable look. The two designs here appear often in portraiture and fashion plates, both with the same function but quite different styles. The first is a V-neck chemisette with a ruffle. You can wear it pinned shut for a super ruffly look, or pull it open for a casual-does-medieval appearance.

MATERIALS

- *½ yard (0.5 m) cotton voile, 54" (137.1 cm) wide*
- *Silk thread (#30 for seams and gathers and #50 for hemming)*
- *1½–2 yards (1.5–2 m) thin cord or tape for drawstring*

ASSEMBLY

1. Cut out the pieces according to the pattern (page 196). Hem the side seams, fronts and neckline of the front and back pieces (8 to 10 stitches per inch [2.5 cm]) before hemming the bottom of the chemisette to create a ½-inch (1.3-cm) drawstring channel.

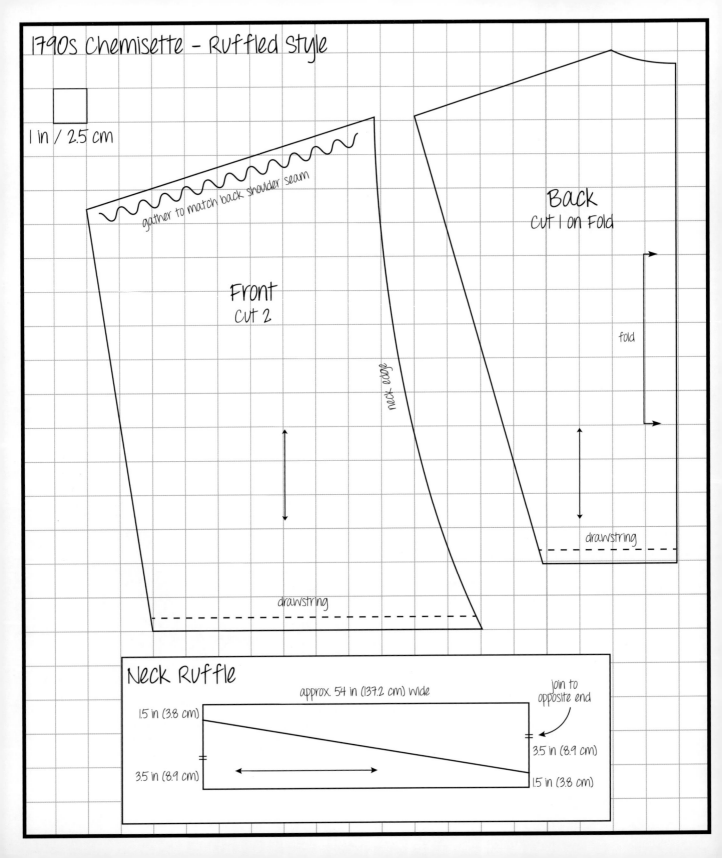

1790s Chemisette - Ruffled Style

1 in / 2.5 cm

Front
Cut 2

gather to match back shoulder seam

neck edge

drawstring

Back
Cut 1 on Fold

fold

drawstring

Neck Ruffle

approx. 54 in (137.2 cm) wide

join to opposite end

1.5 in (3.8 cm)

3.5 in (8.9 cm)

3.5 in (8.9 cm)

1.5 in (3.8 cm)

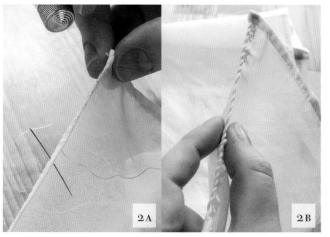

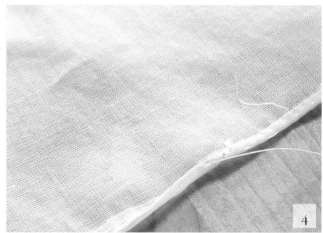

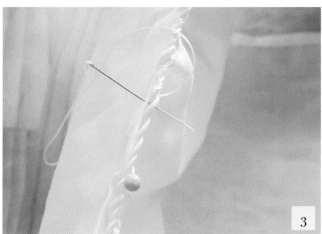

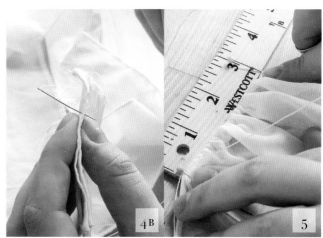

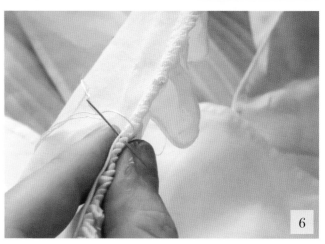

2. Whip over the front shoulder edges and pull the thread to gather this edge to fit the back shoulder edges.

3. Match the front to the back at the shoulder edges, right sides together, and pin. Then whipstitch the shoulder pieces together, catching every bump of the gathers.

4. Finely hem all the edges of the ruffle pieces. With right sides together, whipstitch the finished 3.5 inch short ends together to make one long ruffle piece. Open flat, then press.

5. Whipstitch over the straight edge of the ruffle 9 inches (22.9 cm) at a time, pulling up the thread to gather the ruffle down to 3 inches (7.6 cm) and knotting the thread before continuing on. Gather at intervals until the ruffle fits the neckline of the chemisette.

6. Right-sides together, pin the ruffle to the chemisette neckline. Using #30 silk thread, attach the ruffle using a whipstitch, making sure to catch every bump of the gathers.

7. Insert the drawstring through all pieces. Pull even, then tack the drawstring at the center back to secure it.

1790s
Shirt-Style Chemisette

This second chemisette is inspired by menswear. Very simply made, when worn with the softness of the round gown, it gives off that artistic *je ne sais quoi* attitude of the "coolest" 90s gals.

MATERIALS

- ½–1 yard (0.5–1 m) fine linen or cotton shirting
- Silk thread (#30 for seams, gathers and prick stitching and #50 for hemming) or linen thread (60/2)
- 1½–2 yards (1.5–2 m) candlewicking or narrow tape

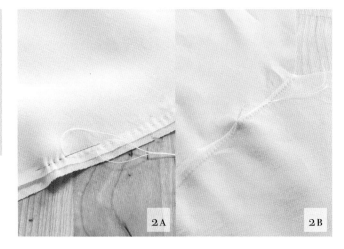

ASSEMBLY

1. Cut out the pieces according to the pattern (page 200). Hem the side seams and fronts of the front and back pieces (8 to 10 stitches per inch [2.5 cm]) before hemming the bottom of the chemisette to create a ½-inch (1.3-cm) drawstring channel. Leave the neckline raw.

2. Fell the shoulder seams (page 13).

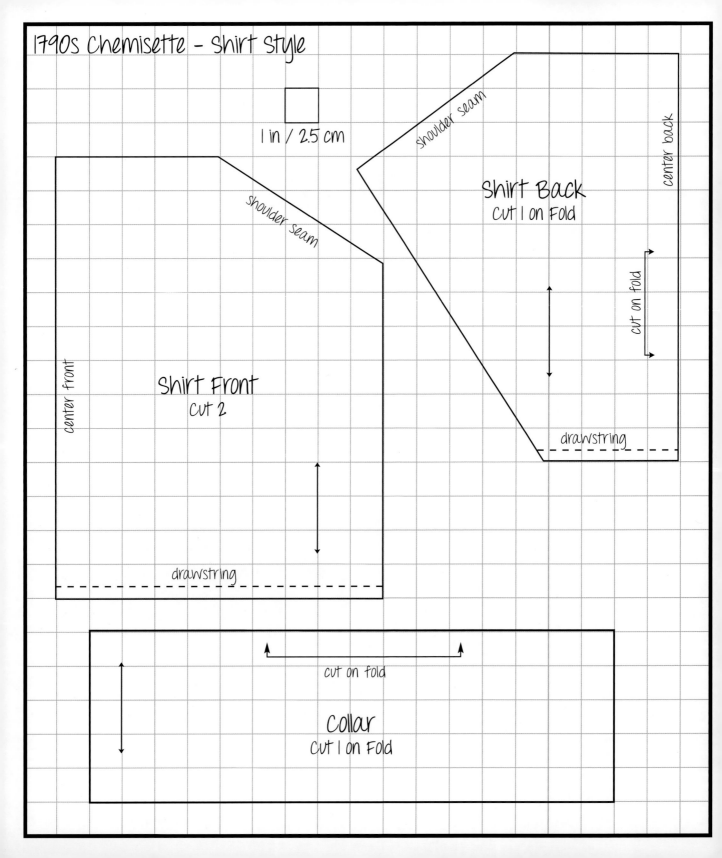

1790s Chemisette - Shirt Style

1 in / 2.5 cm

Shirt Back
Cut 1 on Fold

shoulder seam

center back

cut on fold

drawstring

Shirt Front
Cut 2

shoulder seam

center front

drawstring

Collar
Cut 1 on Fold

cut on fold

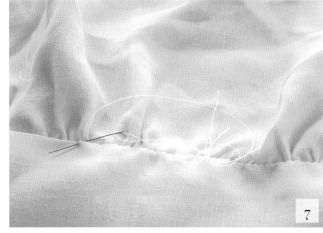

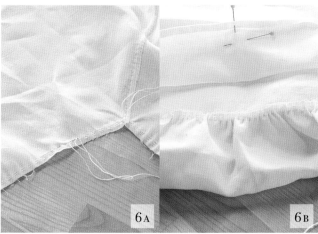

3. Next, prep the collar. Baste up ¼ inch (6 mm) at the bottom and the short sides of the collar.

4. Fold the collar in half lengthwise, lining up the basted edges and prick stitch the collar together ⅛ x ⅛ inch (3 x 3 mm) starting approximately 1 inch (2.5 cm) from the base of the collar, going all the way around to 1 inch (2.5 cm) above the base on the other side.

5. Fold the collar in half lengthwise again and press. Mark the length of the collar in quarters with pins.

6. Gather up the neckline of the chemisette using three rows of evenly spaced running stitches in four sections corresponding to the quarters of the collar: left front = first quarter, back half = second quarter, back half 2 = third quarter, right front = fourth quarter.

7. Turn up one bottom edge of the collar and pin it out of the way. Lap the bottom basted edge of the collar over the raw, gathered neckline of the chemisette. Pin and finely hem stitch, making sure to catch every bump of the gathers.

8. Release the remaining edge of the collar, lap it over the other side of the gathered neckline, then finely hem stitch, again catching in every bump of the gathers.

9. Close any remaining openings at the front of the collar with prick stitches.

10. Run the drawstring through the channels made earlier, and secure with a couple of stitches at the center back.

Done!

1790S
"Vigée Le Brun" Turban Cap

This cap was inspired by the portraits by Elisabeth Vigée Le Brun, references from 1790s newspaper advertisements, and the Gallery of Fashion books. A solid definition and clear construction of this headdress is ambiguous in original sources, so we've interpreted it as the eighteenth-century milliner might have: the appearance of a wrapped turban with the construction of a cap. The pattern for this fun bit of millinery produces a moderate-sized cap, but feel free to scale up the pieces for a grander effect.

MATERIALS

- ¼ yard (0.25 m) linen
- ¼–½ yard (0.25–0.5 m) silk organza
- Silk thread (#30 for gathers, seams, eyelets and #50 for hemming)
- Linen thread (60/2 optional for caul)
- 1 yard (1 m) candlewicking or ¼" (6-mm) wide tape

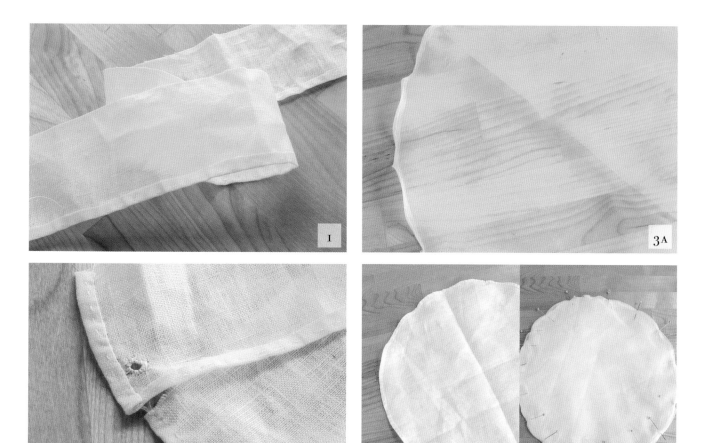

ASSEMBLY

1. Cut out the pattern pieces. Baste up all sides of the band, and hem stitch the short sides and top edge.

2. Use an awl to work an eyelet at both ends of the band just above the basting. Using #30 silk or linen thread, whipstitch the eyelet open. Rework the hole with the awl after sewing, to open the eyelet up again. Turn the bottom edge of the band up again, over the eyelets, and hem to create the drawstring channel.

3. Turn up ¼ inch (6 mm) and baste around the organza caul. Repeat for the linen caul. Next, center the linen caul in the organza caul and pleat the organza to fit the linen caul. This doesn't have to be precise because the caul is going to be gathered up again later.

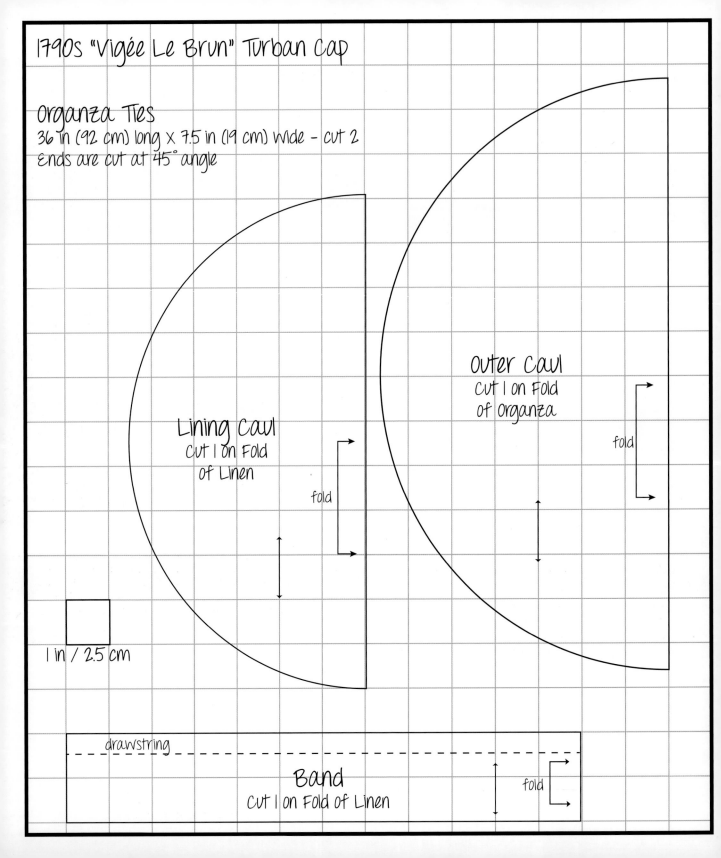

1790s "Vigée Le Brun" Turban Cap

Organza Ties
36 in (92 cm) long x 7.5 in (19 cm) wide — cut 2
Ends are cut at 45° angle

Outer Caul
Cut 1 on Fold
of Organza

fold

Lining Caul
Cut 1 on Fold
of Linen

fold

1 in / 2.5 cm

Band
Cut 1 on Fold of Linen

drawstring

fold

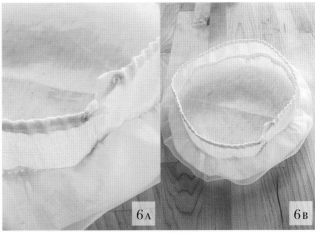

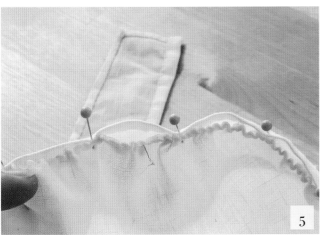

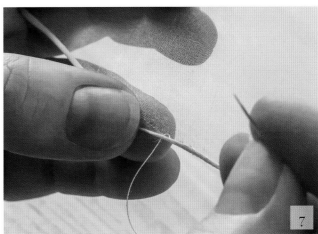

4. Whipstitch the edges of the two cauls together and pull the thread to gather the edge. Gather and adjust to fit the band.

5. With right sides together, pin the caul to the band and whipstitch together, catching all the bumps of the gathers. The short ends of the caul should meet but are not sewn together.

6. Thread narrow tape through the drawstring channel and cut with enough length to tie a small bow. This allows the band to be tightened a little to keep the cap secure.

7. Cut the organza ties according to the pattern, page 204. Roll hem each of the ties on the front and long sides, and stitch a normal basted hem for the back. Gather up or pleat the back of the ties to fit the width of the band and applique stitch them to the band at the back, just above the eyelets. The ties are left free for maximum bow-tying options.

1790s
Linen Turban Wrap

This turban wrap is inspired by the beautiful 1790s portraits of French and Russian aristocrats by Elisabeth Vigée Le Brun. A wrap like this should be no less than 2-yards (2-m) long, but we've made ours 6 yards (6 m). That may seem excessive, but you'll be surprised how quickly this length wraps up. The wrap is made out of a fine lightweight sheer linen. Though silk was used for some turban caps and chiffonets, it can be slippery and difficult to secure to your head as a turban wrap. By using a fine linen or cotton organdy, you can have that gauzy look but still maintain control over your turban.

MATERIALS
- 1–3 yards (1–3 m) of 54" (137-cm)-wide fabric (add more yardage if using a narrower textile)
- Silk thread (#50)

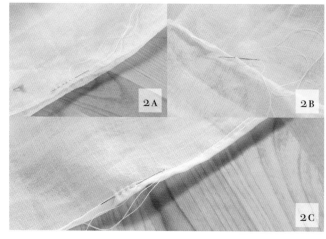

ASSEMBLY

1. Cut enough strips of fabric to create the desired length (2 to 6 yards [2 to 6 m]) of your turban. Your turban can be between 10 and 20 inches (25.4 and 50.8 cm) wide.

2. Fell (page 13) the edges of the fabric together to create one long piece. When all pieces are joined, hem the long edges with a fine running stitch. This takes time.

1790s Turban Wrapping

Turbans of the 1790s are fun and creative. Wrapping styles are endless, and fashionable women of this period tied their turbans all manner of ways. There's no right or wrong way to wrap these turbans—up, down, around, over, under, twisted, tucked, looped, you name it. Have fun!

1. Start with the turban at the center front or center back of your head and wrap it. Cross and twist the fabric to give it texture and dimension. Keep doing this around your head until you're happy with how it looks.

2. As you wrap, don't forget to pull out your curls from the spaces. Securely pin the turban in place using straight or stick pins.

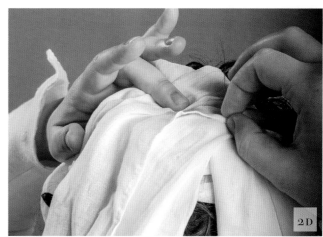

3. If you have extra length after the initial turban wrapping you can do a few different things with it. We love draping the turban around the neck and face, with the length hanging down the back. You can also have it draped over your shoulder, and/or tucked into your sash.

1790s
The Caroline Hat

Hats: we *love* them, but good historical shapes can be hard to find. While a decorated or covered straw hat will serve you well, learning to construct your own *chapeaux* in buckram and wire opens a world of possibilities in any century. This hat is inspired by the Caroline Hat from the Gallery of Fashion, November 1795.[7] While newspapers advertise millinery wire in the eighteenth century and buckram was commonplace, we don't know for certain if these materials were used in the same way as we demonstrate here. There is evidence of buckram, wire and wadding being used in the 1830s for bonnets,[8] but that does not mean that it was used in the 1790s. So, in pursuit of full disclosure, the techniques used for this hat qualify as modern millinery. Since we don't have the hat options that our ancestors did, we have to make do and utilize the options that are available to us.

MATERIALS

- ½–1 yard (0.5–1 m) heavy millinery buckram
- 2 yards (2 m) #19 gauge millinery wire
- 1–2 yards (1–2 m) cotton flannel
- 2 yards (2 m) silk for the top of the hat
- 1 yard (1 m) silk for the under brim (if not the same)
- ¼ yard (0.25 m) linen or cotton
- 1 yard (1 m) candlewicking or cotton tape
- Silk thread (#30 for all construction and #50 for hemming)
- Feathers, ribbons, fake flowers, fruit and whatever else inspires you.

1790s Caroline Hat

☐ 1 in / 2.5 cm

Seam Allowance Guide

Top Fabric Pieces - Add 1 in / 2.54 cm to all edges
Under Brim Fabric - Add 2 in / 5.08 cm to brim pattern edges
Hat Lining - Add 1 in / 2.54 cm to long edges for seam allowance
        on bottom edge and drawstring casing
        on top edge. Add 1/2 in / 1.27 cm to short edges for seam.

Cut Buckram and Flannel with 1/2 in / 1.27 cm seam allowance.
-or-
Adhere Buckram and Flannel together, then
cut pieces without seam allowance.

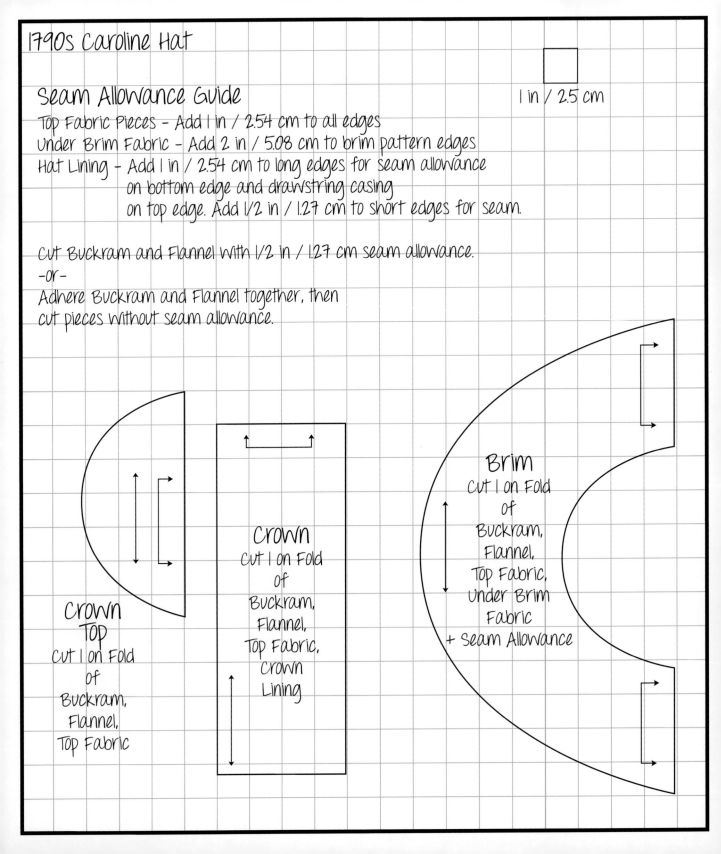

Crown TOP
Cut 1 on Fold
of
Buckram,
Flannel,
Top Fabric

Crown
Cut 1 on Fold
of
Buckram,
Flannel,
Top Fabric,
Crown
Lining

Brim
Cut 1 on Fold
of
Buckram,
Flannel,
Top Fabric,
Under Brim
Fabric
+ Seam Allowance

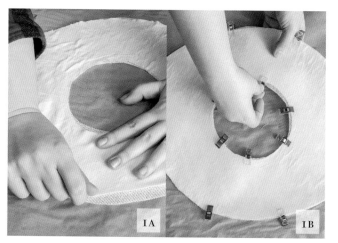

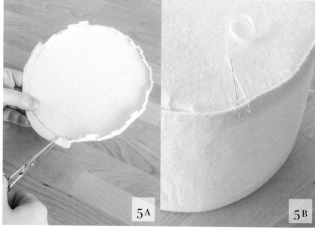

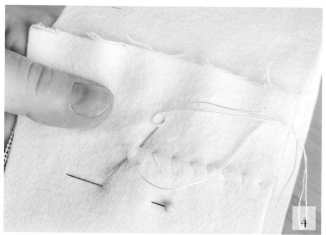

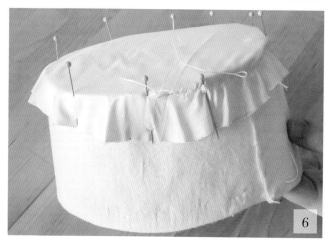

ASSEMBLY

1. First: cut the brim, crown and top pieces out of heavy millinery buckram. Cut the same pieces out of flannel but with a larger seam allowance, marked with a pencil. Dampen the flannel and smooth to adhere to the buckram, making sure that the seam allowance markings are still visible on the flannel. Clip the materials together to keep in place. Let dry overnight and carefully iron the pieces flannel-side up to flatten the buckram. Or simply adhere the yard of flannel to buckram yardage before cutting out the pieces using the method explained above.

> *The damp flannel activates the glue in the buckram, which is how they can stick together. When we worked on this project, we had a slight problem with shrinkage, which is why we suggest the second option of pasting the flannel and buckram together first before cutting out the pattern pieces.*

2. Whipstitch millinery wire around the outside edge of the brim, carefully wrapping and covering the cut wire edges with thread. You want the wire to be on or as close to the edge of the brim as possible.

3. Cover the edge with a long strip of ½-inch (1.3-cm)-wide flannel using large running or prick stitches through both sides to hold it into place and cover the wire. Set aside.

4. Line up the side seam allowance of the crown band and whip down the outside and inside edges. It's okay if the flannel is raw—it will be covered up.

5. Cut the notches through the flannel and buckram of the top crown and fold them so they fit into the crown band. Quickly whip around the edge of the circle to secure the two pieces together, adjusting the notches if needed.

6. Cut out the silk for the top crown and crown band with about a ¾- to 1-inch (1.9- to 2.5-cm) seam allowance for both pieces. Center and pin the silk top crown piece to the buckram. Smooth it from the center outward, over the edge of the crown band, and pin in place. Stitch the silk on the side of the crown band with large basting stitches.

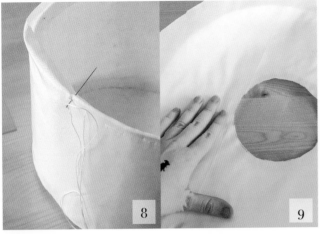

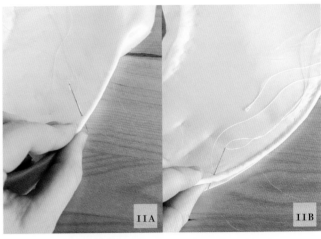

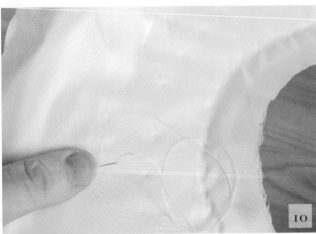

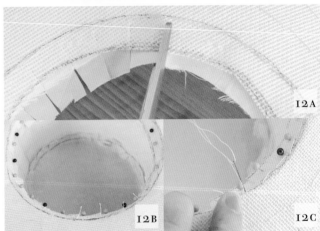

7. On the silk crown band piece, baste the short edge that will form the finished side seam on the outside. In the round, line up the silk crown band piece right sides together at the top of the constructed buckram crown and pin. The silk piece will stick up above the buckram crown. Backstitch into place, keeping your stitches right on the edge.

8. Fold down and pin the silk band over the buckram band. Lap the basted short edge over its corresponding raw edge and applique stitch through all layers to secure. At the bottom, fold the seam allowance to the inside and baste it into place to keep the crown smooth. Set aside.

9. Cut out the silk upper for the brim with an extra 1-inch (2.5-cm) seam allowance on the outside edge. Line up the fabric over the buckram and running stitch in place around the crown opening.

10. Where the brim will sweep up, prick stitch the silk to the buckram working outward in rows with the stitches about 1 inch (2.5 cm) apart. You only need to stitch where the brim curves upward. Test the upward curve and stitch anywhere the fabric needs to be held to the buckram.

11. Around the edge of the brim, smooth the silk fabric around the wired edge and pin in place until you are ready to prick stitch the layers together along the wired edge. Trim the excess brim fabric to ½ to 1 inch (1.3 to 2.5 cm).

12. On the brim, clip and fold up the seam allowance for the crown to the marked line. With the crown open-side up, place the brim atop, continuing folding the tabs into the crown. Pin around the inside. From the inside, carefully stitch the crown to the brim with tiny applique stitches. The interior stitching can be messy, but the outside stitches will be small and fine.

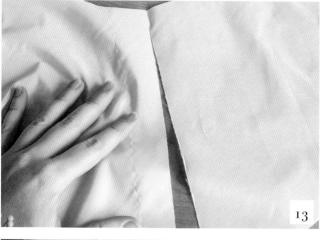

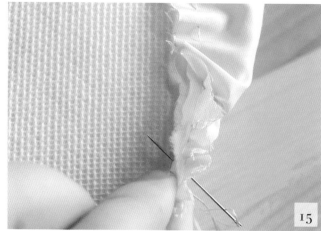

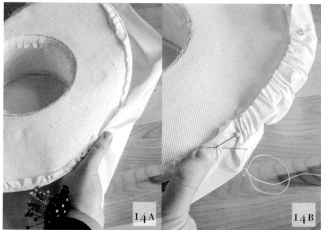

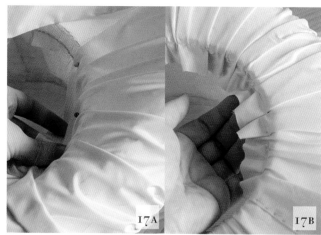

13. Cut out your under-brim fabric with double the width of the original brim pattern on the outer edge. This will provide the extra volume to be gathered up. Cut the oval open on one of the long sides of the brim, and baste one edge up ¼ inch (6 mm).

14. Right sides together, pin the under-brim fabric to the center sides, center front and center back points along the hat brim. Starting at one of these points, tack the point in place and then continue with a running stitch about ¼ inch (6 mm) from the edge of the under-brim fabric. When you've reached the next anchor point, draw up the running stitch to match the hat brim, then tack stitch again and carry on to the next anchor point.

15. When the brim lining is completely gathered and anchored, adjust the fullness through each section, pinning as needed. Finely running stitch the lining fabric to the seam allowance next to the wire that was folded over from the top with a fine running stitch, only catching the fabric and staying right next to the wire.

16. With the outer edge gathered and stitched, turn the under-brim fabric outside-in, over the hat brim completely, so it now lays over the underside of the brim. Stitch the cut seam that you basted earlier in place using fine applique or prick stitches.

17. Bring the under-brim lining to the crown and arrange into pleats, pinning as you go. Running stitch the lining to the crown, your stitches will go through the crown, but you will cover this part up with ribbon to hide all the sins. You will add the final linen lining to the crown after you've decorated your hat. It is easier to decorate the hat when you don't have to pull the crown lining out of the way. Additionally, the lining will cover up all the ugly sewing that will occur when you're attaching your trim.

18. Now you need to decorate your hat. Start by wrapping ribbon around the crown, seaming at the center back with applique stitches. This will cover up the stitching from earlier.

19. There are many different ways to decorate a hat, and we believe it is best to follow a period image for inspiration. To make poufs and 4-loop bows, refer to pages 65, and for 5-loop bows, see page 90. Don't forget that ostrich feathers, veils and faux flowers/fruit were really popular for hat decoration. Apply, arrange and roughly tack stitch feathers and other decorations in place to hold their positions. The variations are endless and completely up to your whims.

20. After decorating your hat, add the lining to the crown. Cut a long rectangular piece of linen following the band pattern, subtracting 1 to 2 inches (2.5 to 5 cm) in width before adding the seam allowance. Baste all sides of the band.

21. Hem the short sides and top edge of the lining, making sure you can insert a drawstring at the top. Match up the short sides and whipstitch together, leaving the top ½ inch (1.3 cm) open for the drawstring. Run the drawstring through the channel.

22. Pin the lining into the inside of the crown, matching the basted bottom edge to the bottom of the crown. Applique stitch (8 to 10 stitches per inch [2.5 cm]) the bottom edge of the lining to just the under-brim fabric. Pull up the drawstring to adjust the fit.

1790s
Giant Fur Muff

While muffs were popular throughout the century, the 1790s seemed like the best place to explain how to make one. Not only were muffs super popular during the decade, they were super big as well! The large size of the muffs during this decade make them great hand and arm warmers for men and women alike...and for the occasional pillow fight. If you'd like to adapt this muff for earlier decades, shrink the diagram measurements to suit.

Muffs can be covered in fur or silk and can be lined in silk or a more utilitarian fabric. While we've made ours out of faux fur, the techniques—razor cutting, taping the edges, etc.—may be applied to working with real fur, too.

Materials

- *1 yard (1 m) faux fur*
- *1 yard (1 m) silk taffeta*
- *2 yards (2 m) ½–1" (1.3–2.5-cm)-wide cotton or linen tape*
- *Down feathers, cotton or wool stuffing*

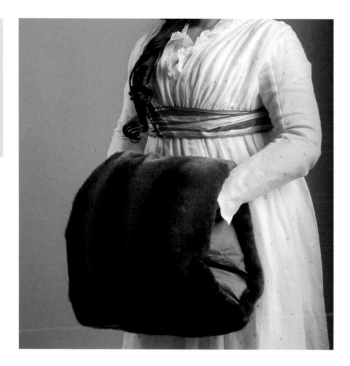

1790s Giant Fur Muff

Muffs could be made small or large, of fur or silk and filled with down feathers or wool. Experiment with different sizes and materials.

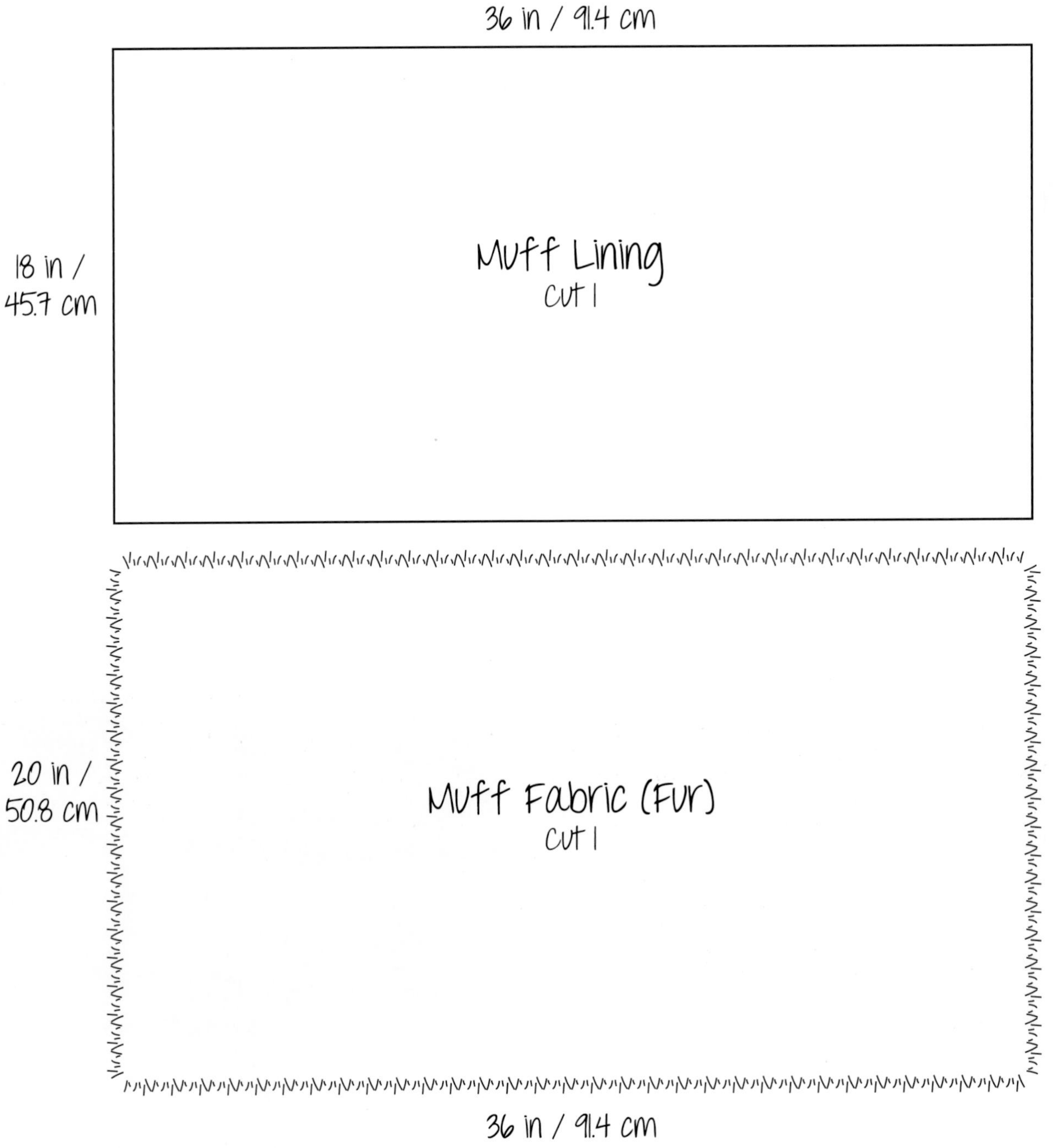

36 in / 91.4 cm

18 in / 45.7 cm

Muff Lining
Cut 1

20 in / 50.8 cm

Muff Fabric (Fur)
Cut 1

36 in / 91.4 cm

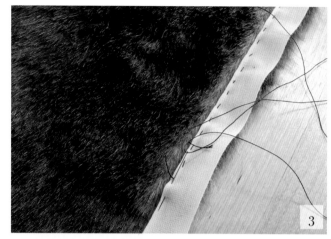

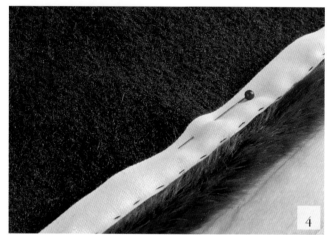

ASSEMBLY

1. Cut out your materials according to the diagram. You will probably need to join pieces of fur together. To cut the fur, gently slice along the hide side with a razor. Do not cut the fur with scissors unless you want hair all over everything you own. Cutting with a razor allows you to pierce just the hide/back side without cutting the hairs, which makes the joining nearly invisible.

2. To join the fur, lay the raw edges flat, hide-side up, so they touch each other, and whipstitch (12 to 14 stitches per inch [2.5 cm]). Do not whip the edges right sides together, as this will catch too much fur. By abutting the edges, you will make a small ridge for the join and minimize the look of the join on the exterior. Once joined, use a pin to "scratch" out any caught hairs.

3. Lay the tape along the edge on top of the fur, and running stitch in place (8 to 10 stitches per inch [2.5 cm]) through the hide. Trim the fur away under the tape to reduce bulk.

4. Turn the tape to the inside. Allow the edges of the fur to roll in by about an inch (2.5 cm) or more to create a seam allowance. Hem stitch the edge of the tape to the backside of the fur.

> *When using real fur, cut a piece of thin, tightly woven fabric the same size as the fur piece and lay it against the hide side of the fur before turning the edges. Turn the taped edges to the inside and hem stitch to this fabric interlining instead of to the hide itself. This is also advisable for loose-knit backing on faux fur to prevent the down feathers from poking through.*

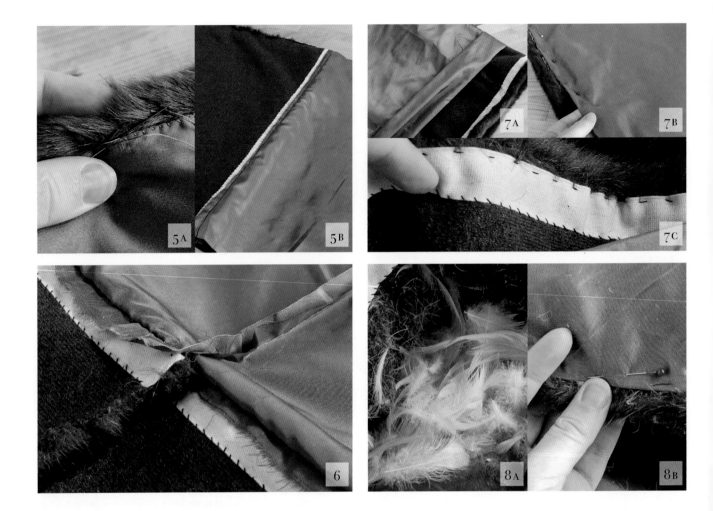

5. For lining, baste the silk up ¼ inch (6 mm) on one long edge. Lay it against the hide side of the fur piece, matching the basted edge up to the tape, and hem stitch in place (6 to 8 stitches per inch [2.5 cm]). Open the lining piece out to the side.

6. To join the muff together, abut the short edges of the fur piece and whipstitch from the back. Then backstitch the short edges of the lining together (6 to 8 stitches per inch [2.5 cm]). Be careful to fully stitch to the edge where the lining meets the fur piece.

7. Turn the muff inside out and pull the lining over the fur piece. Turn and pin the edge of the lining under to meet the taped edge of the fur. Hem stitch the lining to the tape, leaving open about 12 inches (30 cm) for stuffing (8 to 10 stitches per inch [2.5 cm]).

8. Stuff the muff with feathers or your filling of choice. Be sure not to overfill, and if you're using feathers, it's best to do it outside. Finally, hem stitch the remaining 12 inches (30 cm) closed, then turn the muff right-side out.

1790s
The "Sundae Best" Reticule

The 1790s is the decade where the reticule, a small purse—sometimes ridiculously small, hence the name "ridicule" or "reticule"—really comes into fashion. Reticules could be large, small, boring, whimsical, complicated or extremely simple. For this book, we've created two styles for your amusement. First is the hard-bottom "Sundae Best" Reticule, and the second is a soft-bodied "Frog" Reticule (page 226). Trims, embroidery and colors are up to you. Remember that the 1790s loved colorful and bold accessories, so be brave and have *fun* with your color choices!

MATERIALS

- *½ yard (0.5 m) silk in 1 or 2 colors*
- *1 Old American Duchess shoe box*
- *1 yard (1 m) of ¼" (6-mm)-wide silk ribbon for tie*
- *Silk thread (#30 seams and #50 hems)*
- *2 yards (2 m) metallic lace trim*
- *1–2 fringe tassels*

Two 1790s Reticules

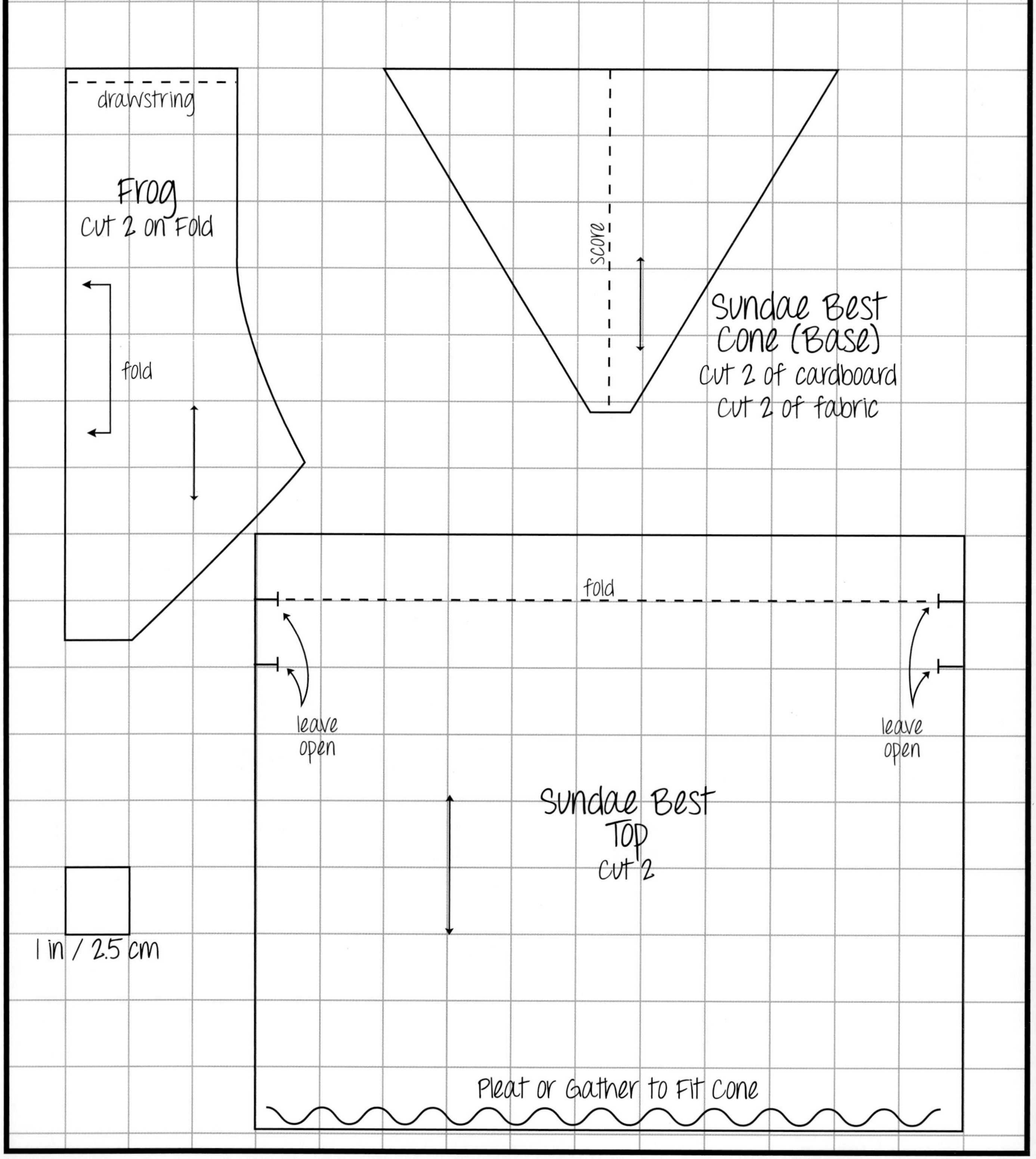

drawstring

Frog
Cut 2 on Fold

fold

score

Sundae Best Cone (Base)
Cut 2 of cardboard
Cut 2 of fabric

fold

leave open

leave open

Sundae Best TOP
Cut 2

1 in / 2.5 cm

Pleat or Gather to Fit Cone

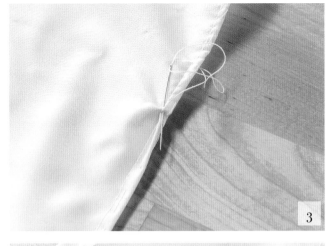

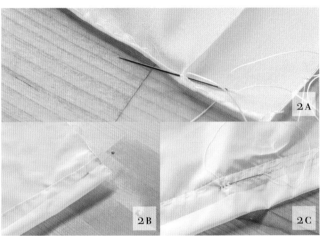

ASSEMBLY

1. Cut out the top pieces according to the pattern. Measure down 2.75 inches (7 cm) from the top, and mark with a pin on both sides of both pieces. Finely hem both edges of that 2.75 inches (7 cm).

2. Fold down the top ¼ inch (6 mm) and baste. Fold down, again, 1 inch (2.5 cm) and hem (10 to 12 stitches per inch [2.5 cm]). From that hemmed edge, measure up ¼ inch (6 mm) and do a fine running stitch to create the drawstring casing.

3. Seam up one side of the bag using the mantua maker's seam, and prep the second seam by basting down the sides so they can be felled together after the bag is attached to the bottom.

4. Fold the bottom up ¼ inch (6 mm) so the raw edge is on the right side of the bag and baste. The raw edge will be protected by the hard bottom of the reticule if done this way. If you baste the opposite, the raw edge will be exposed to your hand and whatever else you put in the reticule. Set aside.

5. Cut out the cardboard and silk bottom pieces according to the pattern. Be sure to add ½ inch (1.3 cm) seam allowance for the silk pieces.

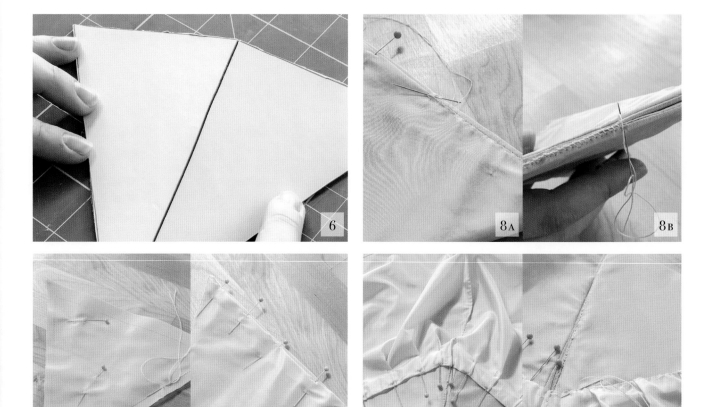

6. Score the middle of the triangular pieces so they will bend, but do not break. (If they do break, it's OK. You will just have to make every piece up individually, but the outcome will be the same!)

7. Right sides together, backstitch the silk pieces together, leaving the top open, to create two pouches for the cardboard. Turn right sides out and press the seams smooth. Insert the cardboard pieces into their covers.

8. Fold the seam allowance inward and whip closed. You want the silk to be tight and smooth over the cardboard. Whipstitch one side seam of the hard bottom pieces together (10 to 12 stitches per inch [2.5 cm]).

9. Now let's bring the pieces together. With the interior of the hard bottom open, lay the top of the reticule ½ to ¾ inch (1.3 to 1.9 cm) down from the top edge of the cardboard, lining up the side seams, and pinning tucks to ease the rest of the top of the bag to the cardboard bottom. Hem stitch the top to the bottom, making sure to catch all layers of the tucks. This is a bit tricky, and it's okay if it's messy. No one will ever see it.

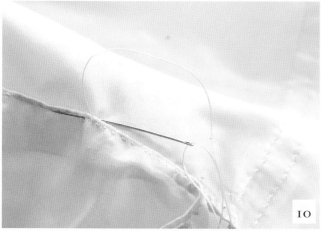

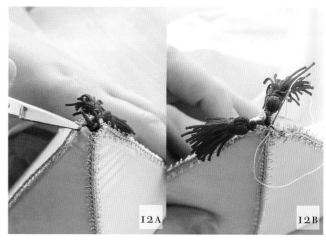

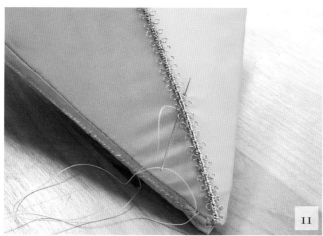

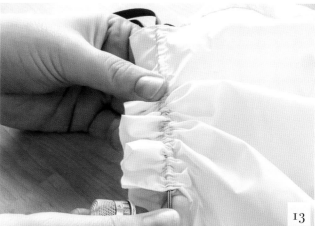

10. Close the reticule and carefully whip the hard bottom side seam closed from the outside. Then, line up and pin the side seam of the top together and stitch closed with either an applique stitch or fine running stitches (10 to 12 stitches per inch [2.5 cm]).

11. Take your metallic lace and cut a length that will cover one of the four edges of the bottom of the reticule including seam allowance. Fold the seam allowance over the top of the cardboard and stitch into place. Carefully couch the trim to the back, taking great care to keep your stitches as invisible as possible. When you reach the bottom, tuck the extra lace into the hole. Repeat on all edges of the bottom of the reticule.

12. Now, take your tassels and insert the loop into the hole at the bottom of the cone, making sure that all the seam allowances from the trim and silk covers are also inserted. Whip the hole closed to secure the tassels and trim.

13. Insert your two lengths of ribbon at the top, so you can pull the bag closed, and knot the ends.

1790s
The "Frog" Reticule

Though "Frog" is not a technical name for this bag, the green silk reminded us of a cute little frog and we couldn't help ourselves! This small and soft reticule can be scaled up for a larger size, and you can also embroider a pretty design on the body of the reticule before putting it together.

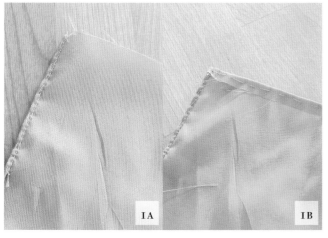

1A   1B

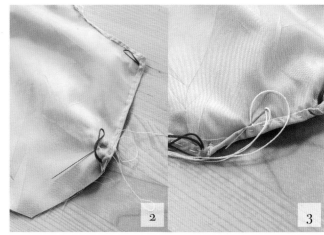

2   3

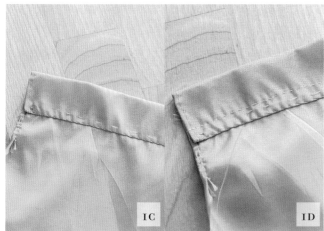

1C   1D

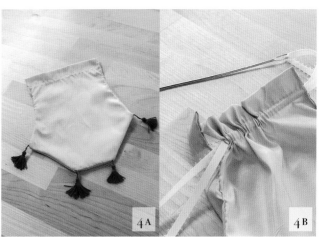

4A   4B

ASSEMBLY

1. Cut out the pieces from the provided pattern (page 222) and measure down 3 inches (7.6 cm) on both sides of both pieces at the top of the reticule, mark, and finely hem. Fold and baste the top ¼ inch (6 mm) of the pieces down. Fold the top down another 1 inch (2.5 cm) and finely hem stitch (10 to 12 stitches per inch [2.5 cm]). Measure up ¼ to ½ inch (6 mm to 1.3 cm) from the hemmed edge, and do a fine running stitch to create the ribbon channel and ruffle for the top of the reticule.

2. Lay both pieces right sides together and pin.

3. Mantua maker's seam the reticule together, and while you're basting the seam, at each point where you want the tassels, insert them between the layers before you make your baste stitch. You'll want the tassel to be inside the bag (because it's the right side) and you'll see the loop that holds the tassel together when you're sewing. Fold and baste the edges and the tassel loop. Finish the mantua maker's seam of your bag, being sure to catch your tassel loops as you sew. This keeps the tassels secure and keeps the strings out of your way when you use the bag.

4. Turn the bag right side out and press everything smooth. Insert the ribbon drawstrings at the top of your bag.

Done!

Getting Dressed and Wearing
Your 1790s Ensemble with Style

Assembly

1. Put on your shift, stockings, shoes and stays.

2. Next, put on your under-petticoat by tying the drawstring at the center front, just below the bust.

3. If you are wearing a chemisette, now is the time to put it on, tying it at the center front.

4. Put on your gown and pin the under-bodice of the gown into place at the center front, then tie the gown drawstring at the center front and tuck the tails into the skirt front opening. Adjust the bodice and chemisette to suit your tastes.

5. Put on your Turban Cap, Caroline Hat or wrap your turban.

6. If you are wearing a sash, put it on now. You can tuck the edges of your turban into the sash. There are endless ways to wear a long sash like this one. Wrap it around and around and tie with a big bow at the back or side. Wrap it around the high waist and up and over the shoulders for a different look. Allow the ends to trail or loop them up. Most importantly, have fun!

7. Grab your reticule and muff and head on out the door!

Now you're ready to go look at art at the Salon!

Troubleshooting

GAPING NECKLINE

Cause: The shoulder straps are too loose, too long or on the bias and stretching out.

Solution: Be sure the shoulder straps are cut on the straight of grain. Recut if necessary. Refit the shoulder straps through the back shoulder seams, pulling up the excess tight. If the neckline still gapes at the front, adjust the seam or take a small tuck to smooth the fit.

BODICE FRONT SIDE WRINKLES

Cause: The front bodice pieces are cut on the straight, and the stays are curvier in the front.

-or-

The waist edges are too long.

Solution: Double-check that the front bodice pieces are cut on the slight bias, recut if necessary, or see if you can adjust the fit of the center front seam to have more bias.

-or-

Clip and turn up the raw waist edge on the body and over all your underpinnings, pulling down toward the waist and smoothing the pieces from armpit to waist.

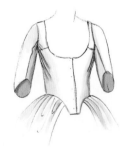

BODICE FRONT ARMPIT WRINKLES

Cause: The armscyes are too tight.

Solution: Carefully clip the armscye to release the tension and smooth the wrinkles upward into the armpit. *Do not overcut or you might have more problems down the road!*

BUBBLY BODICE FRONT

Cause: The bodice front pieces are cut on the straight, and your stays are "thrusty."

-or-

The bodice needs smoothing over the bust.

Solution: First try smoothing the excess fabric from the side to the center front, pulling taught. Pin and redraw the center front line. This may result in a curved front edge, especially for larger busts and "thrusty" stays.

-or-

Recut your bodice pieces so the center front is on the slight bias.

BUBBLY OR LOOSE BACK PIECES

Cause: The center back pieces are cut on the straight.

-or-

Your model is sway-backed.

Solution: Check that the back pieces are on the slight bias. Recut if necessary.

-or-

On the body and over all the underpinnings, smooth the pieces toward the center back seam, pinching up the excess. Mark the new seam line.

SIDE BACK WRINKLES

Cause: The side back pieces are slightly twisted where they are joined and are pulling.

Solution: Release the side back seams prick stitches. On the body and over all the underpinnings, smooth the side back pieces downward to smooth out the wrinkles. Overlap the turned edge of the side back seam and repin. Remove from the body and prick stitch the new seam in place.

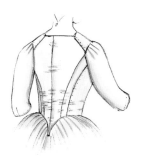

WRINKLED BACK—STRESS LINES

Cause: The bodice is overfitted and too tight.

Solution: Loosen up! Adjust your pinning at the center front closure or, if necessary, loosen the side seams. Refit the side seams on the body and over all the underpinnings.

SHOULDER STRAPS FALLING DOWN

Cause: The shoulder straps are set too wide.

-or-

The sleeve head is too shallow and is pulling the shoulder strap off the shoulder.

-or-

The shoulder straps have accidently been cut on the bias and have stretched out.

Solution: At the back shoulder seams, release and reset the shoulder straps at a narrower angle, closer to the center back seam.

-or-

Remove the sleeves and recut or piece with a higher sleeve head. Remember, it's always better to have a bit more in the sleeve head than not enough.

-or-

Recut and refit the straps on the straight of grain.

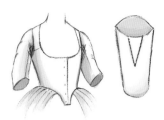

SLEEVES ARE TOO TIGHT

Cause: The sleeves are cut/sewn too narrow.

Solution: Restitch the seams, or recut the sleeves with more ease.

-or-

Add a triangular gore at the underarm either at your sleeve seam or cut into the sleeve at the underarm and add the gore there.

SLEEVES ARE TWISTED

Cause: The sleeve is pinned or stitched on twisted at the armscye.

Solution: Release the sleeve and reset, working the fitment until the twists are worked out.

STRAIGHT SLEEVES ARE STACKING AT THE ELBOW

Cause: The sleeves are too long, causing stacking up at the crook of the arm.

Solution: Take a tuck upward at the crook of the arm, shortening just the front of the sleeve, and prick stitch into place.

-or-

Recut the bottom of the sleeve to shorten it.

SACQUE SILHOUETTE IS ROUND AND BUBBLY

Cause: The sacque front skirt panels are cut straight at the front and side edges.

Solution: The sacque front skirt panels must be cut on the straight of grain but with the side seam at an angle and the front edge cut or folded back at an angle to expose the decorative petticoat. The correct silhouette is trapezoidal rather than rounded or bulbous.

SACQUE TRAIN BUCKLES

Cause: The train folds up on itself due to too little fabric in the skirt circumference at the hem combined with misplaced side pleats.

Solution: Add a gored panel at the side seam, between the front skirt panel and the back breadth, then re-pleat the skirt, working the fullness of the skirt toward the side-back seam. The side pleats that control volume over the pocket hoops should be placed further back than the true side-seam.

SAGGY SAD SACQUE BACK

Cause: The fabric is too heavy and is pulling downward.

-or-

The pleated back lacks the third pleat so collapses in on itself against the back instead of flowing outward.

Solution: Reinforce the binding at the top edge. Also securely stitch the outer fabric to the bodice lining under the pleats at the side back.

-or-

Repleat the back to include the third, hidden pleat as shown on page 98.

FRONT SKIRT PANELS BUCKLING AT WAIST

Cause: The skirt needs fitting at the curved waist edge. There is too much volume just below the waist edge.

Solution: Release the top edge of the skirt panel. On the bodice and over all underpinnings, pull upward until the skirt hangs smoothly. Fold the excess over or cut it off, then restitch the skirt to the waist edge.

SAGGY HOOPED SILHOUETTE

Cause: The width of the top of the hoop is too long and is drooping, and/or the hoops are tied too low on the waist.

Solution: Tie the hoops at your true waist.

-or-

Shorten the top of the hoops to bring them up higher on the hips. See page 76 for our hoop pattern.

PETTICOAT IS TOO SHORT IN BACK OR ON THE SIDES

Cause: The petticoat breadth is cut all one length instead of with a shaped top to fit over underpinnings (bum, pads, hoops, etc.).

Solution: Measure over the bum or hoops, waist to floor. Cut the petticoat and skirt panel according to the longest measurement. Then cut or fold at the waist edge to level the hem over the underpinning. Petticoats may be leveled on the body or on a dress form. For leveling over hoops, see page 81. For leveling over a split bum, see page 134.

Appendix

CITATIONS

HISTORIC STITCHES AND HOW TO SEW THEM

1. Rasmussen, Pernilla. *Skräddaren, sömmerskan och modet: Arbetsmetoder och arbetsdelning i tillverkningen av kvinnlig dräkt 1770-1830*, pg. 188-189, Nordiska Museet Handlinger, 2010.

2. *A Lady, The Workwoman's Guide: A Guide to 19th Century Decorative Arts, Fashion and Practical Crafts 1838*, page 2, Piper Publishing LLC, 2002.

CHAPTER 2: THE ENGLISH GOWN, 1740S

1. Waugh, Norah. *Cut of Women's Clothes 1600–1930*, MPG Books Group, 1968.

2. Crowston, Clare Haru. *Fabricating Women*, pg. 40, Duke University Press, 2001.

3. *The Complete Vocabulary in English and French, and in French and English...*, pg. 85, 1785. Eighteenth-Century Collections Online, November 2016.

4. Boyer, Abel. *Boyer's Royal Dictionary abridged. In two parts. 1. French and English 2. English to French*, "Fourreau," 1777, Eighteenth-Century Collections Online, November 2016.

5. *The Compleat French Master for Ladies and Gentlemen*, pg. 173,1744, Eighteenth-Century Collections Online, November 2016.

6. Buck, Ann, *Dress in Eighteenth-Century England*, pg. 187, Holmes & Meier Publishers, 1979.

7. Montgomery, Florence. *Textiles in America: 1650–1870*, W.W. Norton & Company Inc., 2007.

8. American Sheep Industry Association, "Fast Facts, About American Wool Industry" https://www.sheepusa.org/ResearchEducation_FastFacts, November 2016.

9. Buck, Ann. *Dress in Eighteenth-Century England*, pg. 187, Holmes & Meier Publishers, 1979.

10. *May,* John June,1749, British Museum,1850, 1109.32.

CHAPTER 3: THE SACQUE GOWN 1760S-1770S

1. *A Portrait of a Lady,* 1768, Francis Cotes, Tate Museum London, N04689.

2. Arnold, Janet. *Patterns of Fashion: Englishwomen's Dresses and Their Construction c. 1660–1860,* pg. 25, Macmillan/QSM, 1964.

3. The works of Laurence Sterne M.A. In seven volumes, Sterne, Laurence (1713-1768), London: printed for the proprietors, 1783, Volume 7.

4. This information is a summarization of three to four years of careful study of original images, and period hairdressing manuals, magazines and newspapers.

5. When studying original silk gowns, skirt panels were often sewn selvage to selvage. Their measurements consistently range from 18 to 24 inches (45.7 to 60.9 cm) wide.

6. *The Unwelcome Customer,* John Collet & James Caldwell, August 17,1772, Colonial Williamsburg Foundation, 1953-205.

7. *The Love Letter,* Jean Honoré Fragonard, c. early 1770s, Metropolitan Museum of Art, New York, 49.7.49.

CHAPTER 4: THE ITALIAN GOWN, 1770S-1790S

1. Wenman, J. *The Magazine à la mode, or Fashionable miscellany*, October 1777, Eighteenth-Century Collections Online, November 2016.

2. Cruttwell, R. *The new Bath guide; or, Useful pocket companion ... A new edition, corrected and much enlarged*, First Edition: 1777, Reprinted 1784, Eighteenth-Century Collections Online, November 2016.

3. Queen Charlotte wore an "Italian night-gown and petticoat of white sattin and silver gauze, trimmed with Vandykes of green foil of rich gold trim and tassels." March 28–30, 1792, The Evening Mail, Burney Papers Digital Archive, November 2016.

4. *The Town and Country Magazine,* December 1776, pg. 650, Oxford University via Google Books, March 2017.

5. Watt, Melinda. "Textile Production in Europe: Printed, 1600–1800." In *Heilbrunn Timeline of Art History.* New York: The Metropolitan Museum of Art, 2000–. http://www.metmuseum.org/toah/hd/txt_p/hd_txt_p.htm (October 2003)

6. Sardar, Marika. "Indian Textiles: Trade and Production." In *Heilbrunn Timeline of Art History.* New York: The Metropolitan Museum of Art, 2000–. http://www.metmuseum.org/toah/hd/intx/hd_intx.htm (October 2003)

7. Goadby, R. *The Weekly Miscellany; Or, Instructive Entertainer: Containing a Collection of Select Pieces, Both in Prose and Verse; Curious Anecdotes, Instructive Tales, and Ingenious Essays on Different Subjects*, Volume 7, December 16, 1776, New York Public Library, March 2017.

8. The Bum Shop, c. 1785, Metropolitan Museum of Art. New York, 1970.541.12.

9. Van Cleave, Kendra, and Brooke Welborn. "Very Much the Taste and Various are the Makes: Reconsidering the Late Eighteenth-Century Robe à la Polonaise," *Dress* Vol 39 No. 1, 2013, Costume Society of America.

10. *The Fair Penitent,* 1781, British Museum, 2010, 7081.1022.

11. *Plenty/L'Abondance,* c. 1780, Colonial Williamsburg Foundation, 1980-232.

CHAPTER 5: THE ROUND GOWN, 1790S

1. Bissonette, Anne, and Sarah Nash. "The Re-Birth of Venus: Neo-Classical Fashion and the Aphrodite Kallipygos,"*Dress:* Vol 41 No. 1, 2015.

2. The study of original garments shows the subtle rise in waistlines over the late 1780s and early 1790s. For example: Printed Cotton Jacket and Petticoat, c. 1790, Colonial Williamsburg Foundation, Accession No. 1990-10 shows alterations of raising the waist approx. 1 inch (2.5 cm) from the previous construction, with what appears to be keeping everything else about the garment intact.

3. Huenlich, R. *How to Distinguish Quickly Cotton from Linen,* The Melliand, Vol. 2, No. 11 (February 1931), 2 pages. Posted December 11, 2002, University of Arizona.

4. England, John. *Irish Linen, The Irish Linen Story*. http://johnengland.com/irish-linen-story/, March 2017.

5. Arnold, Janet. *Patterns of Fashion: Englishwomen's Dresses and Their Construction c. 1660–1860*, pg. 46, Macmillan/QSM, 1964.

6. Snowshill Wade Costume Collection, Gloucestershire, Dress Skirt, 1790-1800, NT 1348737.1.

7. Heideloff, N. *Gallery of Fashion*: Volume 2, 1795, Bunka Gakuen Digital Archives of Rare Materials, Accessed January 2017.

8. *A Lady, The Workwoman's Guide: A Guide to 19th Century Decorative Arts, Fashion and Practical Crafts 1838*, pg. 158, Piper Publishing LLC, 2002.

WORKS CITED

Countess Ekaterina Vasilievna Skaronskaya, Élisabeth Louise Vigée Le Brun, 1790, Institut de France, Musée Jacquemart-André, Paris (MJAP-P 578)

Lady Mary Cunliffe, Francis Cotes, 1768, Walker Art Gallery, WAG 1514

Maria Luisa di Borbone, Princess of the Two Sicilies, Élisabeth Louise Vigée Le Brun, 1790, Museo di Capodimonte, Naples (OA 7228)

May, John June, 1749, British Museum, 1850, 1109.32

Plenty/L'Abondance, Carington Bowles, 1780, Colonial Williamsburg Foundation, 1980-232

Portrait of a Lady, Francis Cotes, 1768, Tate Museum, N04689

Portrait of Marquise d'Orvilliers, Jacques-Louis David, 1790, Louvre Museum, RF 2418

Princess Louisa and Princess Caroline, Francis Cotes, 1767, The Royal Collection, RCIN 404334

Self-Portrait, Élisabeth Louise Vigée Le Brun, 1790, Gallerie degli Uffizi, Corridoio Vasariano, Florence, 1890, n. 1905

September, Thomas Burford, 1745, Colonial Williamsburg Foundation, 1988-291,9

EXTANT GOWNS CITED

Note: The garments listed below are a selection of the original museum pieces that have been carefully studied and examined in person by the authors. These garments were not on public display at the time, giving the authors unprecedented access to construction and design details. This list does not include the assortment of original pieces that have been studied that are held in private collections.

LOS ANGELES COUNTY MUSEUM OF ART

LACMA Cotton Italian Gown M.80.138

LACMA Pink/Green Sack M.2007.211.720A-B

LACMA Silk Redingote M.57.24.9

LACMA Riding Habit M.82.16.2a-c

THE COLONIAL WILLIAMSBURG FOUNDATION

CWF 2009-43.3

CWF 1996-95

CWF 1991-449 A-C

CWF 1989-446

CWF 1989-330

CWF 1991-520

CWF 1991-520

CWF 1991-519

CWF 1983-230

CWF 2000-86

CWF 1947-511 (4464)

CWF 1988-223

CWF 1990-10

CWF 1991-450

CWF 1991-470

CWF 1951-150

CWF 1991-466 A&B

CWF 1991-474,A

CWF 1983-233

GLASGOW MUSEUMS/ THE BURRELL COLLECTION

1932.51.o

E.1940.47.c

NORDISKA MUSEET, STOCKHOLM

NM.0186311

NM.0222648A-E

NM.0020602

NM.0158629

BIBLIOGRAPHY AND FURTHER READING

"American Sheep Industry | Fast Facts." American Sheep Industry | Fast Facts. Accessed January 10, 2017. http://www.sheepusa.org/ResearchEducation_FastFacts

"What Makes Wool So Special?" Accessed January 10, 2017. http://www.woolrevolution.com/virtues.html

A Lady, The Workwoman's Guide: A Guide to 19th Century Decorative Arts, Fashion and Practical Crafts, Piper Publishing LLC, 1838/2002.

Akiko Fukai, Tamami Suoh, Miki Iwagami, Reiko Koga, and Rii Nie. *Fashion: A History from the 18th–20th Century*, Taschen, 2005.

Alden O'Brien, *An Agreeable Tyrant: Fashion After the Revolution Exhibition Catalogue*, DAR Museum, 2016.

Anne Buck. *Dress in Eighteenth-Century England*, Holmes & Meier Publishers Inc., 1979.

Bianca M. Du Mortier and Ninke Bloemberg, *Accessorize! 250 Objects of Fashion & Desire*, Rijksmuseum & Yale University Press, 2012.

Clare Haru Crowston. *Fabricating Women: The Seamstresses of Old Regime France 1675–1791*, Duke University Press, 2001.

Cristina Barreto, Anita Lawrence, Martin Lancaster, Elizabeth Tauroza, and Michael David Haggerty. *Napoleon and the Empire of Fashion: 1795–1815*. Milano: Skira, 2010.

Florence M. Montgomery, *Textiles in America 1650–1870*, W.W. Norton & Company, 2007.

Gail Marsh. *18th Century Embroidery Techniques*, Guild of Master Craftsman Publications Ltd, 2006.

Harold Koda and Andrew Bolton. *Dangerous Liaisons: Fashion and Furniture in the Eighteenth Century*, Metropolitan Museum of Art & Yale University Press, 2006.

Janet Arnold. *Patterns of Fashion: Englishwomen's Dresses and Their Construction c. 1660–1860*, Macmillan/QSM, 1964.

John Styles. *The Dress of the People: Everyday Fashion in Eighteenth Century England*, Yale University Press, 2007.

John Styles. *Threads of Feeling: The London Foundling Hospital's Textile Tokens 1740–70*, Synergie Group UK, 2010.

Joseph Baillio, Katharine Baetjer, Paul Lang, and Ekaterina Deryabina. *Vigée Le Brun*. New York: Metropolitan Museum of Art, 2016.

Kimberly Chrisman-Campbell. *Fashion Victims: Dress at the Court of Louis XVI and Marie-Antoinette*. New Haven: Yale University Press, 2015.

Linda Baumgarten. *Eighteenth-Century Clothing at Williamsburg*, Colonial Williamsburg Foundation, 1993.

Linda Baumgarten, John Watson, and Florine Carr. *Costume Close-Up: Clothing Construction and Pattern 1750–1790*, Colonial Williamsburg Foundation/QSM, 1999.

Linda Baumgarten. *What Clothes Reveal: The Language of Clothing in Colonial and Federal America*, The Colonial Williamsburg Foundation and Yale University Press, 2002.

Marika Sardar. "Indian Textiles: Trade and Production." In *Heilbrunn Timeline of Art History*. New York: The Metropolitan Museum of Art, 2000–. http://www.metmuseum.org/toah/hd/intx/hd_intx.htm (October 2003).

Melinda Watt. "Textile Production in Europe: Printed, 1600–1800." In *Heilbrunn Timeline of Art History*. New York: The Metropolitan Museum of Art, 2000–. http://www.metmuseum.org/toah/hd/txt_p/hd_txt_p.htm (October 2003).

Nancy Bradfield. *Costume in Detail, 1730–1930*. Hollywood, CA: Costume & Fashion Press, 2009.

Norah Waugh. *Cut of Women's Clothes 1600–1930*, MPG Books Group, 1968.

Pauline Rushton. *18th Century Costume in National Museums Liverpool*, National Museums Liverpool, 2004.

Pernilla Rasmussen. *Skräddaren, sömmerskan och modet: Arbetsmetoder och arbetsdelning i tillverkningen av kvinnlig dräkt 1770–1830*, Nordiska Museet Handlinger, 2010.

Sharon Sadako Takeda and Kaye Durland Spilker. *Fashioning Fashion: European Dress in Detail 1700–1915*, Los Angeles County Museum of Art and Delmonico Books, 2012.

Sonia Ashmore. *Muslin*, Victoria and Albert Publishing, 2012.

Victoria and Albert Museum, *British Textiles 1700 to the Present*, V&A Publishing, 2010.

Supplier List

SHOES, STOCKINGS AND BUCKLES
American Duchess Inc.,
www.AmericanDuchess.com

FABRICS, SILK RIBBON AND THE BEST SILK THREAD FOR DRESSMAKING
Britex Fabrics, San Francisco,
www.britexfabrics.com

FABRICS, NECK-HANDKERCHIEFS, THREADS, PATTERNS AND ASSORTED NOTIONS
Burnley & Trowbridge Company,
www.burnleyandtrowbridge.com

FABRICS, PATTERNS AND SOME NOTIONS
William Booth, Draper, www.wmboothdraper.com

FABRIC
Silk Baron, www.silkbaron.com

Pure Silks, www.puresilks.us

Renaissance Fabrics, www.renaissancefabrics.net

Mood Fabrics Inc, www.moodfabrics.com

Acknowledgments and Biographies

ABBY'S ACKNOWLEDGMENTS

I would not have been able to coauthor this book if it wasn't for my experience working for the Colonial Williamsburg Foundation, specifically the Margaret Hunter Millinery Shop. Janea Whitacre, Mark Hutter, Brooke Welborn, Neal Hurst, Sarah Woodyard and Mike McCarty are not only my friends but fellow scholars in the field. The exchange of information between us throughout my years at Colonial Williamsburg have helped shape this book. Also, my gratitude goes out to Linda Baumgarten, the former curator of Costume and Textiles at Colonial Williamsburg, and Angela Burnley for being my mentors and friends. A huge thank you to our editor, Lauren Knowles, and the incredible staff at Page Street Publishing for working with us through this process. My deepest love and gratitude to my family for their love and support, specifically to my mother, Susan Meeks, for all the Starbucks gift cards and small gifts to keep up morale, and to my coauthor, Lauren, for including me in this once-in-a-lifetime opportunity. Finally, to Maggie Roberts, because you are a rock star, and we couldn't have done this book without your support.

ABBY'S BIO

Abby's passion for dress history and sewing started in college while studying art history, theatre and history. From there she pursued her passion, studying Decorative Arts and Design History at the University of Glasgow (MLitt 2009), and was able to begin putting her passion into her work while employed at the Colonial Williamsburg Foundation. Her final three years working for the Foundation were spent at the Margaret Hunter Millinery Shop, serving as an apprentice milliner/mantua maker. There she learned and studied eighteenth-century dressmaking techniques. Abby now serves as Vice-President of American Duchess and Royal Vintage Shoes in Reno, NV.

LAUREN'S ACKNOWLEDGMENTS

I would like to thank the amazingly supportive historical costuming community across the world, without which none of this would be possible or needed. Also, thank you to Chris Stowell, who put up with our messes; Maggie Roberts, for helping us make them; and Albert Roberts for graciously letting us have her. We would also like to acknowledge the Metropolitan Museum of Art and Los Angeles County Museum of Art for their supportive and progressive policies in sharing their collections and making them available for public use. Additionally, we'd like to thank the authors and researchers of our collective pasts—Janet Arnold, Nancy Bradfield, Linda Baumgarten, Norah Waugh—whose works we constantly refer back to, and the team at Page Street Publishing for giving us the opportunity to join the ranks.

Finally, I would like to thank Abby Cox, who has been a teacher, friend and partner throughout my historical costuming journey.

LAUREN'S BIO

Lauren Stowell started blogging in 2009 as a fun way to document learning historical costuming. While she loves a great many periods of dress, from the sixteenth century all the way through the early 1960s, Lauren's true love has always been eighteenth-century clothing. In 2011, together with her husband, Chris, Lauren began designing and offering reproduction eighteenth-century shoes for historical costumers and reenactors, which quickly grew into a full-time business manufacturing shoes, boots, silk stockings, shoe buckles and other accessories for all periods from the Renaissance to the Edwardian era. Throughout this time, Lauren continued to sew and blog about historic costume, experimenting, failing, succeeding and always learning more about old clothing and how it was worn and lived in.

Index